WOMEN
OF THE
REFORMATION

WOMEN
OF THE
REFORMATION

in Germany and Italy

by Roland H. Bainton

AUGSBURG PUBLISHING HOUSE
Minneapolis, Minnesota

WOMEN OF THE REFORMATION

IN GERMANY AND ITALY

To the mothers-in-law
of my children

> Lulu Robison
>
> Mary Brown
>
> Dorothy Peck
>
> Leta Ford
>
> Pearl Lunt

Contents

Part I.

WOMEN OF THE REFORMATION
IN GERMANY

Part II.

WOMEN OF THE REFORMATION
IN ITALY

Preface

This work aims to give brief biographical sketches of women who played a prominent role in the Catholic and Protestant reform movements in the early years of the 16th century. The term *Reformation* is used in the title because it designates a recognizable reform, but the word is here employed in a broad sense to include not only Protestantism but also evangelical Catholicism. The arrangement is geographical. The present volume has eight sketches for Germany and six for Italy.

The reasons for undertaking this work are several. I have always had an interest in those who have not had their due, and devoted my earliest studies to the heretics of the Reformation, who were persecuted alike by the Catholics and the Protestants.

The second reason is to observe the way in which the reform was disseminated. The women constituted a half of the population, and had they boycotted the movement, one may be sure that would have been the end.

The third is to assess the impact of the Reformation on the social order. This involves the character of the family, the position of women in society, and the role of women in the church. The reform, in my judgment, had greater influence on the family than on the political and economic spheres. The reform did not extinguish the power drive nor eliminate the acquisitive instinct. It did affect domestic relations at first indirectly by the elimination of monasticism. In consequence the home became the area *par excellence* for the exemplification of the gentler Christian virtues: love, tenderness, sharing of goods, self-effacement, humility, reconciliation, compassion, and the bearing of one another's burdens. If Reinhold Niebuhr's book *Moral Man and Immoral Society* had been written in the Middle Ages, the contrast would have been between man in the world and man in the monastery. Only after the Reformation did it become a contest between city hall and the stock exchange, on the one hand, and the home on the other.

The reader of these sketches may feel that the data presented do not validate the thesis, and certainly the reformers themselves did not state the case in these terms. They were dealing with concrete situations, and reflection came only later. At the outset, they stressed marriage as the cure for concubinage. The abuse was rife, and the bishops collected taxes on the women and the bastards. The reformers argued that in the case of the clergy not endowed with the gift of chastity marriage was the *remedium peccati,* the remedy for sin. But after the point had been made and clerical marriage established, the emphasis shifted and the stress was placed on marriage as the school for character. Luther so regarded it and Butzer said that the only defect of his second wife was that she did not criticize him, for criticism is a necessity.

A further emphasis which was present at the beginning, but came increasingly to the fore was that marriage is a partnership in the common endeavor of rearing children in the fear of the Lord and of working together in his vineyard. Thus husbands and wives were drawn more closely together through a common loyalty. On the other hand, if this mutual commitment was not there, the marriage was often severely strained, if not disrupted. After Protestantism became established, care was taken to keep marriage within the fold, but in the first generation one member might be converted and the other not. We shall encounter more than one example of acute friction.

With regard to the role of women in western society and the church, the common assumption all along has been that the female sphere is the home—not politics and literature. The great statesmen, warriors naturally, but also philosophers, scholars, poets, and composers have been men. All along the line, however, there have been notable exceptions; to picture woman in the West as in a continuous state of subjection is a gross exaggeration.

One can readily reel off the names of famous women: in the Old Testament we think of Sarah, Rachel, Miriam, Rahab, Hanna, Ruth, Naomi, Esther, Judith, and Jael, not to mention Eve. Likewise in the New Testament we have Mary and Martha, Mary Magdalene, Phoebe, Lydia, Chloe, Rhoda, Lois, Eunice, Priscilla, who is usually mentioned ahead of her husband, and of course Mary, the mother of Jesus.

In the classical world one thinks of Aspasia and Sappho. In the Homeric pantheon the goddesses are as powerful as the gods. In Roman history we have Lucretia and Virginia, Tullia and the daughter of Cicero, and Arria, who when her husband Paetus received the order from Nero to commit suicide, plunged the dagger into her own breast and then handed it to him with the words, "Paetus, it does not hurt." The women of the Caesars appeared with their husbands on the coins, and Ferrero devoted an entire volume to *The Women of the Caesars*.

Famous queens in antiquity were Cleopatra and Zenobia of Palmyra. Helena, the mother of Constantine, was held by her son in high esteem. Eudoxia, the empress in the time of Chryssostom, proved to be a formidable opponent of the saint. Theodora, the empress of Justinian, exerted strong political influence in the sixth century and the Empress Irene in the eighth restored the images after the Iconoclastic controversy.

In the West the barbarian invasions retarded all cultural life, and military progress was held in chief esteem. Yet even in such an age women could be prominent in political life, as were Brunhild and Fredegund. Literary life flourished only in the monasteries. Here we find a Hroswitha of Gandersheim. In the 11th century important roles were played by Agnes, the mother of Henry IV, and the Countess Mathilda. The emergence of a lay culture in the late Middle Ages engaged men more than women. But in the Renaissance there was a large number of highly educated women in all countries, though only among the aristocracy. Women were involved in politics only as the widows or mothers of rulers or as rulers themselves in default of a male heir.

The attitude toward women throughout exhibited the *querelle des dames,* the controversy between the defenders and the detractors of women. Detraction was a male sport, and since the men did most of the writing, those trained to the distaff were deprived of a rebuttal. Two sources fed into the detraction. One was the Platonic disparagement of the flesh as an impediment to the spirit. Sex was viewed as an aspect of the flesh, and woman regarded as a seductress. Even more extreme was Manicheanism which condemned sex as evil *per se*. The church stoutly resisted this view, even though it shared in the distrust of sex as defiling. The second source was the New Testament which combined the theme of the fall of man through woman and the expectation of the speedy end of the age, making marriage inadvisable. In 1 Timothy 2:11-15 Eve rather than Adam is blamed for the fall; therefore she should be submissive and silent. Because he expected the end to come soon, Paul would not encourage any change of status whether from slave to free or unmarried to married (1 Cor. 7). He, too, says that woman is subordinate to man and should not speak in church (1 Cor. 14:33-36).

In the Christian literature of the early centuries one finds at times a strange ambivalence. A Tertullian can call woman the gateway to hell and at the same time compose a charming picture of husband and wife sharing in their devotions. The church did not admit women to a full ministry but did have orders of widows and virgins and deaconesses perhaps earlier than the third century. Women martyrs such as Blandina, Perpetua, and Felicitas were honored. Julian the Apostate testified to the influence of the women of the Galileans. A man, said he, goes to bed as a pagan and wakes up a Christian.

Monasticism did not begin as a revolt against sex or against women. The cry of the early monks was not "flee women," but "flee mankind." The revolt was against the secularization of Christianity that came with the influx of hordes of nominal Christians after the Constantinian revolution. But since the early monks lived as hermits apart from any human association, sex became an obsession. In time, however, the radical separation of the sexes was relaxed. Jerome was glad to avail himself of the assistance of the learned Paula and Eustochium in the translation of the Scriptures.

In the West the disparagement of the female sex was accentuated by the Gregorian reform of the eleventh century which imposed clerical celibacy. The propaganda literature disparaged marriage and womanhood. Over against this attitude two extremes emerged. One was the revival of Manicheanism in the Albigensian heresy which repudiated sex altogether. The other was the emergence of romantic love which made a religious cult out of devotion to the lady. The expression of this love was extramatrimonial. Eleanore of Aquitane said that love and marriage are incompatible. She had had some experience. In the late Middle Ages romantic love and marriage were brought into conjunction.

The *querelle des dames* continued. The *Quinze Joyes de Mariage* of about the 15th century dealt satirically with the five plagues of marriage with appropriate scurrility for women. An entire volume has been devoted to the disparagement of women during the Renaissance. On the other side were Boccaccio, Symphorien Champier, Erasmus, Vives, and Rabelais. But whatever men said about women, they listened to them, often yielded to them, allowed themselves to be governed by them and gave them little credit.

How greatly the Protestant Reformation affected the role of women in society and the Church is difficult to assess. The suggestion has been made that the Protestant Reformation gave women an opportunity to step out of the home into public life. There was no need for that. Witness the career of Catherine de Medici, a Catholic. The political role of women depended largely on circumstance. All of the English queens of the 16th century were involved in the issues whether they were Catholic or Protestant, for the simple reason that they were already queens. In general one may say that any revolutionary period may cause persons of any faith, age, or sex to be precipitated into a more active role. The charge has sometimes been made that the Reformation restricted the role of women because of the decline of monasticism. By way of compensation, however, in the late 16th century, the Protestants revived the diaconate for the distribution of alms and for nursing.

With respect to the role of women in the church the Counter-

Reformation may have meant more than the Protestant Reformation. Evenett in his book *The Spirit of the Counter-Reformation* (Cambridge, England, 1968) calls attention to the "hidden influence of so many remarkable women in the Italian contemplative convents," as well as of the Spanish *beatas* and the French mystics, and suggests the need for a work on "the spiritual influence of women in the Counter-Reformation." Yet all of this has to do with piety rather than with a ministerial role for women. Neither Catholics nor Protestants were ready to ordain women.

There is one respect in which the Reformation had a profound influence on women and they in turn upon the church. The translation of the Scriptures into the vernaculars and their dissemination through the printing press stimulated literacy and the will to read. The women who are sketched in these pages were steeped in Scripture and even the comparatively uneducated, who appear in the martyrologies and the heresy trials, gave their judges a terrific run at any point involving the word of God.

I have indicated a number of reasons for undertaking this study. Not the least is that we have here magnificent examples of courage. When I read to a woman Luther's statement that the death of his little daughter Elizabeth had left him "as weak as a woman," she repeated the expression with scorn. Well she might after reading these vignettes!

Most of the information about the women discussed in this book appears in languages other than English. The reader will notice that oftentimes English quotes are attributed to works with non-English titles. In these instances the translations are my own.

BIBLIOGRAPHY

Role of Women in the West (and elsewhere):
Maurice Bardèche, *Histoire des Femmes,* 2 vols., (1968).

The Renaissance:
Ruth Kelso, *Doctrine for the Lady of the Renaissance,* (Urbana, 1956).

Role of Women in the Church: the Diaconate:
Freiherr von der Goltz, ed., *Der Dienst der Frau in der christlichen Kirche,*
2 vols. in one (Potsdam, 1913).

Women in the Reformation:
Käthe Stricker, "Die Frau in der Reformation," *Quellenhefte zum Frauen-leben,* Heft II (Berlin, 1933). A collection of sources.

Detraction of Women in the Renaissance:
Katherine M. Rogers, *The Troublesome Helpmate* (Seattle, 1956).

Part I

WOMEN OF THE REFORMATION IN GERMANY

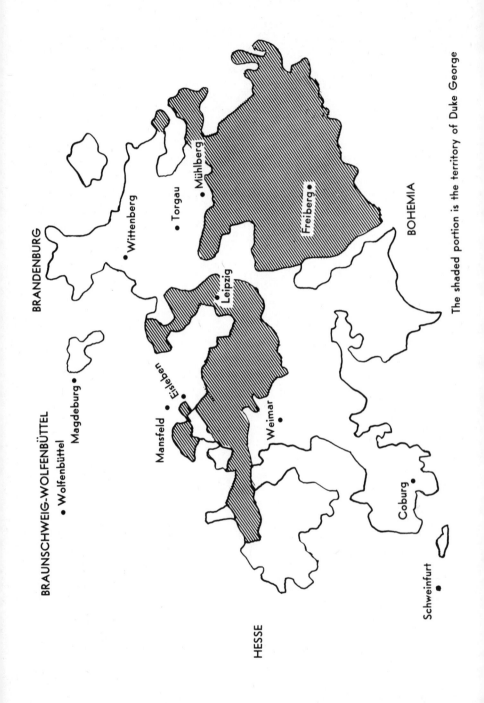

BRANDENBURG

BRAUNSCHWEIG-WOLFENBÜTTEL

• Wolfenbüttel

Magdeburg •

• Wittenberg

• Torgau

• Mühlberg

Freiberg •

Leipzig •

Mansfeld

Eisleben •

Weimar •

HESSE

Coburg •

Schweinfurt •

BOHEMIA

The shaded portion is the territory of Duke George

The Reformation in Germany

A number of events in the Reformation in Germany recur in these pages. Curiously the indulgence controversy started by Luther with the publication of his Ninety Five Theses in 1517 had largely dropped out of the picture by the time these women came to be involved. The doctrine of justification by faith continued, however, to give great comfort to troubled spirits.

Luther's views of clerical and monastic marriage and his own marriage were at first to the fore. In the summer of 1520 in his *Address to the Christian Nobility of the German Nation* he had already declared that clerical marriage should be allowed. In the spring of 1521 he was placed under the ban of the church and the empire by the Edict of Worms. Only the protection of his prince, Frederick the Wise, saved him from the stake. For a year he was hidden at the castle of the Wartburg. During his absence from Wittenberg even monks began to marry. This led him to examine the whole question of monastic vows and to bring out a tract calling for their abolition. In 1522 he was recalled in order to bring order into the turbulent progress of the Reformation at Wittenberg.

His own marriage came in 1525, the year of the Peasants' War. During the Diet of Augsburg in 1530 he was not able to be present since he was under the ban of the church and the empire. He was secreted nearby at the castle of the Coburg. At this diet the Augsburg Confession was presented and rejected by the emperor who gave the Lutherans a year in which to submit on pain of war. Because of his own involvement in wars with the French, the pope, and the Turks, the emperor was unable for a quarter of a century to carry out his threat.

In the 1520s other reformatory movements had sprung up in Switzerland and South Germany involving Zwingli, Oecolampadius, and Butzer along with Capito and Zell. In 1546, after Luther died, the emperor found himself free to deal with the German question. In 1547 he won the battle of Mühlberg and took prisoner John Frederick of Saxony and Philip of Hesse. The Augsburg Interim, which gave the Protestants a few concessions until the meeting of a general council, was promulgated in 1548. In consequence, Butzer and Fagius were exiled from Strasbourg. In 1552 Moritz of Saxony, having driven out the emperor, concluded the Peace of Passau. In 1553 he was killed in the battle of Sievershausen in which Erich II of Braunschweig and others were involved. The Peace of Augsburg, which accorded toleration to Lutherans in designated areas, followed in 1555.

The literature on the Reformation in Germany is very extensive. A few brief treatments may be mentioned:

Roland H. Bainton, *The Reformation of the Sixteenth Century* (Boston, 1952).

Owen Chadwick, *The Reformation* (Penguin, 1968).

A. G. Dickens, *Reformation and Society in Sixteenth-Century Europe* (London, 1966).

THE HAPSBURGS

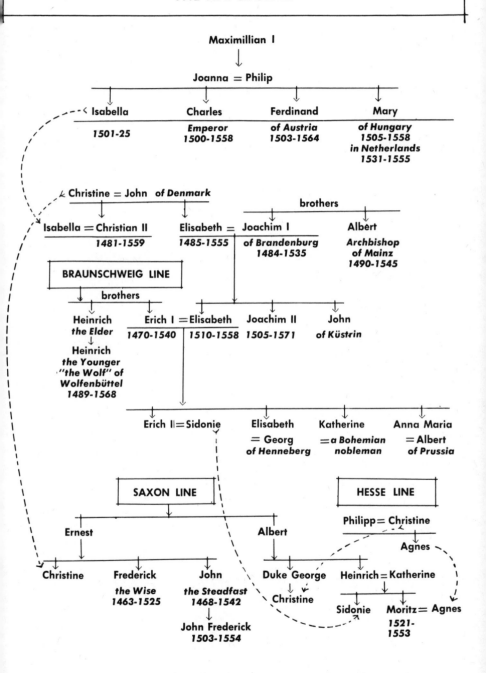

Dotted curved lines denote: SAME PERSON

1.

Katherine von Bora
(1499-1550)

Katherine von Bora is best known of all the women of the Reformation because she was Luther's wife. Kierkegaard suggested that she had no other claim because, said he, Luther might just as well have married a plank. Kierkegaard's point was that Luther had nothing more in mind than to demonstrate his approval of clerical marriage. The case was by no means so simple. If Katherine was no more than a plank the wood was oak, polished on one side, left rough on the other.

Katherine von Bora, born in January 1499, at the age of 10 was placed in a nunnery at Nimschen when her father remarried. She took the vows at the age of 16. In the early 1520s the writings of Luther began to infiltrate even into monastic houses. The sisters at Nimschen, nine of them, disquieted in conscience, sought his counsel. Luther advised escape and undertook to make the arrangements.

This was difficult because Nimschen lay in the territory of Duke George. Saxony was divided into two sections: one part was ruled by Frederick the Wise, Luther's friend; the other by Duke George, Luther's foe. The duke had executed a man for assisting the escape of nuns. Luther turned to a highly trusted layman, Leonard Kopp, who on occasion delivered barrels of smoked herring to the nuns and returned with the empties. Arrangements were made that on the very night when Christ rose from the tomb, the nuns should rise from their couches. They are frequently alleged to have escaped inside the herring barrels, but the chronicle says that they were hidden in a covered wagon "as if they had been the barrels."

Like the Holy Family fleeing into Egypt, by dawn they were beyond the confines of the king who sought the young child's life and on Tuesday after Easter their wagon rumbled into Wittenberg.[1] A student wrote to a friend: "A wagon load of vestal virgins has just come to town all more eager for marriage than for life. May God give them husbands lest worse befall." [2]

Luther felt responsible that worse should not befall. He corresponded with relatives who declined to take the renegades. One was placed in a teaching post, several in homes, some in matrimony. Katherine von Bora spent two years in a Wittenberg home where she received admirable training in household economy. She was evidently attractive; the King of Denmark in exile spent some time in Wittenberg and gave her a gold ring. More promising for the future was the attention of a handsome young patrician of Nürnberg, 25 years old. Katie was 24. Attraction was mutual. He went home intending to return for Katie, but his family so stoutly objected that he dallied. Luther wrote him that he had better make up his mind, else he would lose her.[3] He did make up his mind and married another. There were no recriminations and in later years Luther, who always believed that the wishes of parents should be respected, could send him friendly greetings from "his old flame." [4] Luther now suggested to Katie that she marry Dr. Glatz. Loath to offend her benefactor, Katie enlisted the mediation of Dr. Amsdorf, Luther's trusted friend, then visiting Wittenberg. She asked him to convey the word to Luther that under no circumstances would she marry Dr. Glatz, but she would be willing to consider Amsdorf himself or Luther.[5] Presumably she mentioned these two because she was dealing with them and regarded them both as ineligible by reason of age. Luther was 16 years her senior.

On receiving this news Luther began to question his ineligibility. His resolve never to marry had been softening of late. Had he been told at the Diet of Worms that in seven years he would be married and would also be a father he would have roared.[6] When he was in hiding at the Wartburg and word came

Luther and Katherine
after Cranach

to him that monks at Wittenberg were marrying, he ejaculated, "Good God, will our Wittenbergers give wives even to monks? They won't give one to me." [7] As late as 1524, when word came to him from a woman whom we shall meet again, Argula von Grumbach, urging him to seal his testimony by marrying, he answered that he was of no such mind, "not because I am a sexless log or stone, but because I expect daily the death of a heretic." [8] But in June of 1525 on hearing that Albert the Archbishop of Mainz, against whom the Ninety Five Theses were directed, was contemplating matrimony, Luther wrote to say that if his own marriage would be an encouragement, he was ready.[9] Then, though 42, he went dutifully to consult his parents as to Katie's hint. The father, who had been deeply disappointed by Luther's monastic vow, depriving him of the hope of progeny, was now highly enthusiastic.[10] Luther had then an arsenal of reasons: his marriage would please his father,[11] rile the pope,[12] make the angels laugh and the devils weep,[13] and would seal his testimony.[14]

Luther made no pretense that this was a romantic match. The Reformation in general was not romantic. Couples married for conviction or convenience. In Luther's case it was conviction; in Katherine's, partly convenience. They fell in love afterwards. Compare his references to his wife over the years. At the outset he confided to a friend, "I am not madly in love, but I cherish my wife." [15] "I would not change Katie for France or for Venice, for God has given her to me and other women have worse faults. She has a few but her virtues outweigh them." [16] A year after his marriage he could say, "My wife is compliant, accommodating, and affable beyond anything I dared to hope. I would not exchange my poverty for the riches of Croesus." [17] He referred to her as his *carissima* [18] and addressed her as *Meine Herzliebe*.[19] In 1538 he could say, "If I should lose my Katie I would not take another wife though I were offered a queen." [20] When he thought her on the point of death he pleaded, "Stirb mir ja nicht," ("Don't die and leave me"). His designation of her as "The Morning Star of Wittenberg" has been taken to be a facetious reference to her rising at four in summer and five in winter, but the tribute was unalloyed when he called his beloved

Pauline Epistle to the Galatians "my Katherine von Bora," [21] and even more when he ruefully confessed that he relied more on Katie than on Christ. [22] "In domestic affairs," said he, "I defer to Katie. Otherwise I am led by the Holy Ghost." [23]

Having once made up his mind and obtained Katie's consent, he pushed wedding plans with the utmost speed tolerable to a bride.[24] He wanted to choke the ejaculations of friends who were bound to say, "Oh no, not this one!" [25] and to scotch the reproaches of enemies who were already circulating the slander that he was living with Katie before marriage,[26] though, as a matter of fact, they considered this less reprehensible than that a monk should marry a nun.[27] Luther was naive if he supposed that either a deed or a denial would silence this rumor. Two years after marriage a printed pamphlet addressed Katie in these terms:

"Woe to you, poor fallen woman, not only because you have passed from light to darkness, from the cloistered holy religion into a damnable, shameful life, but also that you have gone from the grace to the disfavor of God, in that you have left the cloister in lay clothes and have gone to Wittenberg like a chorus girl. You are said to have lived with Luther in sin. Then you have married him, forsaking Christ your bridegroom. You have broken your vow and by your example have reduced many godly young women in the cloisters to a pitiable state of body and of soul, despised of all men." [28]

Luther was more realistic when he told Katie that if he were burned, she would not escape his fate.[29] Well did a friend in later years write him that Katherine was "the partner of his calamities." [30] The betrothal, which constituted the official marriage, took place on June 13, 1525, in the presence of four witnesses. Two weeks later came the public celebration with a parade through the streets to the music of fifes, followed by a great banquet. Luther's father and mother were in attendance.

Married life brought many changes for the pair. Unhappily we have only Luther's version. Katie is seen through a glass darkly or standing in the offing like Joseph at the Nativity. Her feelings have to be deduced from those of her husband. He reported his amazement on waking in the morning to find pig-

Dancing at
a wedding

tails on the pillow.[31] He may have been even more surprised to find a pillow, since he confessed that for a year at a time he tumbled into an unmade bed till the straw decomposed.[32] Katie took all that in hand and so much else that he sensed a curtailment of his liberty. He wanted to go to Torgau for the marriage of a friend, but the intervening territory was still infested with marauding bands of peasants. Katie said no and Luther stayed.[33]

More galling was the curb on his prodigality. He said that God divided the hand into fingers so that money would slip through,[34] and whatever was given God would replenish.[35] Short of a miracle God would have had a hard time without Katie. Luther was loath to accept anything not absolutely necessary and would give away anything not absolutely required. When the Archbishop of Mainz magnanimously sent 20 gold gulden, they would have been returned by Luther had they not already been accepted by Katie,[36] and when Luther wrote to a friend that he was sending him a handsome present, he had to append a note to say that it had been hidden by the "crafty Katie." [37] He began to refer to her not as My Lady *(Domina)*, but as My Lord *(Dominus)*.[38] Sometimes he punned on her name Kethe as *Kette*, chains.[39] To a friend whose wife was also Katherine he might send greetings "from chains to chains," [40] though the more customary salutation was, "I and my rib send greetings to you and your rib," [41] and even with the addition "and all the little ribs." [42]

Katherine ministered to her husband's diseases, depressions, and eccentricities. She had great skill with diet, herbs, poultices, and massages. Her son, later a distinguished physician, praised her as half a doctor.[43] Luther frequently suffered tortures from the stone. On one such occasion he would neither eat nor drink, and Katie besought him to take some sustenance. "Very well," said he, "roast beef, peas, and mustard and be quick before my fancy fades." She complied and he ate heartily. His doctors called and were aghast. They returned in the morning to see the corpse and found him at his desk. He had passed a stone.[44] The help of Katie in this instance could scarcely have been more than psychological. Often it was only that.

He suffered from acute depressions, interpreted as assaults of

Satan. They were more severe in the night watches. He would then turn over and say to Katie, "Forbid me to have such temptations." [45] One may regard it as an eccentricity that on occasion when in health he would abstain from all food and drink for four days. This we learn from the testimony of his intimate friend Melanchthon.[46] Hence we are not to regard as incredible the tale that once he locked himself in his study and did not emerge for three days. Katie had the door removed, whereupon he looked up in bewildered innocence and asked what harm he was doing.[47] She was undoubtedly pleased that he carried over from his monastic days the practice of mending his own clothes, but she was emphatically annoyed when to obtain cloth for a patch he cut up little Hans' breeches.[48]

Katherine was involved in vastly more than curbing her husband's unbridled munificence and curing his maladies of flesh and spirit. She came to be the mistress of a household, a hostel, and a hospital. The Augustinian Cloister, where Luther had lived as a monk, was first loaned and then given to the couple by the Elector.[49] It had on the first floor 40 rooms with cells above. The day was to come when not a single room was unoccupied.[50] The reason was not that Katie bore 40 children. There were only six. But Luther brought in some six or seven nephews and nieces, and when a friend lost his wife in the plague, Luther brought home the four children. Katie also took in some of her relatives. One of them, a very great help, was her aunt Magdalene, who had been with her in the cloister. The Luther children called her *Mumme Lena* and were so fond of her that Luther was a trifle jealous.[51] For the children there were tutors and then as many student boarders as the quarters would accommodate. Luther would have charged them nothing, but not Katie.

Foreigners came from as far as England and Hungary for protracted stays. Refugees arrived unpredictably and remained unpredictably. There was, for example, the Duchess Ursula of Münsterberg, who together with two other noble nuns escaped from a convent in the territory of her cousin Duke George and turned up penniless in Wittenberg. The Duke said that Luther was conducting an asylum for renegades.[52] Then there was the

Wie ein iglicher
Chrift gegen allerley le-
re/gut vnd böfe/nach
Gottes befelh/fich gebür-
lich halten fol.
Juftus Menius.
Mit einer Vorrhede
D. Mart. Luther.

Wittemberg
M D XXXVIII

A wedding dance

Electress Elisabeth of Brandenburg, a Swedish princess of Lutheran persuasion, married to the rabidly Catholic Joachim I.[53] Their daughter betrayed to the father that the mother was celebrating communion in both kinds. He locked her up, but she escaped and sought a refuge with the Elector of Saxony. While he was renovating a castle for her residence, she stayed, sick now in body and in mind, with the Luthers. Her daughter, the one who had betrayed her but now of her faith, offered to come and do the nursing. There was no room for another in the Black Cloister and Katie took over.[54]

So large an establishment was more than one person could handle alone. Katie herself herded, milked, and slaughtered the cattle, made butter and cheese, brewed, planted, and reaped, but help was indispensable. There were maid servants and men servants, sometimes faithful, sometimes unreliable. Luther remarked, "The eyes of the wife cook better than the maid, the man, the fire, and the coals." The hubbub in the household of babies, children, students, guests, refugees, and servants was so great that Luther sent his son Hans early away to school where he could study in quiet.[55]

The noise was the least of it. How was this community to be supported? In addition to the routine expenses there were special occasions. Promotions to the doctorate and weddings called for banquets which the Luthers provided for their friends. On such occasions Katie set places for 120 guests. Mere attendance at a wedding called for a substantial present and so did standing sponsor for a child at baptism. Where did the money come from? Luther and Katie brought no endowments or dowries from their monastic careers. The Black Cloister, placed at their disposal, had by way of equipment little beyond pots and pans. Luther as a professor had a salary, but not adequate for such an establishment. Students were expected to pay for their keep, but were continually in arrears and to the great annoyance of Katie would raid the garden or the orchard. She concealed from her husband the vexation of minor infractions. Gifts came from affluent admirers, but all too often in the form of rings, goblets, medals, and bejewelled chains, fit only for a museum, where they now are.[56]

Katie resolved to make the household self-sustaining. She did some remodelling in the Black Cloister, making three cellars with an extra stairway. A bath was installed, which served presumably also as a laundry, and there was a brewery. The Black Cloister carried with it a small garden yielding peas, beans, turnips, cabbage, lettuce, cucumbers, and melons. An orchard was developed which supplied cherries, pears, apples, peaches, nuts, grapes, mulberries, and figs. Katie, having extracted her husband's consent by eloquence and tears, acquired another garden through which ran a brook. To Luther's delight she hooked from it pike, trout, perch, and carp. Her livestock included various horses. A precise count in 1542 listed eight pigs, five cows, nine calves, besides chickens, pigeons, geese, and of course the immortal dog Tölpel, whom Luther fully expected to meet in heaven.[57] The supplies that Katie couldn't raise herself may be inferred from a letter written by her husband requesting a friend to purchase some viands for a doctoral banquet: "My Lady Katie, the chief cook, desires that with the enclosed sum you purchase birds, all manner of denizens of the aerial realm. No crows please, and all the sparrows there are we can swallow at a gulp. Whatever extra you spend will be reimbursed. Oh yes, rabbits and the like, whether bought or caught."[58]

Luther's wife foresaw the day when, in view of the discrepancy of age, she would be left without a husband and with the care of a young brood. She realized that his salary would cease, student boarders would drop off, gifts would diminish. The soundest investment in her eyes was real estate, and she sought to acquire as much as possible. Luther was not so happy over her expansionism, for he thought that land was wealth only if sold or worked. "Grain," said he, "has more value than gold."[59] If land is merely held, it becomes an encumbrance.

Katie did come into possession of a farm at Zulsdorf, two days distant from Wittenberg. A short trip did not warrant the effort so she would go for three weeks and on her return would still be thinking of Zulsdorf. Luther addressed her as "The rich lady of Zulsdorf, Frau Doktor Katherine Luther, who lives in the body at Wittenberg, in the spirit in Zulsdorf, *meine Herzliebe*."[60] Zulsdorf was her project and her release. She had building operations under way. The Elector gave her oak logs and his chaplain supplied dray horses. And then if Katie didn't want to secure another farm at Wachsdorf, only an hour from Wittenberg! It would have been more manageable if Zulsdorf had been relinquished. Luther was spared a clash because Wachsdorf went off the market.

Katie's greatest victory was that she taught her husband to say no. When a friend and former student asked the Luthers to provide him a wedding banquet according to their wont, Luther brought himself to write, "My dear fellow, we just can't manage it. I would suggest that you have your banquet at Freiberg or later on here on a very modest scale." [61]

The coming of the children and the events of family life receive notice in Luther's letters and *Table Talk* with allusions naturally to Katie. Here is a little chronicle of the children's births and sometimes deaths. On October 21, 1525, Luther reported to a friend, "Katie is fulfilling Genesis 3:8 where the Lord God said to the woman, 'In pain shall you bring forth children.' " [62] On June 7 of the following year she gave birth to a son, named Hans for Luther's father. By January Luther could write to a friend, "Little Hans salutes you. He begins to cut teeth and blithely scolds every one. Such are the fruit and joy of marriage, of which the pope is not worthy." [63] In October Luther reports that Hans relieves himself in every corner.[64] What this meant for Katie is left to inference. When Hans was two his father, on his behalf, sent thanks for a rattle,[65] and when he was ten and a half wrote him a letter in Latin.[66]

The next child was Elisabeth, who lived less than a year.[67] Two days after her death Luther wrote to a friend, "My little daughter Elisabeth is dead. I am left as weak as a woman. I would never have believed that the hearts of parents are so moved toward their children." [68]

On May 4, 1529, Magdalene arrived, named for Mumme Lena and called Lenchen. Luther wrote to Amsdorf, "Honorable and noble sir, God the Father of all grace has given to me and my dear Katherine a little daughter. I beseech you for God's sake to assume the Christian office of father in God to bring this poor little heathen into the Christian fold through the Holy

A German farm in the days of
Katherine von Bora

Sacrament of Baptism." [69] Two days later he wrote, "Katie is as well as if she had never had a baby." [70]

Martin came on November 9, 1531.[71] "The love of parents," said Luther, "always gravitates to the youngest. My Martin is my dearest treasure. Hans and Lenchen can talk now and don't need so much care." [72] Seeing Martin at the breast Luther observed, "The enemies of this child are the pope, bishops, Duke George, Ferdinand, and all devils, and yet he sucks away without the least concern. Truly Christ said, 'We must become as little children.'" [73] Again watching Katie fondle him, Luther remarked, "Surely God must talk with me even more fondly than my Katie with her *Martinichen*." [74]

Paul, named of course for the apostle, arrived on January 29, 1533. Luther proclaimed to a friend, "This night my Katie has born to me a son. I hope you will assist to bring him from the old birth in Adam to the new birth in Christ through the Holy Sacrament of Baptism that he may become a member of the Christian fold, and perhaps God may make him an enemy of the pope and the Turk. I'd like to have the baptism at vespers that he may be no longer a heathen." [75]

Margareta, named for Luther's mother, was the sixth, born on December 17, 1534. Luther in his correspondence gave her the pet name of *Margaretula*.[76] He remarked on the sweetness of her voice at the age of five, as she took part in musical evenings with the family.[77]

To one of the children Luther apostrophized, "Child what have you done that I should love you so? What with your befouling the corners and bawling through the whole house?" [78] When the baby cried for an hour and father and mother sat disconsolate, he remarked, "This is the trial of marriage which makes men shun it. But God has restored marriage, the magistracy, and the ministry." [79] After Elisabeth had died and Martin was born he could say, "God has given to me greater gifts than to any bishop in a thousand years. I have three children. I have lost one. They are more precious to me than all the kingdoms of Ferdinand: Hungary, Bohemia, and Germany." [80]

Luther was especially fond of Lenchen. When he was secreted at the castle of the Coburg during the Diet of Augsburg, which he could not attend because he was under the ban, Katie sent him a painting of the little girl, which he set up above his table, deriving from it great comfort in his despondencies.[81] In her fourteenth year she was taken. Luther knelt by her bedside in prayer and tears. Then he took her in his arms, while Katie stood a little aside. As she was laid away, he said, "My dear Lenchen, you will rise and shine as the stars and the sun. . . . How strange it is to know that she is at peace and all is well and yet to be so sorrowful!" [82]

The *Table Talk* of Luther introduces Katie on numerous occasions. The conversation was a blend of German and Latin, which Katie could handle, having received instruction in the cloister.[83] Mumme Lena, who had been there with her, when asked by Luther whether she would like to go back, answered not in German *Nein,* but in Latin *Non.*[84] Katie was a lively conversationalist. Luther said she could teach an Englishman German better than he ever could.[85] But he suggested that she curb her volubility by saying the Lord's Prayer before opening her mouth.[86]

She was quite deferential toward him and addressed him as *Herr Doktor* and in the polite speech rather than with the familiar *Du.* As a pupil she invited instruction and asked for the meaning of dialectic. "Dialectic," said Luther, "is knowing how to do the washing. Rhetoric is getting it done." [87] She posed a more difficult question when she asked, "How could David say, 'Judge me according to my righteousness,' when he didn't have any?" [88] At the same time she did not hesitate to rebuke her husband, and on the occasion of an indecorous remark about Schwenckfeld broke in, "Oh come now, that's too raw." [89] And she could be recalcitrant. Her husband kept prodding her to read through the Bible, and promised her 50 gulden if she finished by Easter.[90] She already knew the Psalms, he acknowledged, better than ever the papists had done.[91] Eventually she balked, "I've read enough. I've heard enough. I know enough. Would to God I lived it." [92] Once she disagreed with him flatly. He was speaking of the agony of Abraham when commanded by God to kill Isaac. "I don't believe it," said Katie. "God would not have done that to his son." Luther answered, "But Katie, he did." [93]

Though protesting against coarse invective, Katie by no means sought to deter her husband from sharp polemic. That he should have replied to Erasmus has seemed puzzling, since Melanchthon informed Erasmus that his tract against Luther had created no stir at Wittenberg.[94] And then Luther came out with his blast. The *Table Talk* discloses that Luther was at first minded to pass over the attack in silence, until a colleague enlisted Katie to prod him into an answer.[95] Another time she angered Chancellor Brück, the legal adviser to the Elector. Brück tried to dissuade Luther from an attack on Heinz of Wolfenbütel, lest there be political repercussions. Luther usually paid no attention to political repercussions, but this time he showed an inclination to be obliging, until Katie stiffened his spine and he came out with the tract *Wider Hans Wurst,* that is, *Against Hans Baloney.*[96]

Luther liked to tease his wife and pointed out to her that polygamy was allowed in the Old Testament. "Yes," she answered, "but Paul said that each should have his own wife." "His own, yes," said Luther, "but not just one." "Well, if it comes to that," retorted Katie, "I'll leave you and the children and go back to the cloister." [97] When she struck her side and ejaculated, *"Ave Maria!"* Luther asked, "Why don't you ask Christ to help you?" [98]

Certain of his asides mention her. "To tell a German," said Luther, "that an olive crop has been spoiled doesn't mean a thing. It's something else to say that the hops and malt have been ruined, as Katie's were." [99] Again said the doctor, "If I might advise God, I would suggest that he charge for what he gives men: for a wife, child, eye, foot, hand, mouth, nose, teeth, stomach, etc., each time 100 florin. I'd pay 100 florin if he'd give Katie more milk." [100]

From the correspondence of Luther and Katie nothing is extant on her side. But we have a number of his letters.

February 7, 1532. *"Meine herzliebe* Katie. If Dr. Brück will release me [from business for the Elector] as he gives me to hope, I will come with him tomorrow or the next day. Pray God he may bring us home well. I sleep six or seven hours and then afterwards two or three. The beer does it, I suspect. I am sober as at Wittenberg. The Elector's body is as healthy as a fish, but the devil has bitten his foot. Since our servant John is leaving and has been so faithful, as others you know have not, I'd like to give him ten gulden. Don't give him less than five, and if there is anything at all in the house, don't let him go away empty. I leave it to your discretion. Kiss little Hans for me. Ask Hänschen, Lenchen and Mumme Lena to pray for our dear princes and for me. I can't find any suitable presents for the children in this town, although it is the annual fair. See if you can dig up something at home for me to give them." [101]

July 29, 1534. "Grace and Peace in Christ, dear Lord Katie! Yesterday I had a good drink. I thought of what good wine and beer I have at home and a lovely wife, or should I say lord? You'd do well to send me our whole cellar full of wine and a flask of your beer as soon as you can. I commend you to God with all the young ones and relatives. *Dein liebchen. . . ."* [102]

July 26, 1540. "To the rich Lady at Zulsdorf! The conference at Hagenau [with the Catholics] was a waste of time. My gracious lord the Elector has lost 1000 acres of wood through fire in the Thuringian forest. Christ, our Lord, will come and light such a fire under the devils that they won't be able to put it out. I don't know whether this letter will reach you at Wittenberg or Zulsdorf, else I would have written more." [103]

September 18, 1541. From Wittenberg to Katie at Zulsdorf: "I wonder that you don't write. We're worried about you. Sell what you can and come home. It looks to me as if God will empty the viols of his wrath upon us [i.e. war will break out]." [104]

July 28, 1545. Luther in his last days, sick in body and in mind, left Wittenberg in a panic of disgust and wrote to Katie: "To my dear wife Katherine von Bora, preacher, brewer, gardener, and whatsoever else she may be: I don't want to come back to Wittenberg. My heart is cold. Give the Black Cloister back to the Elector. Sell everything else. Move to Zulsdorf. My salary will help to fix it up, if the Elector will let me keep it for my last year. The women at Wittenberg dress so shamelessly. The Word of God is despised. Only to get out of this Sodom! I just can't stand the wrath and the loathing any longer." [105]

On seeing this letter, Melanchthon and a few friends went

after him and brought him back to Wittenberg. His spirit rallied. The dukes of Mansfeld, quarreling over mining rights, asked Melanchthon to mediate. He was too sick to go. Luther was too sick to live, but went in his stead.

February 1, 1546. From Eisleben where the conference with the dukes was held: "I was very weak as we approached Eisleben. I am better now, but I haven't enough vitality to look at pretty women, so I'm in no danger of going astray. The boys are at Mansfeld. [Katie had sent them to this spot nearby that they might be at hand should the end come for their father.] [106]

February 10, 1546: "To the saintly, worrying Lady Katherine Luther, doctor at Zulsdorf and Wittenberg, my gracious dear wife: We thank you heartily for being so worried that you can't sleep, for since you started worrying about us, a fire broke out near my door and yesterday, no doubt due to your worry, a big stone, save for the dear angels, would have fallen and crushed us like a mouse in a trap. If you don't stop worrying, I'm afraid the earth will swallow us. Haven't you learned the Catechism, and don't you believe? Pray and let God worry. 'Cast your burden on the Lord.' We are well except that Jonas banged his ankle. He is jealous of me and wanted to have something the matter with him too. We hope soon to be released from this assignment and come home." [107]

February 14, 1546. "We can come home this week. The dukes have made up. I'm going to invite them as guests that they may talk to each other. I am sending you some trout which the Duchess of Hohenstein sent me. She is very happy over the reconciliation. The boys are still at Mansfeld. We are so well treated here that we are in danger of forgetting Wittenberg. The bladder stone, praise God, is not bothering me. Dr. Jonas is having trouble again with his leg. There are rumors of wars. We'll wait and see what God will do. God be with you. Amen." [108]

The end did come and the boys were at hand. With Luther's death the fears of husband and wife were both realized. She foresaw a reduction of income and desired more real property. He foresaw that the land unworked would be a millstone, and war might sweep everything away. The farm at Wachsdorf came again on the market and she went after it, but Chancellor Brück

A wife greeting her husband

opposed. His advice was that she retrench, send all the boys to school, dispose of property, return the Black Cloister to the Elector, and live with her daughter modestly on an allowance from the Elector. She insisted on keeping the cloister. She would again take in students and rent rooms. She fought for Wachsdorf and got it and did the planting and harvesting herself.

And then were unleashed the horsemen of the Apocalypse. The emperor, who in 1530 had given the Lutherans a year in which to submit under penalty of war, had been unable to fulfill his threat because he was involved in conflicts with the French, the Turks, and the pope. Now he was able to come with Spanish troops, reinforced by Hungarians under his brother Ferdinand, and even by Saxons. Wittenberg was besieged. Katie fled with the children to Magdeburg. When the invasion receded, she returned to find her lands scorched, buildings burned, livestock devoured, fodder consumed, and gardens ravished. The Black Cloister fortunately was intact. Then another invasion, another flight, another return, another desolation. Once more she set herself to rebuild.

Then came the fourth horseman, pestilence. Two of the boys were at school. With Paul and Margaret, Katie set out to drive to Torgau. The horses bolted over a rough road. She jumped to check them from the side, but landed on her back and rolled into a ditch of cold water. Taken to Torgau, she was nursed by Margaret, now 18. The end came after three months on December 20, 1550, in her fifty-first year. Her last words were, "I will stick to Christ as a burr to a top coat." [109]

She emerges as a woman of character and courage, sensible, non-sentimental, hard-headed, tender, determined, and usually right. She discussed with her husband the issues of the Reformation and supported him in his polemical endeavors. Yet the public arena was not her proper sphere. Her contribution to the Reformation is not on that account to be disparaged. She presided over the first well-known Protestant parsonage and did much to give the tone to German domestic life—authoritarian, paternalistic, with no nonsense, and at the same time tenderly affectionate and marked by utter devotion.

Luther's views of marriage were profoundly affected by his own experience. "Nothing," he said, "is more sweet than harmony in marriage, and nothing more distressing than dissension. Next to it is the loss of a child. I know how that hurts." [110] "Marriage offers the greatest sphere for good works, because it rests on love—love between the husband and the wife, love of the parents for the children, whom they nourish, clothe, rear, and nurse. If a child is sick, the parents are sick with worry. If the husband is sick, the wife is as concerned as if it were herself. If it be said that marriage entails concern, worry, and trouble, that is all true, but these the Christian is not to shun." [111]

"Youthful infatuation does not last, just as at the wedding at

Cana, attended by Christ, the wine gave out. There was no beer and the bridegroom stood there like a beggar. Mary then went to Jesus and told him the wine was emptied. He answered, as it were, 'Do you have to drink water, that is do you have trouble in the outward man and is it bitter? See then, I will make it sweet and turn the water into wine. I will not pour out the water, it will have to stay, but I will perfect it. I will not take the vexation out of marriage. I may even increase it, but it will turn out wonderfully,' as they only know who have tasted it.' " [112]

Luther was fond of the saying: "Let the wife make her husband glad to come home, and let him make her sorry to see him leave. [113]

BIBLIOGRAPHY

There are two full length biographies of Katherine von Bora.

Albrecht Thoma, *Katharina von Bora* (Berlin, 1900). Thorough and documented but with references of necessity to older editions of Luther's works.

Ernst Kroker, *Katharina von Bora* (Leipzig, 1906). Careful scholarship by the editor of Luther's *Table Talk* in the Weimar edition, but unfortunately not documented. Kroker has also an excellent article: "Luthers Werbung um Katharina von Bora," *Lutherstudien* (Weimar, 1917), 140-50.

Heinrich Boehmer, "Luthers Ehe," *Lutherjahrbuch* VII (1925), 40-69 is detailed on Luther's marriage.

Ratzeberger refers to *Die handschriftliche Geschichte Ratzeberger's*, ed. Chr. G. Neudecker (Jena, 1850).

Schottenloher refers to Karl Schottenloher, *Bibliographie der deutschen Geschichte*.

NOTES

Abbreviations:
ADB *Allgemeine deutsche Biographie.*
BR Luther's *Briefwechsel* in the Weimar edition.
EA Erlangen edition of Luther's Works.
EE *Erasmi Epistolae,* ed. P. S. Allen.
TR *Tischreden,* edition of Luther's *Table Talk* in the Weimar edition.
WA Weimar edition of Luther's Works.

1. Thoma and Kroker. BR spring 1525
2. Beatus Rhenanus, *Briefwechsel* p. 319
3. BR 782
4. BR 3676
5. Boehmer, *Luther's Ehe.*
6. TR 3177
7. BR 426
8. BR 800
9. BR 883
10. TR 881
11. BR 900 and TR 623
12. BR 911 and TR 2129a
13. BR 892
14. BR 900
15. *Ibid.*
16. TR 49
17. BR 1032
18. BR 1043
19. BR 1908
20. BR 3253
21. TR 7264b, 2772, 146
22. TR 980, 1352, 2458
23. Thoma 182
24. TR 1657
25. *Ibid.*
26. BR 890, 892
27. Thoma 57
28. Enders VI, No. 1368, pp. 334 f.
29. TR 3504
30. BR 1501
31. TR 1656
32. TR 5117
33. BR 615-7
34. TR 2731b
35. TR 5181
36. BR 999
37. BR 1009
38. BR 1844 & 2106

39. BR 394, 1040 TR 5202
40. BR 1007
41. BR 952, 1252
42. BR 1757
43. Thoma 177, Kroker 233
44. Ratzeberger 61 f.
45. TR 1557
46. Melanchthon, *Vita Lutheri* (1564) 12 verso
47. Thoma 176
48. TR 4531
49. BR 1902
50. Kroker 218
51. TR 4569
52. Thoma 71 and 106
53. See ADB & Schottenloher
54. Thoma 126-7
55. Kroker 194 and Thoma 71
56. Kroker 89
57. *Ibid.* 102-7
58. BR 2234
59. BR 3146
60. BR 3519
61. BR 3056
62. BR 932
63. BR 1067
64. BR 1160
65. BR 1303
66. BR 3129
67. BR 1183, 1303
68. BR 1303
69. BR 1415
70. BR 1417
71. BR 1886
72. TR 2754b
73. TR 1631
74. TR 1237
75. BR 1997
76. BR 2226
77. BR 3300

78. TR 1004
79. TR 2867b
80. TR 5494, 2590b
81. BR 1595, 1582
82. TR 5494, p. 191
83. TR 4860
84. BR 2589
85. TR 4081
86. TR 1975 & 1978
87. TR 5987
88. Ps. 7:8 TR 2787b, 6280
89. TR 5659
90. BR 2267
91. TR 5008
92. TR 3835
93. TR 1033, 2754b
94. EE, 1500
95. TR 5069
96. Thoma 220
97. TR 1461
98. TR 1449
99. TR 798c
100. TR 1626
101. BR 1908
102. BR 2130
103. BR 3519
104. BR 3670
105. BR 4139
106. BR 4195
107. BR 4203
108. BR 4207
109. Thoma
110. TR 250
111. EA2, III, 513 f.
112. Sermons on John 2:1-11 in Erwin Mülhaupt, *Dr. Martin Luthers Evangelienauslegung* (Göttingen, 1954) IV.
113. TR 6320

2.

Ursula of Münsterberg
(Born 1491-5, died after 1534)

The case of Ursula of Münsterberg, already mentioned as a refugee with the Luthers, gives us a fuller picture than does the flight of Katherine von Bora of what was involved in leaving the cloister. The escape of Ursula is the more fascinating because we have not only her own account but also the testimony of the sisters left behind, who were examined one by one by a visitation committee that recorded their answers verbatim. We also have the correspondence between the prince who gave her asylum and the princes who demanded her extradition.

She was the granddaughter of King George Podiebrad of Bohemia and, on her mother's side, the cousin of Duke George and his brother Heinrich. During her very early years, after the death of her parents, she lived with them, being cared for by her aunt, their mother. Somewhere between the ages of nine and fifteen, the limits for admission, she was placed in the convent of Mary Magdalene the Penitent.

We have her own account of why she found the life distasteful, quite apart from any doctrinal considerations. She was frail in health and could not stand getting up in the middle of the night for vigils and then spending the day in singing and reading. The prescribed readings in medieval works of piety and theology were to her entirely unedifying, and the fasts were more than her frame could endure.[1] She was irked by an atmosphere of legalistic restraint. Twenty-four times a year she was required to

45

take the sacrament of the Lord's body. But such a sacrament, said she, requires a hungering soul, and of what profit is it if the heart be not ready?[2] The prioress, distinguished for her efficiency and strictness, may have been the less inclined to be indulgent, because Ursula did not bring with her a sufficient endowment to cover her expenses. We have two of Ursula's letters to her cousin, the princess Margaretha of Anhalt, the one thanking her for a gift, the other requesting six *florin* to defray the extra expenses incurred through a sickness. When Ursula breached the regulations the sister called her an apostate, a heretic, a violator of her vow, unworthy to live on earth.[3]

They were not so far wrong when they suggested heresy, for two chaplains in turn were assigned to the sisters, each preaching Lutheran doctrine. They were appointed without the knowledge and consent of Duke George, Luther's intractable opponent and the ruler of all ducal Saxony, but apparently with the connivance of his younger brother Heinrich, who in a subordinate role, administered the little town of Freiberg and the adjacent nunnery. With his consent the Lutheran chaplain was appointed. Duke George protested that he should have been consulted and predicted trouble, but did not countermand the appointment,[4] presumably because he did not know but merely surmised the leanings of the chaplain. When after two years the chaplain died, another of like mind was installed.[5] One of the sisters, testifying later, declared that this man was assigned at the request of Ursula of Münsterberg and through the intervention of the Duchess Katherine, the wife of Duke Heinrich.[6]

This is a very significant disclosure. Duke Heinrich and his wife, being the underlings of the older brother George, were not in a position to engage in overt obstruction of his policies. But when George died in 1539 and Heinrich succeeded, he proceeded at once to Lutheranize the whole region at the instigation of his wife Katherine. We have a few other glimpses of Katherine's undeviating Lutheranism. When Duke George lost his son and realized that the succession would go to Heinrich and after him to Moritz, the son of Heinrich and Katherine, George set about to get the young man married to a sound Catholic. Katherine warned her son of the Duke's machinations, and he married the daughter of the Protestant Philip of Hesse. And when nine years later Moritz had succeeded his father, Katherine besought him to allow no "devilish tares" in his vineyard, meaning of course popery.[7] The above revelations make it apparent that she was carrying on clandestine activity in the cloister of Mary Magdalene the Penitent already in 1528.

We have a further illustration of her tactics in the case of the infiltration of Luther's books. One of the sisters testified that at the instance of Ursula, the duchess had sent works of Luther to Freiberg to be bound and smuggled into the convent. When this was reported to the duchess, she denied that she had sent the books to be bound. The sister responsible for the allegation was interrogated again and confessed an error. Sole responsibility was placed on Ursula, but how could she have had Luther's books bound in Freiberg? The duchess in her denial admitted that she had corresponded with the sisters, and she and her husband had done their best to fulfill their requests. One of the requests was that of Ursula for the Lutheran chaplain.[8]

We learn more from the sisters of what the chaplain said and did and of what books were smuggled in and how. What did the preacher preach? He preached that good works are hypocrisy, that life in the cloister is worthless, and that we are saved by faith alone. Good works are the fruit of faith and are without merit. He railed at the bishops and decried the cult of the saints.[9] What he did in private may well have made more of an impact than his sermons. He had talks with Ursula and conversed often with the subprioress, Martha von Schönberg, through the window of the choir, for as long as two hours. Her sister Barbara was also addicted to the new doctrine. The new prioress, Katharina Freibergin, had a room near the gate through which she allowed the chaplain to enter and lodged him in the room next to her own. They had long conversations,[10] presumably after the manner of Pyramis and Thisbe.

As for Luther's books, the only one specifically mentioned was the *Postila* from Easter to Advent, described by one of the sisters as a "right poisonous and damaging book." [11] The volumes were smuggled in through the window in the choir. But of course some one had to be on the outside to push them through.

Philip, the barber who tonsured the sisters, was incriminated; so also were the overseer, his wife, and the fire tender. Ursula herself had taken advantage of the excitement attendant upon a previous visitation to smuggle in a corn sack full of subversive publications. The recipient at the window was the subprioress, who had the works copied.[12]

The sisters were frank in admitting that the impact of all these infiltrations had been great. One of the conservatives estimated that of the 77 nuns, one third were Catholic, one third Lutheran, and one third wavering. She thought only 15 were entirely sound, though another sister set the figure at 20.[13] The question was put whether some of the remaining sisters were restless. "Oh yes, and if scolded would say, 'All right, then I'll leave.'"[14] One sister declared that she had never kept her vows because she did not know what she had vowed. "If the books are taken away, I will not stay, because only the Word brings us to God." She wept. "If you knew what anguish of spirit I have gone through these last few days."

One sister said that she had not taken the vows willingly and was sorry she ever had. Her mother wanted her to wear the crown of a virgin that she might be able to intercede for her in heaven forever, and if she refused she would be cut off from any support on earth. She would gladly go to another convent if there were an evangelical preacher. If this were denied, she had a breadknife in her bosom, and she'd use it on herself in front of them all.[15]

Such was the state of the convent. Evidently Ursula was successful in clandestine subversion. Why then did she decide to leave? Because, said she, the spirit of contention had become unbearable.[16] How was it possible to leave? This was not too difficult because the new prioress was so lax that she even let the sisters chant in their cells. Her ideal was that of the Cluniacs in the early Middle Ages, who far from being sequestered became entertainers extraordinary. She would let anyone come into the convent, men, women and children. A family nearby with children would stroll in even at meal times. The keys were left where anyone could pick them up. Even with everything locked, a sister testified, the convent was not escape-proof. The

Frederick the Wise and John

prioress not only let the world in but went out to it. She herself would visit the secular city and took sisters to visit relatives. On Saturdays some of the lay sisters were allowed to go to market.

The regular nuns, however, were not allowed to wander off without supervision, and escape did require some subterfuge. Ursula frequently absented herself to play with the children nearby and often busied herself in the garden so the sisters would not find it unusual if she were not in her cell. On the evening of October 6, 1528, between the hours of six and seven, some pushing was heard at the cloister door but nothing was thought of it until in the morning a veil was found near the garden door through which flour was brought in. Then it was discovered that Ursula had escaped with two companions. They went first to the pastor at Leisnig and then to Wittenberg, arriving on October 16th.[17]

Then followed a correspondence between the Dukes George and Heinrich on the one hand and the Lutheran Elector John on the other. The communications may be summarized. All were written in the year 1528.

October 10. George and Heinrich to John: "Our cousin, Ursula, and two other nuns have left the convent. They were for a few days at the parsonage at Leisnig. We suspect that they are in your territory and beg you to send them back." [18]

October 13. John in reply: "We assure you that we shall do our best to find a Christian and proper solution for this matter. We will send our official to Wittenberg and Torgau to find out what has happened." [19]

October 18. Ursula to John: "Your official has arrived and told me that I am not to leave your territory. I assure you I do not need to be admonished not to leave your territory, and I am quite willing to relate all the anxiety, danger, and misery I have experienced in my escape. I have already written my apology. I ask nothing of this world and were I in this hour to stand before the judgment seat of God I would die of joy." [20]

November 6. John to George and Heinrich: "The nuns are at Wittenberg. We suggest that you send some one to Wittenberg to inquire of our kinswoman and her two companions why they left." [21]

November 11. George and Heinrich to John: "If we send some one to Wittenberg to inquire of them, the whole Lutheran synagogue will rise in their defense and we shall be involved in an interminable wrangle, which is not to our liking. We intend to stand by the Christian practice of our forefathers. Send them back and punish those who abetted their escape." [22]

November 20. John in reply: "If you are not disposed to send someone to Wittenberg to confer with the ladies, we are not disposed to send them back." [23]

November 27. Heinrich to George: "Since John won't send them back we've done our bit and we are excused before God Almighty. [And no doubt Heinrich would be much better excused before his wife if the case were dropped]." [24]

November 27. George and Heinrich to John: "Our concern is to save the soul of our kinswoman, but since you will not return her, there is nothing more we can do, but we beg you to keep the matter quiet. Please don't let her publish her apology, as we hear she intends to do. It may upset many of the sisters and cause others to embrace a godless life." [25]

December 7. John replied: "We would like you to know that in our school at Wittenberg nothing is preached but the pure word of God and the gospel. It is a Christian synagogue. We assure you that we had no hand in her escape, and we do not know whether she is still in Wittenberg. As for your request that her defense be not published, before the arrival of your letter we had already received copies of the printed apology. We have read it and see in it nothing offensive, but only that which would afford comfort and help to those in like bondage. In case you have not seen it we are sending you two copies." [26]

The tract appeared with a preface by Luther.[27] In it Ursula defends herself and her companions.[28] Here are her words:

We were constrained by conscience that we might escape the inescapable judgment of God upon all who reject his eternal and true Word. We have not acted lightly nor without consideration. Our defense will not impress those who take offense at the crucified Christ, whom we confess to be the power and the wisdom of God (1 Cor. 1:23-24). The reasons for our leaving are the texts: "Go ye into all the world and proclaim the Gospel" (Mark 16:5); "God so loved the world that he gave his only begotten Son that whosoever believeth on him should not perish but have eternal life" (John 3:16); "The just shall live by faith" (Heb. 2:4); "I am the way, the truth and the life" (John 14:6); "He who does not believe is damned" (Mark 16:16). You see that our salvation rests only on faith. Our consciences have been greatly troubled and our flesh corrupted. The only hope lies in faith. By baptism we have been received into the kingdom of Christ. To say that the monastic vow is a second baptism and washes away sins, as we have heard from the pulpit, is blasphemy against God, as if the blood of Christ were not enough to wash away all sins. We are married to Christ and to seek to be saved through another is adultery. The three monastic vows are the work of men's hands. There is only one way to relieve our consciences and that is to make a clean break. We have suffered such torments of spirit that we could no longer hold on. Who can withstand God's wrath? We had hoped for relief from the princes. None came. We had hoped for help from the preacher, but we were told not to heed what he said. This has been going on for two years. We are as sheep without pasture save through Christ the Shepherd. Our salvation is not so light a thing that we should sell it for human favor, for we know that we have here no abiding place (Heb. 13:14). We must go out to him who was crucified before the gate (Matt. 27:31-32) and bear his shame. We await the time when the same crucified and rejected Christ will come again in the glory of his Father (Matt. 16:27) and we trust we shall not be among those to whom he will say, "I know you not" (Matt. 7:22-23). Dear friends, brothers and sisters in Christ, these are the reasons we are ready to let go body, life, honor, and goods.

Ursula forfeited a secure abiding place, and when and where she died we do not know. In the cloister the prioress confessed that she was old, weak, and weary and would gladly be relieved.[29] She was, by death. The sisters then elected Barbara Schönberg,[30] one of the leaders of the Lutheran sympathizers. One may find it very surprising that she should have been willing to remain, but one is to bear in mind that Luther did not demand that all leave the cloisters, only that those who remained should not think thereby to contribute to their salvation. A bar was placed across the window in the choir.

BIBLIOGRAPHY

Biography of Ursula.

Hubert Ermisch, "Herzogin Ursula von Münsterberg," *Neues Archiv f. sächische Gesch. u. Alterthumskunde* III (1882), 290-333.

Biography of Katherine, the wife of Duke Heinrich.

Karl von Weber, "Zur Lebensgeschichte der Herzogin Katharina von Sachsen, Gemahlin Herzog Heinrichs des Frommen," *Archiv f.d.* Sächs. Gesch. VI (1868), 1-35.

Ursula's Apology.

Frau Ursulen Herzogin zu Münsterberg, christliche Ursachen des verlassen Klosters zu Freiberg. Luthers *Werke* Walch 2d. ed. XIX, No. 178.

Luther's preface. *Weimarer Ausgabe* XXVI, 623-

Correspondence and Records of the Visitation

"Urkundenbuch der Stadt Freiberg in Sachsen," ed. Hubert Ermisch, *Codex Diplomaticus Saxoniae Regiae* (Leipzig, 1883).

Documents 702 through 714.

NOTES

1. Walch, sec. 60.
2. *Ibid.*, sec. 48.
3. *Ibid.*, sec. 62.
4. *Urkund.* Nos. 702, 703.
5. *Ermisch* p. 301.
6. *Urkund.* No. 714, sec. 9, p. 490.
7. Weber.
8. *Urkund.* No. 715.
9. *Ibid.*, No. 714, sec. 8, pp. 489-90.
10. *Ibid.*, No. 714, sec. 6.
11. *Ibid.*, No. 714, sec. 5.
12. *Ibid.*, sec. 6.
13. *Ibid.*, sec. 15.
14. *Ibid.*, sec. 5.
15. *Ibid.*, sec. 5, p. 488 note.
16. Walch sec. 50.
17. Ermisch p. 305.
18. *Urkund.* No. 705.
19. *Ibid.*, No. 706.
20. *Ibid.*, No. 707.
21. *Ibid.*, No. 708.
22. *Ibid.*, No. 709.
23. *Ibid.*, No. 710.
24. *Ibid.*, No. 711.
25. *Ibid.*, No. 712.
26. *Ibid.*, No. 713.
27. Luther, *Weimarer Ausgabe* XXVI, 623 ff.
28. Walch 2 XIX, No. 178, pp. 1694-1723.
29. *Urkund.* No. 714, sec. 18.
30. *Ibid.*, No. 718.

3.

Katherine Zell
(1497/8-1562)

Katherine Zell described herself as "a splinter from the rib of that blessed man Matthew Zell." [1] He would have called her at least two ribs. He referred to her as "Mein Helfer." [2] The first help she gave him was when he was under excommunication by the bishop for having married her. Opponents of the Reformation circulated the tale that she had caught him with the maid and that, when she protested, he had thrashed her. Katherine published a refutation in which she said: "I have never had a maid. I have had the help only of a little girl, too young for that sort of thing, and as for thrashing me, my husband and I have never had an unpleasant 15 minutes. We could have no greater honor than to die rejected of men and from two crosses to speak to each other words of comfort." She not only refutes this particular slander but makes a vigorous defense of clerical marriage and denounces the "celibate" priest who gets seven women pregnant at the same time. "You remind me," she says, "that the Apostle Paul told women to be silent in church. I would remind you of the word of this same apostle that in Christ there is no longer male nor female and of the prophecy of Joel: 'I will pour forth my spirit upon all flesh and your sons and your *daughters* will prophesy.' I do not pretend to be John the Baptist rebuking the Pharisees. I do not claim to be Nathan upbraiding David. I aspire only to be Balaam's ass, castigating his master." [3]

A defense of clerical marriage was very much in order in Strasbourg in the year 1523. Seven priests including Katherine's husband were under excommunication for having married. The man who had taken the lead in this matter was Martin Butzer. He was not the first evangelical minister at Strasbourg—that honor falls to Zell. Butzer came already married. An ex-Dominican, he had taken to wife an ex-nun, Elizabeth Silberstein. Cast out in every quarter, Butzer and his wife had taken refuge in his native Strasbourg. Zell set him up in his own house to give lectures on the Epistle to the Romans and later succeeded in placing him in a parish. Butzer began urging marriage upon his colleagues and even endeavored to find a partner for his fellow priest, Wolfgang Capito.

To that end Butzer addressed "The noble, honorable, Christian Lady, Ottilie von Hohenheim" of Basel. He informed her that marriage was not a necessity for many priests as a remedy for sin, since they were capable of continence. For the sake of those not so gifted, however, those who were capable of celibacy were duty bound to render the marriage of the clergy reputable. This they could not do without partners. All of the eligibles for Capito had been reviewed and none was deemed more suitable than Ottilie. "Your deportment hitherto has been exemplary. You will crown your witness by assuming a reviled and crucified marriage. I beseech you in the name of Christ, crucified and accursed." But Ottilie did not feel that this was her cross.

Capito did succeed in marrying a daughter of one of the chief magistrates of Strasbourg.[4] Her father's consent to such a union shows the degree to which the members of the government supported the reform. Without this aid the reformers would never have been able to withstand the bishop.

Another priest married. Anthony Firn married his concubine. The officiating priest was Matthew Zell, and he took advantage of the occasion to deliver a homily on the validity of clerical marriage. "Hitherto it has been the custom," said he, "for the minister at a wedding to say, 'If any know just cause why these two may not lawfully be joined together let him now speak. . . .' This is a wholesome practice, but there are those who come forward with very unjust causes, claiming that priests should not marry. Such a union is not an innovation but simply a return to the word of God who instituted marriage at the creation, and now, because we have not heeded God's ordinance, we are worse than Sodom and Gomorrah. Wherefore, dear brother Anthony, fear not. Blessed are you because this day you are breaking the power of Antichrist. If you are banished or put to death this cannot hurt you, because you are doing what God has commanded, and many more brothers, God willing, will follow your example, who until now have been intimidated. Antichrist has established his kingdom by lies. Let us establish the truth that Christ may reign forever and ever." [5]

The next priest to follow the example of Anthony Firn, after only three weeks (December 3, 1523), was this same Matthew Zell. The vows were administered by Martin Butzer.[6] The bride was no previous concubine, but the intrepid Katherine Schütz, who had been delivered from dire anguish of spirit by reading the tracts of Martin Luther.[7] On the occasion of her marriage Luther sent her a letter of congratulation.[8] She was 25 or 26 years old and her husband was 20 years older. This union brought the number of married priests to four. Three more followed. The bishop then excommunicated them all. As a group they defended their action to their superior.[9] Katherine sent him a letter which admittedly "smoked," [10] and in addition brought out a tract that the bishop complained about to the council, calling it abusive.[11] The council forbade like fulminations, but at the same time upheld the married priests.

In consequence, until 1529 Catholic and Evangelical services took place side by side in the cathedral of Strasbourg. The bishop's appointee preached from the high pulpit, Zell from a pulpit improvised by his parishioners and trundled on wheels to the center of the nave, where he addressed the auditors to the number of about 3,000.[12]

Since Katherine and her husband were so completely a team we must first glance at the stand taken by the husband. One cannot say, as some insinuated, that he was led by apron strings, since he had been a vigorous reformer before he married. He had come to Strasbourg three years earlier in 1520 when he was about 42, and was assigned to the staff of the cathedral with

Church of St. Thomas at Strasbourg

the special office of *poenitentiarius,* authorized to levy fines and grant or withhold absolution for sins. In the discharge of this office he was deemed by the bishop and his treasurer to be egregiously lax. Zell would absolve peasants without a fine for eating butter on fast days, and he would not levy a fee on a woman who came for purification after a miscarriage. Why did she need to be purified or absolved? [13] While the bishop grumbled, the cathedral chapter often gave Zell support.

Worse was to come. In the 1520s the tracts of Luther were circulating, and Zell's sermons betrayed their influence. He was charged with a long list of heresies to which he made a lengthy reply, the first manifesto of the reform in Strasbourg. "We are told," he began, "to make no innovations but to wait for the decisions of a general council. If the apostles had waited for a general council of the Jews to endorse Christ, they would have waited a very long time. I am accused of having read Luther. To be sure I have. How is a shepherd to know where to pasture his sheep if he has not tried out the pastures? If Luther is guilty of some errors, that does not make him a heretic. Which of the church fathers was ever free from all error? Men say that Luther's language is too rough. I agree, but the question is not whether he is rough or gentle but whether he is right. He is being read all over Germany and am I alone to be forbidden to read him? I follow Luther in so far as he follows the Scripture. . . . What a shame to be ashamed of the eternal Word of God! A noble work it would be if the bishop himself were to preach in his own cathedral instead of spending his time with falcons and hounds. . . . Scripture, Scripture, my Lords, I say, not the iron sword. Send out preachers. If you do not, they will come anyway. And though you issue a thousand bulls against them, though you use up the whole Schwarzwald to burn them, though you scatter them over the earth, it will do you no good. If you root them out, from their roots will grow others." [14]

This was the man to whom Katherine Zell was a "Helfer." Throughout his lifetime she was able to devote herself almost exclusively to this role, because of the deaths of two infants and the arrival of no more. She was prone to think of her childlessness as a mark of divine displeasure over her sins.[15] Her spirit

Matthew Zell

was frequently overcast by a sense of guilt, though one who did not know the secrets of her heart might well have numbered her among the saints. The doctrine of justification by faith did not bring her an unbroken assurance any more than it did Luther. Both were subject to depressions and recurrent wrestlings with the angel. Perhaps she was thereby all the more impelled to engage so unfailingly in works of mercy. Her days and nights were abundantly filled with such ministries.

Strasbourg became a city of refuge because it was a "free city," not immediately under the control of the imperial house of Austria, bent upon enforcing the Edict of Worms against Luther and his followers. Neighboring towns did not enjoy such immunity. At Kensingen in Breisgau the minister was forced to leave. One hundred and fifty men of the parish accompanied him for several miles. When they returned, the gates were closed and guarded by the troops of Austria. One man was caught and executed. The rest fled to the river and secured passage to Strasbourg.[16]

Katherine bedded 80 in the parsonage and fed 60 for three weeks, while finding provision elsewhere for the remainder. She also wrote a letter, published as a tract, to the wives left behind in Kensingen. "To my fellow sisters in Christ, day and night I pray God that he may increase your faith that you forget not his invincible Word. 'My thoughts are not your thoughts, saith the Lord' (Isa. 55:8). 'Whom I make alive I kill' (Deut. 32:39). The Lord would wean you from the world that you may rely only on him. Has he not told us that we must 'forsake father and mother, wife and child'? (Luke 14:26). 'He who denies me him will I deny in the presence of my father,' (Matt. 10:33). 'Those who would reign with me must also suffer with me' (2 Tim. 2:12)."

"Had I been chosen," said Katherine, "to suffer as you women I would account myself happier than all the magistrates of Strasbourg at the fair with their necklaces and golden chains. Remember the word of the Lord in the prophet Isaiah (54:8) 'In overflowing wrath for a moment I hid my face from you, but with everlasting love I will have compassion on you.' 'Can a woman forget her suckling child? Even these may forget, but I

Den leyden-
den Chriſtglaubigen
weybern der gemain zů
Kenzingen meinen
mit ſchweſtern in
Chriſto Jheſu
zů handen.

❦   ❦

❦

Katherina Schützin

M. D. xxiiij.

Katherine Zell's tract for the
women of Kensingen

will not forget you' (Isa. 49:15). Are not these golden words? Faith is not faith which is not tried. 'Blessed are those that mourn.' Pray, then, for those who persecute you that you 'may be perfect as your Father in heaven is perfect' (Matt. 5:4, 44, 48)." [17]

A calamity more dire befell the city not long thereafter. The Peasants' War broke out in 1525. Contingents from different parts of Germany were clustered around Strasbourg. The ministers Capito and Zell, accompanied by Katherine, visited their encampments and pleaded for the avoidance of violence.[18] The pleas went unheeded and the peasants were massacred. Survivors, together with the wives and children of the slaughtered, flocked into Strasbourg to the number of 3,000. This influx put a tremendous strain on the economy of a city of only 25,000.

Strasbourg, at the moment, was in the throes of revamping the whole system of poor relief. Luther taught that almsgiving did not facilitate entry into heaven. In consequence he proposed to suppress begging. Those able to work should work, and those unable should be supported by the community. Strasbourg was introducing this practice but extended the relief only to citizens. Here now were 3,000 who were not citizens. The problem was tackled by two persons. The first was Lucas Hackfurt, an ardent member of the municipal directors of relief and, incidentally, at the time an Anabaptist. The second was Katherine Zell. Presumably, since Hackfurt was involved, the city must have relaxed in some measure the rule limiting aid to citizens. The bulk of the refugees were lodged en masse in the Franciscan church, but much of the feeding and housing must have been handled privately, and here the lead would fall to Katherine. The emergency lasted for half a year until the war subsided and the families were able to return to their farms. Out of this experience came two lessons: that Strasbourg in times of persecution abroad and famine nearby must enlarge her bounty, and that congestion of refugees in one lodging was a hazard to health, and distribution in homes was to be preferred.[19] The role played by Katherine throws light on the remark of Butzer, "She is a trifle imperious." [20]

The Reformation in Strasbourg was assuming a form midway

between the Lutheran in Germany and the Zwinglian in Switzerland. The big difference concerned the interpretation of the Lord's Supper. Luther understood the words "This is my body" to mean that Christ is physically present in the sacrament. Zwingli declared that in this sentence the word *is* means *signifies*. The rite is a memorial to Christ's death. Butzer and the Strasbourgers believed in a spiritual presence. The matter assumed political proportions in 1529 when Philip of Hesse sought to unite the Germans and the Swiss in a league of mutual defense. To that end he invited theologians from the three areas to assemble at his capital city, Marburg. Zwingli of Zürich and Oecolampadius of Basel passed on their way through Strasbourg and were entertained by the Zells. "For 14 days I was their cook and maid," [21] said Katherine.

Butzer went with the group to Marburg. The theologians failed to reach agreement. Philip of Hesse suggested that they practice intercommunion nevertheless. Luther was so inclined until Melanchthon pointed out to him that to come to terms with the Swiss would close the door to the Catholics.[22] When the news reached Strasbourg that Luther had declined, Katherine sent him a remonstrance pleading that love is above all else. "Yes," replied Luther, "except where God's Word is at stake." [23]

The entertainment of distinguished personages fell more than once to Katherine. In 1538 Calvin was in Strasbourg, having been expelled from Geneva. He was frightfully upset when the Strasbourg ministers gave a letter of confidence to Pierre Caroli, a very vacillating person of whose unreliability Calvin had had painful experience. Unwilling to sign the letter and loath to dissent from his ministerial hosts, he took his distress to the magistrate Jacob Sturm, who brought him to Butzer, by whom he was taken to the home of the ever reconciling Zells. There, as he later confessed, Calvin blew up disgracefully until he was mollified. How much Katherine had to do with the cooling we do not know. She was the hostess.[24]

While the Protestants were seeking to close their ranks, negotiations were also in progress in the hope of reunion with the Catholics. A preliminary interchange among the theologians of both confessions took place in 1540 at Hagenau near Strasbourg.

At one time or another Katherine entertained 30 of the delegates coming from Wittenberg, Saxony, Hesse, Nürnberg, Swabia, and other areas.[25] Katherine and her husband were at other times the guests. Together they traveled 600 miles in 1538 to visit Luther and Melanchthon at Wittenberg. Other trips were made together to Switzerland, Constance, Swabia, Nürnberg, and the Palatinate.[26]

The years 1529 to 1533 were very trying to the reformers of Strasbourg because of the great influx of a veritable swarm of sectaries.[27] The reformers objected to their views but even more to their behavior. They were secessionists who threatened to split the reformed community. Grave consequences might well ensue because even the free city of Strasbourg might be attacked by the imperial forces if the reformers were too drastic or anarchic. Most of the outstanding leaders of what is sometimes called the left wing of the Reformation or the radical Reformation were in Strasbourg at this time: Carlstadt, Denck, Haetzer, Marbeck, Hofmann, Servetus, Schwenckfeld, and Sebastian Franck. The ministers were in favor of persuasion rather than coercion, but when persuasion failed they had recourse to banishment and imprisonment and condoned even death, though there were only two executions and these for reasons other than belief. Zell, among the reformers, was the most liberal. "Any one," said he, "who acknowledges Christ as the true Son of God and the sole Savior of mankind is welcome at my board." [28] Behind Matthew Zell was Katherine, who was suspected of giving the pitch.[29]

She secured permission from the council to visit Melchior Hofmann in prison.[30] He was one of the most troublesome of the sectaries, who had come to Strasbourg because of a prophecy that he would be imprisoned there for six months and then, at the coming of the Lord, lead the 144,000 saints in the slaughter of the ungodly. Only the first part of the prophecy was fulfilled and at that not exactly. He languished in prison not for six months but for 10 years, until his death. Katherine's visit implied no approval of his views. She visited anyone in prison. An entry in the record of the council grants her permission "to visit a poor prisoner under sentence of death." [31] Neither did she endorse the theology of Michael Servetus, but when he was executed in Geneva she spoke of him with great compassion.[32]

There was, however, one dissident for whom she had a genuine sympathy. He was not a deliberate secessionist, though his attitude made for secession. This was Caspar Schwenckfeld, a Silesian nobleman of gracious demeanor and courteous manner. He taught that Christ's body on the altar is his celestial body and that a moratorium should be declared on the Lord's Supper until it could be observed without contention. Butzer claimed that Schwenckfeld imposed on Katherine with his courtly manners and saintly deportment.[33] After his retirement from Strasbourg she corresponded with him to the end and on occasion defended him stoutly.[34]

The Zells were sometimes at odds on matters of church unity with Butzer and the other ministers, who wanted organic unity through theological agreement. The Zells were concerned rather for brotherliness despite theological disagreement. Butzer felt that Matthew lagged because Katherine dragged.[35] Matthew devoted himself to composing squabbles. For example, the congregation at Schaffhausen was wrangling over whether the chalice should be of silver or gold, and whether the bread in the sacrament should be a wafer or a chunk broken each time from the loaf.[36] A dispute arose at Strasbourg over whether to continue the custom of having godparents at baptisms. Among the Catholics the sponsors contracted spiritual relations so that their children could not marry the godchildren without dispensations. The new marriage ordinance at Strasbourg had abolished the whole system of spiritual consanguinity.[37] The Zells feared nevertheless that superstition would linger. Butzer argued that the assumption by friends of responsibility for the religious upbringing of children was in itself wholesome and should be continued. The Zells did not disrupt the unity of Strasbourg over a matter of no great consequence.[38]

Matthew Zell died in January of 1548. After the eulogy by Butzer, Katherine delivered an address,[39] thereby feeding the allegation that she aspired to be "Doctor Katrina." "I am not usurping the office of preacher or apostle," she said. "I am like the dear Mary Magdalene, who with no thought of being an apostle, came to tell the disciples that she had encountered the risen Lord."

After having braced herself for this ordeal, Katherine collapsed. She was persuaded to go to Basel to stay for a while with Pastor Myconius. Butzer, who had on occasion spoken somewhat slightingly of Katherine, now wrote to her host, "The widow of our Zell, a godly and saintly woman, comes to you that perchance she may find some solace for her grief. She is human. How does the heavenly Father humble those endowed with great gifts! Her zeal is incredible for Christ's lowliest and afflicted. She knows and searches the mysteries of Christ. Because she is resentful of their dispensation, she heaps upon herself frightful reproaches. She is all too human. Truly this is a trial from the Lord and it is astounding. Comfort her patiently for the love of her husband, a sincere and faithful servant of Christ, even if, like the rest of us, he did not perfectly fulfill all that he might." [40]

From Basel Katherine went to Zürich for a visit in the home of the distinguished Hebraist, Conrad Pellikan. Back in Strasbourg on January 9, 1549,[41] she sent him a letter of thanks which speedily broke into a lament because of the introduction of the *Interim*. This term was applied to a compromise adjustment of the dispute between Catholics and Protestants to be imposed by the emperor during the interim pending a definitive solution by the Council of Trent. The compromise granted to the Protestants only that the Mass might be celebrated in both kinds and clerical marriages already contracted would be recognized. Katherine informed Pellikan that the Mass had been reinstated in the whole land of Württemberg, in Ulm, Augsburg, and other places. In some cases Spanish priests had been installed. "We do not know what is in store for Strasbourg. Jacob Sturm [the magistrate] came to see me so choked that he could not speak. . . . I am sending your wife and your daughter-in-law each a pound of flax for spinning shawls. I would have sent more if I had had a carrier. I have been allowed to keep the parsonage which belongs to the parish. I take any one who comes. It is always full. I don't know how long I can keep it. [She was permitted for nearly three years.] "One thing I have asked of the Lord. That will I seek after, that I may dwell in the house of the Lord' to behold my noble husband with all the saints in the vision of God."

She was not long in finding out what the *Interim* would mean for Strasbourg. The Mass was to be restored in the cathedral and in all the churches save three, where evangelical preaching would be allowed provided it were not controversial. The two leading ministers, Butzer and Fagius, were exiled. They prepared to go to England whither they had been invited by Cranmer, the Archbishop of Canterbury. But they overstayed the stipulated time for departure by three weeks. During that period they were hidden by Katherine Zell.[42] They left behind them two gold pieces for Katherine and from England sent a letter of thanks. She responded that whereas in England evidently the harvest was plentiful, the laborers few, in Strasbourg the laborers were plentiful but the harvest scant. As for the gold pieces: "You put me to shame to think that you would leave money for me, as if I would take a *heller* from you poor pilgrims and my revered ministers. I wish I could have done better for you but my Matthew has taken all my gaiety with him. I intended to return the two gold pieces with this letter, as Joseph put the money in the sack of his brother, but a refugee minister has just come in with five children, and the wife of another who saw her husband beheaded before her eyes. I divided the one gold piece between them as a present from you. The other I enclose. You will need it." [43]

Katherine's health began to fail. She suffered from dropsy and several letters were written from the baths.[44] But her incredible zeal did not flag. In 1558 one of the chief magistrates of Strasbourg, Felix Ambrosiaster, was stricken with leprosy or whatever was thus diagnosed. He was required to leave his family and live beyond the walls in a quarantined institution. He petitioned that instead he might be allowed to live in a little hut with a garden. Permission was granted, but his daughter was not given leave to attend him.[45] There was one who visited frequently, however, and that was Katherine Zell. For him she wrote a little treatise of consolation which was published.[46] Here is an abridgement.

"My dear Lord Felix, since we have known each other for a full 30 years I am moved to visit you in your long and frightful illness. I have not been able to come as often as I would like, because of the load here for the poor and the sick, but you have been ever in my thoughts. We have often talked of how you have been stricken, cut off from rank, office, from your wife and friends, from all dealings with the world which recoils from your loathsome disease and leaves you in utter loneliness. At first you were bitter and utterly cast down till God gave you strength and patience, and now you are able to thank him that out of love he has taught you to bear the cross. Because I know that your illness weighs upon you daily and may easily cause you again to fall into despair and rebelliousness, I have gathered some passages which may make your yoke light in the spirit. though not in the flesh. I have written meditations on the 51st Psalm: 'Have mercy upon me, O God, according to thy loving-kindness,' and the 130th, 'Out of the depths have I cried unto thee, O Lord.' And then on the Lord's Prayer and the Creed."

Here in brief is her meditation on the Lord's Prayer.

"*Our Father, who art in heaven.* He is called not Lord or Judge, but Father. And since through his Son we are born again we may call him grandfather, too. He may be likened also to a mother who has known the pangs of birth and the joy of giving suck.

"*Hallowed be thy name.* May we hold it in reverence, nor by our behavior cause others to hold it in irreverence.

"*Thy kingdom come.* Reign thou in our hearts, soul, body and conscience.

"*Thy will be done.* Save us from murmuring against any cross laid upon us.

"*Give us this day our daily bread.* Bless the labor of our hands that we may have food for ourselves and others. Give us of the bread and the water of life, of which if a man eat and drink he shall never more hunger or thirst. As the grains of wheat become in the loaf one bread, so may we be united in Christ, ready with him to endure want, pain, and shame.

"*Forgive us our debts.* Save us from resentment when we are

Printer's mark
on Katherine Zell's
hymnbook

Hymn
singing
in the
home

maligned and scorned, like Christ who as a sheep before the shearers was dumb and opened not his mouth.

"*Lead us not into the temptation* of believing that we have truly forgiven, while rancor lingers and from the temptation of despairing of thy mercy, forgetting that Peter and Mary Magdalene were forgiven.

"*Deliver us from the evils* of hunger, war, famine, and pestilence, though only if it be thy will.

"*For thine is the kingdom.* May Christ reign in heaven and on earth.

"*And the power.* As thou didst deliver Israel so deliver us.

"*And the glory.* Thou givest breath to every living thing. Wherefore of thy glory there is no end."

Katherine visited Felix Ambrosiaster as a friend. She felt a more direct responsibility for a nephew stricken with syphilis. The disease was in that day a frightful scourge, partly because of the inadequacy of the cure, partly because of ignorance as to the transmission, which can be by any open cut or even by a kiss. When the nephew could not be cared for at home he was placed in the hospital for syphilitics. Katherine went to live with him. She was appalled by the mismanagement of the institution and sent the town council a devastating critique. "The manager and his wife lie in luxury," she said, "and neglect the patients. Beds rot. Water is not heated for baths. Tough and sometimes wormy meat is served indiscriminately, whereas some require a soft diet. There is no religious instruction and some patients do not know the Lord's Prayer. The manager mumbles a grace so that one cannot tell whether he may not be swearing. The mercury cure martyrs the patients. There should be a dedicated couple in charge. The number of maids should be reduced. The fewer, the less quarreling. Get rid of the savage dog which mangles all the cats. Give up swine and goats in favor of a hundred hens. Have religious instruction every morning while the heart is fresh. For medication use only guyac." Her recommendations were adopted almost *in toto,* but were hard to implement. She appears to have discontinued her residence, but not her contribution.[47]

Both Katherine and her husband were interested in popular

education. He put out two simple catechisms for children,[48] and in 1534 she issued a collection of hymns in the form of four little pamphlets that sold for a penny apiece. They were translations already made from Czech into German. In her preface Katherine said, "When I read these hymns I felt that the writer had the whole Bible in his heart. This is not just a hymn book but a lesson book of prayer and praise. When so many filthy songs are on the lips of men and women and even children I think it well that folk should with lusty zeal and clear voice sing the songs of their salvation. God is glad when the craftsman at his bench, the maid at the sink, the farmer at the plough, the dresser at the vines, the mother at the cradle break forth in hymns of prayer, praise and instruction."

The device of the printer, Frölich of Strasbourg, was fortuitously highly appropriate, a singing swan above a viola and a sheet of music. In this instance the swan might also be easily identified with the goose, the symbol of the Czech John Hus, whose name in that language means goose.[49]

Katherine's last days were plagued by strife. The Augsburg *Interim* ended with the defeat of the emperor. The Peace of Augsburg in 1555 granted toleration to the Lutherans in designated areas. Strasbourg committed herself to Lutheranism. Some of the ministers vented the invective formerly bestowed upon the Catholics, now upon the sectaries. One of the chief offenders was Ludwig Rabus, a former resident in the Zell's home and confessedly indebted to Katherine for spiritual counsel. Now in a Christmas sermon he digressed from the text to rail against Schwenckfeld, "Stenckfeld [Stinkfield], that emissary of Satan."

Katherine remonstrated with him in private. Rabus called her a "disturber of the peace of the church." "A disturber of the peace am I? Yes indeed, of my own peace. Do you call this disturbing the peace that instead of spending my time in frivolous amusements I have visited the plague infested and carried out the dead? I have visited those in prison and under sentence of death. Often for three days and three nights I have neither eaten nor slept. I have never mounted the pulpit, but I have done more than any minister in visiting those in misery. Is this disturbing the peace of the church?"[50]

"Why do you rail at Schwenckfeld? You talk as if you would have him burned like the poor Servetus at Geneva. You say that you have left Strasbourg and gone to Ulm because the ministers here are too lenient toward Schwenckfelders, Zwinglians, and Anabaptists. You behave as if you had been brought up by savages in a jungle. The Anabaptists are pursued as by a hunter with dogs chasing wild boars. Yet the Anabaptists accept Christ in all essentials as we do. They have borne witness to their faith in misery, prison, fire, and water. You young fellows tread on the graves of the first fathers of this church in Strasbourg and punish all who disagree with you, but faith cannot be forced. You should read that man Bellius who collected statements from the early reformers on religious liberty from which alas some have since receded. [She is referring to the pseudonymous work of Castellio, *Concerning Heretics,* castigating the burning of Servetus.] [51] You say that Strasbourg by her laxity is a shame and scorn to all Germany. Not yet, my dear fellow. She is rather an example of mercy and compassion. My Matthew testified in private and from the pulpit that he would not be guilty of the crucifixion of these poor folk. The Good Samaritan, when he came upon the man who had fallen among thieves, did not ask him to what denomination he belonged, but put him on his ass and took him to an inn. Remember the words of the Lord Jesus, 'I am meek and lowly of heart.' "

Katherine's last service was in the year 1562 to a disciple of Schwenckfeld, the wife of the distinguished physician, Guinter of Andernach. On her death the husband asked one of the pastors to conduct the funeral. The pastor replied that the superintendent would suffer him to do so only on condition that after lauding her virtues, he should then declare her to have fallen away from the true faith. The husband declined and arranged to have the interment at six in the morning when none would notice. Katherine Zell, now too weak to walk, was taken at that hour in a carriage to the cemetery and herself conducted the service. The town council decreed that if Katherine got well she should receive a reprimand.[52]

It was never delivered, for in that same year Katherine, like Moses, "died of the kiss of God and no man knows the place of her burial."

BIBLIOGRAPHY

This material is reprinted by permission of the Medieval and Neo-Latin Society, copyright owners of *Medievalia et Humanistica*, published by the Press of Case Western Reserve University in December 1970, with the addition of the text of sources not reproduced here. The most frequent reference below is to *Füsslin* which is number five in the works of Katherine Zell. The best study to date was done by William Klaustermeyer, *The Role of Matthew and Katherine Zell in the Strassburg Reformation* (doctoral dissertation, Stanford University, 1965, unpublished). His account is fuller for Matthew than for Katherine, and he has not utilized quite all the material available for Katherine. The works to which reference is made in the following notes are these:

Johann Adam, *Evangelische Kirchengeschichte der Stadt Strassburg* (Strassburg, 1922).

Johann Wilhelm Baum, *Capito und Butzer* (Elberfeld, 1860).

Timotheus Wilhelm Roehrich, *Geschichte der Reformation im Elsass und besonders in Strassburg*, 3 vols. (Strassburg, 1830-32).

—— "Matthaeus Zell," *Beiträge zu der theol. Wissenschaften* II (1851), pp. 144-192.

—— *Kathrina Zell* (Strassburg, 1853), less detailed than the above.

François Wendel, *L'Église de Strasbourg . . . 1532-1535* (Paris, 1942).

—— *Le Marriage à Strasbourg . . . 1520-1692* (Strasbourg, 1928).

Otto Winkelmann, "Das Fürsorgewesen der Stadt Strassburg," *Quellen und Forschungen für Reformationsgeschichte* V (1922).

Abbreviations The letter X signifies that a document is available in xerox in the Yale library.

BSC   *Bulletin de la Société pour la Conservation des Monuments Historiques d'Alsace II Ser., XIX* (1899, Strassburg).

CR   *Corpus Reformatorum, Calvini Opera.*

CS   *Corpus Schwenckfeldianorum*

Oek, B. A. "Briefe und Akten zum Leben Oekolampads," ed. Ernst Staehelin, *Quellen und Forschungen zur Reformationsgeschichte* XIX (1934).

Schiess, *Ambrosius und Thomas Blaurer Briefwechsel*, 3 vols. ed. Traugott Schiess (Freiburg i. Br., 1908-12).

Täufer, *Quellen zur Geschichte der Täufer* VIII *Elsass*, Teil II (Strassburg 1523-35), ed. Manfred Krebs und Hans Georg Rott.

Works of Matthew Zell.

1. Christeliche Verantwortung M. Matthes Zell von Keysberssberg Pfarrherrs und predigers im Münster zu Strassburg / vber Artikel vom Bischöfflichn Fiscal daselbs entgegen gesetzt / vnnd im rechten vbergeben . . . (Colophon). Getruckt in der löblichen Satt Strassburg / durch Wolffgangum Köpffel . . . M.D. xxiij.
   X from the Stadtbibliothek, Zürich.

2. Ein Collation auff die einfuerung M. Anthonij Pfarrherrs zu S. Thomans zu Strassburg / vnnd Katharina seines eelichen gemahls / von Matthes Zeell . . . (Colophon) Durch Wolff Köpffel . . . M.D. xxiij vj Kalen. Decem. X from the Stadtbibliothek, Zürich.

3. Appelatio Sacerdotvm, Maritorvm, Vrbis Argentinae, adversus insanam excommunicationem Episcopi / 1524 / attributed to Capito, signed also by Zell. X from the Stadtbibliothek, Zürich.

4. Doctor Capito Mathis Zellen / vnnd ander Predicanten zu Strassburg wahrhaftige Verantwortung. . . . X Stadtbibliothek, Munich.

Works of Katherine Zell.
1. Entschuldigung Katharina Schützinn / für M. Matthes Zellen / jren Ehegemahel . . . (Strasbourg ?, 1524). X Stadtbibliothek, Zürich.
2. Den leydenden Christglaubigen weybern der gemain zu Kentzingen meinen mitschwestern in Christo Jesu zu handen. Katharina Schützin. M.D. xxiiij. Contoura copy from the Crozer Theol. Seminary. Another copy at the Foundation for Reformation Research, St. Louis, Mo.
3. Von Christo Jesu . . . Lobgsäng. Hymns in four small separate parts. (Strasbourg, 1534.)
4. Klagrede und Ermahnung Katharina Zellin zum Volk bei dem Grab M. Matheus Zellen. Printed from manuscript in W. Horning, *Beiträge zur Kirchengeschichte des Elsasses* VII (1887), 49-79 and 113-21. X.
5. Ein Brief an die genze Bürgerschaft der Stadt Strassburg, betreffend Hern Ludwig Rabus . . . 1557 (Schottenloher, 17593), reprinted in J. C. Füsslin, *Beyträge zur Erläuterung der Kirchen-Reformationsgeschichten des Schweitzerlandes*, V (1753), 191-354. The fullest autobiographical source for Katherine. Copies Yale, Cornell.
6. Den Psalmen Misere/ mit dem Khünig David bedacht/ gebettet/ vnd paraphrasirt von Katharina Zellin M. Matthei Zellen seligen nachgelassne Ehefraw . . . Augstomonat, 1558. X Stadtbibliothek, Zürich.

NOTES

1. Füsslin, p. 200.
2. *Ibid.*, p. 302.
3. K. Zell, No. 1 aij and verso, bvij-ciij.
4. Baum, pp. 263-4.
5. M. Zell, No. 2.
6. Adam, p. 62 and Röhrich, Beiträge, pp. 173-4. Firn was married Nov. 9, Zell on Dec. 3.
7. Füsslin, p. 197.
8. *Weimarer Ausgabe*, Briefwechsel, No. 808.
9. M. Zell, No. 3.
10. Füsslin, p. 238.
11. *BSC* No. 4540.
12. Baum, p. 196; Adam, p. 31; Roehrich, *Beiträge*, p. 160. M. Zell, No. 1b.
13. M. Zell, No. 1 Vij.
14. *Ibid.*, Ciij, diij, qii verso-qiii, yii, yiv.
15. To Ambrosius Blaurer, Sept. 30, 1534, partially in Schiess I, No. 465. Full text in my documentary article.
16. Füsslin, p. 300; Baum, p. 267; Roehrich, *Geschichte* I, 267-8, 405-7. Winkelmann, p. 100.
17. See the title page on p. 62. Copies at Crozer Theol. Sem. and Foundation for Reformation Research, St. Louis, Mo.
18. M. Zell, No. 4, analyzed in Roehrich's *Beiträge*. On Katherine's visitation Füsslin, p. 264.
19. Füsslin, pp. 303-4; Winkelmann, p. 102.
20. Täufer No. 406, p. 119. Butzer to Margareta Blaurer, July 9, 1533.
21. Füsslin, p. 313. Cf. Oek. No. 691.
22. See my article "Luther and the Via Media at the Marburg Colloquy," *Collected Papers*, vol. 2 (Boston, 1963). Katherine herself makes the same comment. Füsslin, p. 270.
23. *Weimar Ausgabe*, Briefwechsel No. 1777.
24. *CR* X, No. 188, p. 398. Calvin to Farel, Oct. 5, 1539.
25. Füsslin, p. 316.
26. *Ibid.*, p. 312.

27. The most recent work on the Strasbourg sectaries is the microfilmed Yale dissertation of Charles B. Mitchell, *Martin Bucer and Sectarian Dissent* (1960).
28. Füsslin, p. 270.
29. Schiess I, No. 397.
30. Täufer No. 451.
31. *BSC* No. 4924.
32. Below, p. 73.
33. Täufer, No. 502, and Schiess II, No. 26, p. 805.
34. *CS* index and my documentary article.
35. Schiess, Nos. 385, 390, 394.
36. *Ibid.*, No. 391.
37. On the Patenschaft Schiess I, Nos. 396, 402 and II Anhang II. Täufer Nos. 455, 622. Wendel, *Église,* pp. 80-81 and 213; *Mariage,* 82.
38. K. Zell, No. 4.
39. Butzer to Myconius, July 16, 1548. Text in my documentary article.
40. Katherine Zell to Pellikan, Jan. 9, 1549. Text in my article.
41. Füsslin, p. 263.
42. Katherine Zell to Butzer and Fagius, March 25, 1549. Text in my documentary article.
43. Johann Adam, "Eine unbeachtete Schrift der Katharina Zell aus Strassburg," *Zeitschrift für die Geschichte des Oberrheins* N.F. XXXI (1916), 451-5.
45. K. Zell, No. 6.
46. Winkelmann, pp. 172-77 and Urkunden, Nos. 33 and 34.
47. Matthew Zell's catechisms are reproduced in Johann Michael Reu, *Quellen zur Geschichte des kirchenlichen Unterrichts,* (Gütersloh, 1904-35).
48. Katherine's hymns are described in Wackernagel's Bibliographie, p. 469, No. 1082. Part of her preface is given in Otto Michaelis, *Elsäsische Gestalten* (Strassburg, 1942). See my documentary article.
49. K. Zell, No. 5.
50. See my Castellio *Concerning Heretics* (reprint Octagon Press, 1965).
51. Details in J. Bernays, "Zur Biographie Johann Winters von Andernach," *Zeitschrift für die Geschichte des Oberrheins* NF XVI (1901), 28-57.

Holbein's *Dance of Death*

4.

Wibrandis Rosenblatt
(1504 - 1564)

The contribution of Wibrandis Rosenblatt to the Reformation, like that of Katherine von Bora, lay in the domestic sphere. Her role was to provide a haven of composure for a harassed spouse, and not simply one, as in the case of Luther's wife. Wibrandis was married in turn to three reformers, architects of the religious revolution in Basel and Strasbourg, and prior to these unions there had been still another. She bore children to them all.

Her experience in this regard was, of course, not related to the Reformation. Any wife in that age might have lost several husbands and many children. The remark of John Bright, during the Crimean War in England, applied to any place and time in the sixteenth century. "The Angel of Death," said he, "is abroad in the land. One can almost hear the beating of his wings." A familiar artistic theme was that of the *Dance of Death*. In Holbein's *Totentanz* the pope and the emperor, the cardinal and the king are summoned by the spectre. Beside the minister in the pulpit stands death holding the hour glass and walks before the priest as he goes to administer the last rites. The farmer is snatched away from the plow, the merchant from the bales, the bride from the groom and while the mother is preparing soup, death takes the babe by the hand.

All this was no fantasy concocted to titillate the jaded. This was the way it was. The average length of life was only 25 years because so many died in infancy. Men considered themselves old

Wibrandis

at 40.[1] Those who passed that frontier might attain longevity, yet thousands of every age were swept away in the great epidemics. Fathers were left with families of young children and no housekeeper, and mothers with perhaps still copious broods were left with no bread winner. The most obvious expedient for meeting such emergencies was remarriage, and that generation saw no impropriety in entering upon new unions within a few months.

Wibrandis, in marrying so many husbands and bearing so many children, shared a lot which might have fallen to any woman in her day, but the strains in her case were greater than for other women because three of her husbands were leaders in a movement fraught with special dangers. If the rulers of the

land favored the reform, the reformers might even enjoy popular esteem, but if the political regime were altered, the result
could be confiscations of goods, exiles, or even executions. The
role of a wife under such circumstances was like that of Aaron
and Hur who upheld the sagging arms of Moses, for only while
his hands were aloft did Israel prevail over Amalek.

Wibrandis, born at Basel in 1504, was named after a saint
whose remains in that year were transferred to the altar of the
cathedral. The father of our Wibrandis was in the service of the
Emperor Maximillian. When just under 20, Wibrandis was married to the Basel humanist, Ludwig Keller, known as Cellarius.
She bore him a daughter who was also named Wibrandis.[2] After
only two years of marriage Keller died—in July, 1526.

The second husband, the minister in St. Martin's church at
Basel, was named Oecolampadius, a hellenized form of the German *Hausschein* (that is House Shine, in Greek *oikos* and *lam-
pado*.) He was at the same time a professor of theology, highly
learned in Greek and Hebrew and had assisted Erasmus in the
publication of his edition of the New Testament. His commentary on Isaiah and his lectures on John's gospel made such an
impression that he had in his classes not only students but
around 400 citizens of Basel.[3] He was unmarried and his house
was tended by his mother until her death. When that happened
he was urged to marry by his old friend Wolfgang Capito of
Strasbourg, who had been enjoined by Butzer to take this step
and now passed on the injunction to Oecolampadius. "Marriage," wrote Capito, "is honorable and especially for a Christian
pastor. Celibacy is not without its cares and dangers. I thought
I was called to it, and I would not have changed my mind had
I not been pressed by friends. Thus I was constrained to take a
wife, the daughter of a magistrate and fairly well off. Her godly
brothers persuaded her to enter upon a maligned marriage. I
have in her a most pure helpmate, intent on hospitality, disposed to almsgiving, diligent in piety, encouraging to good deportment. I am not equal to her in virtue, and I fear my infer-
iority may offend some. I haven't heard that it has, but I am
fearful. Now, if a suitable person is pointed out to you, I think
you should not decline. To have a mate of like zeal will be a

glory to the Lord. But there is no greater cross than to be married to a daughter of Belial." [4]

Oecolampadius replied, "Don't worry about my marrying. I appreciate your concern. Either I shall find a Christian sister like Monica, or I will remain unmarried. Such a woman is a rare bird, but perhaps one can be netted. I cannot stand my present housekeeper. I wouldn't for a moment consider marrying her. But I think I should keep her a little longer lest I seem hard in dismissing her at once." [5]

After slightly more than a year, Oecolampadius was married to Wibrandis (March 15, 1528). She was 24 and he 45. Boniface Amerbach commented unkindly: "A decrepit old man with trembling head and body, so emaciated and wasted that you might well call him a living corpse, has married an elegant and blooming girl of 20, more or less." [6] Erasmus was even more cutting when he wrote, "A few days ago Oecolampadius married a not inelegant girl with intent to castigate his flesh during Lent." [7] Oecolampadius wrote to Farel: "In case you have not heard, let me tell you that in place of my deceased mother the Lord has given me a sister and wife, adequately Christian [presumably he means versed in reformed doctrine], not exactly affluent, well born, a widow with several years experience in bearing the cross. I wish she were older, but I see in her no signs of youthful petulance. Pray the Lord to give us a long and happy marriage." [8] A year later he was able to report to Capito: "My wife is what I always wanted and I wish for no other. She is not contentious, garrulous, or a gadabout, but looks after the household. She is too simple to be proud and too discreet to be condemned." [9]

The turbulent events of the Reformation can scarcely have failed to make life tense in the parsonage. Wibrandis bore a son, Eusebius, on the day before Christmas in 1528, and in the following February Basel was in ferment. The militant reformers, led by her husband, demanded that the Catholics be excluded from the town council, that the images be removed from the churches, and that the celebration of the Mass be everywhere forbidden in any church in Basel. The council hesitated. The mob assembled, a thousand strong, in the *Barfüsserplatz*, the Franciscan Square. When after three days the council still deliberated, the

IOANNES OECOLAMPADIVS
Basiliensis Ecclesiæ Pastor.

Quem coluit Basilea sacrorum clara ministrum:
Sim LAMPAS Domini, quod vocor, opto, DOMVS.

M. D. XXXI.

Oecolampadius

mob broke loose, stormed up the hill to the cathedral, smashed all the images of wood and stone, and left the artistic treasures of the piety of the ages strewn as rubble over the square. The Mass was abolished. Everyone was required to attend the Lord's Supper, interpreted as a memorial after the manner of Zwingli, or else leave the city.[10] Erasmus left. Oecolampadius had triumphed.

While all this was going on, the home provided him a spot of tranquility. "Eusebius," reported Oecolampadius, "is a gentle and quiet child unless hungry, thirsty or in need of a change. He is very subject to colds and coughing. I fear he will not live long." [11] He did live to be 13.[12] Other children came—two daughters, Aletheia (meaning Truth) and Irene (meaning Peace).

Wibrandis was continually entertaining ministers and refugees. Capito was her guest. A delegation from the Waldenses came to confer with her husband. The argumentative Servetus was there. Zwingli was entertained when he came to join her husband, and both went on to the Colloquy at Marburg. Wibrandis was in correspondence with the wives of other reformers, for the leaders of the Reformation in the south German and Swiss cities constituted a close fellowship. She exchanged letters with Anna Zwingli, Agnes Capito, and Elisabeth Butzer. Agnes sent a prayer book exalting the heroines of the Bible.[13]

The death of Zwingli, slain on the field of battle at Kappell in October, 1531, was a severe shock to the Reformed churches. They feared the Lutherans would gloat over his death. Some did. A woman spoke up for him. "Is he dead? Then he died as a hero. I love and honor him." [14] The woman who said that was Katherine Zell of Strasbourg. Oecolampadius was asked to replace him but declined, partly in all probability because he sensed that for him the sands were low. He died the following month, in November of 1531.

Wibrandis was for the second time a widow. In the very same month of November Capito's wife Agnes was taken. Shocked by the deaths of two of his friends and then of his wife, Capito was sorely shaken. A trip was suggested to him. He should visit Basel, Bern, Constance, Augsburg, and Ulm. Butzer, who was always active in finding wives for his colleagues, appraised the forthcoming visits with an eye to a possible mate. Two cities were regarded as auspicious, one as ominous. At Basel there was Wibrandis, who would be ideal; at Constance, Margareta Blaurer, equally ideal if amenable; but at Augsburg there was Sabina, the widow of the one time Anabaptist, Augustine Bader.[15]

Until 1528 Bader had been a travelling apostle of the Anabaptists, but as one after another of his friends were martyred, he gave up his visitations and withdrew to a little community of his own, consisting of only four families. He announced that he was a king and decked himself out in royal regalia. Word came to the authorities who tortured and executed all of the men. Bader was beheaded with his own regal sword. His wife became for a time a refugee in Strasbourg and was harbored by the Capitos.

Butzer confided his hopes and fears to Ambrose Blaurer, the brother of Margareta. "My choice for Capito is the widow of Oecolampadius, but he inclines to Sabina Bader, the widow of the Anabaptist king. She may have been innocent of her husband's designs, but she was the queen, and such a marriage will hurt the evangelical churches. Besides Capito is so mercurial that he needs a demure and not a domineering wife. I thought first of our Margareta (Blaurer's sister), but he cooks up such fantastic schemes, which do him no good and embarrass others, that I think she would be of more service if unencumbered by him. I hope the same consideration will not weigh against me should I ever be in his situation. Capito puts love above everything else and when suffering from insomnia dreams up outlandish philanthropies and then carries them out, despite protest, so that he has run up vast debts. He writes me that he has been very touched by the sight of the widow Wibrandis and the orphaned children. When he comes to Constance, if Providence has destined that the lady be Margareta, they will know it. When he goes to Augsburg, I am afraid Sabina may wrap him around her finger." [16] To Margareta Butzer wrote teasingly, as was his wont with her: "If I had not settled on Wibrandis for Capito, I'd try to pry you loose from your masterless estate." [17] The counsel of Butzer prevailed. On August 11, 1532 Wibrandis was married to Capito.

Wolfgang Capito

If he was really as difficult as Butzer pretended, one wonders whether he should have been foisted upon her, but since she did curb his foibles, balance his budget, and keep his household sweet, her achievement belongs to the annals of unrecorded heroisms. Wibrandis brought with her to Strasbourg her daughter Wibrandis by Keller and the children of Oecolampadius. In addition the household included Wibrandis' mother, Margareta née Strub. The daily round was presumably little different from what it had been with Oecolampadius. Capito, also both a pastor and a professor, was laden with public responsibilities. The energies of Wibrandis were strained by keeping the cradle full. To Capito she bore five children: three girls, Agnes, Dorothea and Agnes, named for the half sister who had died; and two boys, John Simon, and Wolfgang, named for his father. There are records of sicknesses, but all survived until the great plague of 1541 when 2500 died in Strasbourg. Pastor Hedio lost all five of his children. Butzer's wife Elisabeth had borne him 13 children, of whom only about five were alive at the time of the plague. Only one survived, Nathaneal, weak in body and in mind, and Elizabeth herself was taken. She might have escaped had she left the city at the outbreak of the epidemic, but Butzer would not leave his flock and she would not leave her husband.[18] In the home of Capito, the plague took Eusebius, the son of Oecolampadius, and Dorothea and Wolfgang, the children of Capito, and Capito himself. Wibrandis was again widowed.

As Elisabeth Butzer was stricken, Katherine Zell came to bring the news of Capito's death. Elizabeth, aware that for her the bell would shortly toll, asked her husband to assume the place of his colleague as father and husband. Butzer answered only by tears. Elisabeth, presumably through Katherine, then summoned Wibrandis, who having been so shortly widowed hesitated to be seen in public by day. She came by night and received the appeal of Elisabeth to take her place by the side of Butzer.[19]

The wish of Elisabeth was fulfilled, and in April of 1542 the marriage took place. Butzer wrote to a friend: "There is nothing that I could desire in my new wife save that she is too attentive and solicitous. She is not as free in criticism as was my first wife, and now I realize that such liberty is not only wholesome but necessary. . . . I only hope I can be as kind to my new wife as she to me. But oh, the pang for the one I have lost!" [20] The new household, though sorely reduced, was not small. On Butzer's side there was Nathaneal and on Wibrandis' her mother Margareta, Aletheia, Agnes, Irene and John, making a family of eight. Her daughter Wibrandis, by Keller, was 17 and married at this time.[21] More children arrived. She bore to Butzer a son Martin, who appears to have died early and a daughter Elisabeth. In addition a niece of Wibrandis was adopted.

We have a picture of life in the household from the pen of an Italian refugee named Vermigli, a distinguished theologian, esteemed among the reformatory circles of the papal church. He might conceivably have been named a cardinal had not the rigoristic party triumphed. With the establishment of the Roman Inquisition in 1542, he went into exile. Since there was no post for him at Bazel, Butzer invited him to Strasbourg. Vermigli wrote to sympathizers in Italy: "For 17 days after my arrival I was entertained in Butzer's home. It is like a hostel, receiving refugees for the cause of Christ. In his family during the entire time I saw not the least occasion of offense but only ground for edification. His table is not lavish nor sparse, but marked by a godly frugality. No distinction is made with respect to foods on particular days. Thanks is given to God in Christ for all. Before and after the meal a passage is read from Scripture, followed by comment. I never left the table without having learned something. Butzer is constantly occupied in preaching, administration, and pastoral care and in influencing the government. There is scarcely a day when he does not go to the town hall. He devotes his nights to study and prayer, and I have never awakened without finding him still up." [22] In all this praise there is not a word of appreciation for Wibrandis.

Shortly after the visit of Vermigli she was left to manage the household alone for a year. Her husband was called to assist Hermann von Wied, the Archbishop of Cologne, in the reorganization of his entire diocese in accord with the principles of the Reformation. To Wibrandis, Butzer wrote that he would succumb from a diet of salted meat and smoked fish were it not that his secretary, Christoph Söll, had also some skill in the culinary

Abcontrafactur des Ehrwürdigen vnd hochgelehrten Herren / Martin Butzer / Diener des Euangelions Jhesu Christi zů Straßburg.

Ich weyß nichts dann Christum den gecreutzigten / 1. Cor. 2.

Diser fromm vnd gelehrte Mann/   Zůletst das Interim kam zů handt/
   Hat viel gůts der Kirch gethon/   Schiffet er hinweg in Engellandt:
   Mit dem Bapst ein harten streit/   Darinn die Lehr gerichtet an/
   Gehalten hat ein lange zeit/   Mit jm Fagius der gelehrte Mann.
Zůletst hat er gesiget schon/   Darinn ist er in Gott entschlaffen/
   Helffen stellen die Confession.   Der ist sein Burg/Wehr vnd Waassen.

Getruckt zů Straßburg/
Anno 1586.

Martin Butzer

art.[23] As for his mission, the dukes, the nobles, and towns around Cologne supported the reform, but the cathedral chapter opposed.[24] No doubt in time their opposition would have been overcome had not the political situation shifted so that the archbishop himself was deposed and Butzer came home with all tangible results of his efforts expunged.

In February of 1548 a friend wrote of another absence: "Butzer is away on some business. I do not know where. His wife is having to take care of her sick mother and two sick children. Peter Martyr and Ochino [another Italian refugee] have gone to England. Butzer and Fagius [a colleague] have been invited but they are needed here." [25] In February of the next year a friend reports: "Butzer considers leaving because of the *Interim*. I do not know where he will go. He has six children and a decrepit mother-in-law and a wife in poor health." [26] It was then that Butzer and Fagius were hidden by Katherine Zell for two weeks.

On the journey to England Butzer wrote back from Calais to his son Nathanael: "My dear son, if your blessed mother had not worked so hard we might have her with us yet. Take it to heart, my dear boy. I know you are not strong, but even the smallest seed can bear fruit. Study your Bible, practice the catechism, and come to know our crucified Savior. You know that Wibrandis is to you no step-mother but a true mother indeed. If it is the Lord's will that you come to me, you will see that I love you as my son, and all that is left to me of my dear wife." [27]

Arrived in England, Butzer and Fagius were very graciously received by Archbishop Canmer of Lambeth Palace and rejoiced to see again their old friend Vermigli. During the summer the two were engaged on biblical translation. There were some lighter hours. The archbishop arranged musical soirees at the palace at Croydon.[28] "But," wrote Fagius, "we have no taste for court life. Better to live on onion soup and to be quiet by ourselves." [29] In the fall both were assigned to teaching posts at Cambridge. Luckily, Fagius had a son who had been a student there for two years and could interpret.

Healthwise the two suffered severely. Butzer complained of the diet, everlastingly meat, meat, meat, seldom eggs, cabbage or other vegetables. To his doctor he sent a lugubrious recital of his

ailments: severe constipation, fever, lassitude compounded by insomnia, colic, stone, crippling of arm and fingers, presumably by
arthritis, made all the worse by the severity of the English winter with only fireplace heat. He feared he would have to return
to Germany for the sake of thermal baths, which were very infrequent, said he, in England.[30] Fagius sent word teasingly to
Wibrandis that "she had better come to care for Butzer else he
might marry some one else. The Duchess of Suffolk would have
him. She is a widow." [31]

Confronted by the dread prospect of another such winter,
Butzer in August of 1549 ventured to express the hope to Wibrandis that she might come: "How I'd love to have you here,
but we are in the Lord's hands. If you cannot come, I wonder if
a trusty brother and his wife might come and cook for us in the
winter and look after the house. You know what kind of a housekeeper I am. If I could have that hope I could the better spare
you until the times improve, but I am in the Lord's hands. If
you can come, I think it would be better to bring only Agnes
and the maid Anna and Lisbeth. God forbid that I should take
Christophel away from the church. [The reference is to Christoph
Söll, mentioned above as Butzer's secretary at Cologne. He was
now a pastor at Strasbourg and married to Wibrandis' daughter
Aletheia.] Let him who has a pulpit preach, preach, preach so
long as the Lord allows. It would be much less dangerous for you
and for him if you were not together. You can make the journey
in eight days and during that time your absence would scarcely
be noticed. Give the impression that you expect to winter in
Strasbourg. You can come down the Rhine as far as Nimwegen,
then overland 12 miles. Don't let the ship's people know what
it's all about. You ought to have a man with you. Lukas Hackfurt [32] or Katherine Zell will know of someone. I'd like some
paper and a list of books, especially the edition of Eusebius
printed by Herwagen. That's all the advice I have. Our dear
Grandma must not be left alone. Christophel might live in her
house. The children would be in school while he is busied with
parochial duties. I cannot urge that Grandma come. May the
Lord comfort her in her latter days. She has seen so much of
trouble. I would be glad to divide you with her, or to leave you

wholly to her were I sure that God would have it so. May his will be mine. We must bear the cross. We deserve it. Truly it is no light cross to give up such dear churches, schools, children and friends, and one's own household. Söll will do his best for John Simon and Irene."

Then come notes to each of the children and individual thanks for their letters to him. Would that they had been preserved. After a note to Grandma there is a postscript: "At Antwerp you should buy sausages, sugar and plums. Here everything is so expensive and get the doctor at Strasbourg to give you some pills. The price here is ghastly. Bring bobbins and oakum. The barrels can be sent directly to London. Be sure they are properly addressed." [33]

Wibrandis came, and having surveyed the scene, decided to return for the remainder of the family. Agnes Capito stayed to look after Butzer. Once back, Wibrandis reported that the Papists were trying to confiscate her property. Some official had summoned her and Söll to appear. He had answered that they were citizens of Strasbourg and would not appear. Let the official come to them. "Söll confided to me his fear that if we appeared I would say something hot, as indeed I might well have done. I have left for the baths with instructions to Söll to say nothing until I get back." [34]

Then the entire family migrated, the children, Grandma, Wibrandis, and Söll, though only to see them safely arrived and then go back. Preparation for the winter had been made by King Edward VI, who sent a present of 20 pounds for the construction of a German stove, and then a like sum for a second stove for the family.[35] But the installation came too late. Fagius died in November of 1549. Butzer, engaged in indefatigable labors for the structure, liturgy, and program of the Anglican church, survived only until February of 1551. In the final stages of his illness Wibrandis was relieved of incessant nursing by the Duchess of Suffolk. Truly was it said that no man in so short a time as 30 years left such an impression on the Church of England as had Butzer.[36]

The task now fell to Wibrandis to take care of all of the financial matters and get the family back to Strasbourg. She wrote to various persons sometimes in German, sometimes in Latin. Her letter to Archbishop Cranmer has been translated: "I heartily implore for your Reverence the grace and favor of God the Father through our Lord Jesus Christ. Although the rank and dignity of your Reverence would greatly deter me from writing, yet the exceeding benefits bestowed by your Reverence both upon my husband in his lifetime, and on myself since his decease, prevent the possibility of my being silent, unless I would be branded with ingratitude. But though I am unable to recount them as they deserve, or worthily to praise them, I nevertheless thank God, and daily implore him on behalf of your Reverence, that he who is most rich and powerful, may regard you with his unexhausted goodness and infinite beneficence. I remember, Most Reverend Prelate, that when I was yet in England, your Reverence promised me some document in writing, whereby the gift of his most Serene Majesty would be confirmed to myself alone, and remain undivided. . . . Since therefore your Reverence has promised me this document, and I am in hopes that by its authority and efficacy I may be able to obtain for myself and my little daughter, who very greatly needs it, the donation of his most Serene Majesty; I beg and implore, etc."

The Archbishop replied: "The especial favor with which I regarded your husband during his lifetime, is by no means diminished now that he is no more. His remarkable piety indeed, and profound learning, have produced not a transient but an everlasting benefit to the church; whereby he has not only bound all godly persons, but myself more than all of them, under perpetual obligations to him. You must not therefore on my account allow yourself to be deterred from writing to me, should there be anything in which I can be of use to you or to your affairs." The grant of 100 marks is confirmed.[37]

The party returned to Strasbourg, but not to remain. Frau Wibrandis, together with Grandma and the children, went back to the home city of Basel. Here the final days were not unclouded. The son, John Simon Capito, was a student of theology at the newly founded University of Marburg. To him Wibrandis wrote: "I haven't heard from you for some time, but I well know that if I had, the news would not have been comforting. You contrive always to be a cross to me. If only I might live to the day when I have good news from you. Then would I die of joy. Be thrifty, study hard, no drinking, gaming, or wenching. If you would follow in the steps of your father, then Grandma, the sisters, and the in-laws would lay down their very lives for you. But if you won't behave differently, no one will give you a heller. If you will behave yourself properly, come home. If you won't, then do as you will. I advise you to be saving. I wish you a good year. Your faithful mother." [38]

The plague struck again and in 1553 carried off Christoph Söll. We have no further news relating to Wibrandis until a full 10 years later when in 1564 a still more devastating plague took 7,000 lives in Basel. Frau Wibrandis was among them. Most of the bodies were buried in common graves. Hers was laid to rest in the cloister walk of the cathedral beside her second husband, Oecolampadius. Playing upon her maiden name of Rosenblatt, a poet wrote:

> So lovely was our Rose and none more fair than this
> Whether in Alsace or among the Swiss.[39]

Her tribute came at last through the dance of death.

BIBLIOGRAPHY

This sketch has previously appeared with the addition of the German text of a letter in the *Festschrift* for Ernst Staehelin entitled *Gottesreich und Menschenrecht* (Basel, 1969).

There are three excellent brief sketches without documentation:

Ernst Staehelin, *Frau Wibrandis* (Berlin and Leipzig, 1934).

Otto Michaelis, *Elsässische Gestalten* (Strassbourg, 1942).

Maria Heinsius, *Das Unüberwindliche Wort* (München, 1951).

Much documentation is to be found in Ernst Staehelin, *Briefe und Akten zum Leben Oekolampads*, QFRG XIX (1934).
On the marriage with Oecolampadius, Nos. 456, 457, 559, 639.
On the marriage with Butzer: Nos. 989, 1006, 1007. The letter of Aletheia to Christoph Söll, No. 1008, the return to Basel, No. 1011. Wibrandis to her son, No. 1013.

A number of pertinent letters of Butzer are in Traugott Schiess, *Ambrosius und Thomas Blaurer Briefwechsel*, I, No. 929, II, Nos. 931, 940, 948, 951.

Oecolampadius to Zwingli in *Corpus Reformatorum* 96, Zwingli *Sämmtliche Werke* 9, Nos. 699, 704.

Melanchthon's tribute to Butzer's wife in A.-L. Herminjard, *Correspondence des Reformateurs* VII (1886), No. 1053.

On the English period: Andrew Edward Harvey, *Martin Butzer in England* (Marburg, 1906). Reproduces letters of Fagius to his wife, Butzer to Wibrandis, to his physician and others.

Otto Winckelman, "Strassburger Frauenbriefe des 16 Jahrhunderts," *Archiv für Kulturgeschichte* II, 2 (1904), reproduces letters of Agnes Fagius to her husband, Aletheia to Söll (also in BA), Wibrandis to her son (also in BA), and one by Elizabeth nee Butzer.

Vermigli's tribute to Butzer's household is in *Loci Communis D. Petri Martyris Vermilli Florentini* (Zürich, 1577), pp. 1071 and to Wibrandis on the death of her husband 1089-90.

Correspondence of Wibrandis and Cranmer, *Zürich Letters* (Parker Society 1846) Nos. xvi and clxxx, cf. xvii, clxxxi.

Facsimile of a portion of the letter of Wibrandis to her son, Johannes, in Ficker und Otto Winkelmann, *Handschriftproben des sechszehnten Jahrhunderts nach Strassburger Originalen* II (Strasbourg, 1905).

Scattered references in Johann W. Baum, *Capito und Butzer* (Eberfeld, 1860).

NOTES

1. Creighton Gilbert, "When Did a Man in the Renaissance Grow Old?" *Studies in the Renaissance* XIV (1967), 7-32.
2. Staehelin *FW*.
3. Staehelin, "Das theologische Lebenswerk Johannes Oekolampads," QFRG XXI (1939), 189.
4. Staehelin *BA* No. 456.
5. *Ibid.*, No. 457. The reading in CR 96, No. 699 is *Monica*. The original in Staehelin *BA* No. 457 is *Phoenicem*, i.e. Carthaginian and presumably Monica.
6. Amerbach, *Korrespondenz* III, 1253, lines 51-53.
7. *Erasmi Epistolae*, ed. P. S. Allen VII, No. 1977, lines 70-73, March 20, 1528.
8. Staehelin *BA*, No. 559, March 22, 1528.
9. *Ibid.*, No. 639. Cf. No. 576.
10. *Ibid.*, No. 636.
11. *Ibid.*, No. 639. Cf. 618, note 6.
12. *Ibid.*, No. 636, note 26. He died Oct. 12, 1541.
13. Staehelin *FW*.
14. Baum, p. 482.
15. On Bader see the *Mennonitisches Lexikon*.
16. Schiess I, No. 929. The letter in full in German translation. Excerpts in Latin in Staehelin *BA*, No. 965.
17. Staehelin *BA*, No. 965.
18. Melanchthon's testimony in Herminjard VII, No. 1053.
19. Schiess II, No. 940. Staehelin *BA*, No. 989.
20. Schiess II, No. 948 and 951.
21. Staehelin *FW*.
22. Vermigli, *Loci*, see bibliography.
23. Schiess II, No. 987.
24. *Ibid.*, II., No. 1030.
25. *Ibid.*, II, No. 1510.
26. *Ibid.*, II, No. 1606.
27. For the text see my article in the Staehelin *Festschrift*.
28. Baum, pp. 551-2.
29. *Ibid.*, p. 553. Harvey No. 1.
30. Harvey, No. V.
31. Baum, p. 552.
32. Lucas Hackfurt was one of the officials for poor relief in Strasbourg. On him see Otto Winkelmann, "Das Fürsorgewesen der Stadt Strassburg," QFRG V (1922).
33. Harvey, No. 2.
34. Staehelin *BA*, No. 1006.
35. Baum, p. 564. Staehelin *BA*, No. 1007, note 7.
36. Baum, p. 565.
37. *Zürich Letters*, see bibliography.
38. Winkelmann, AKIG, pp. 185-6. See bibliography.
39. Staehelin *FW* and *BA*, No. 1017.

5.

Argula von Grumbach
(1492 - after 1563)

Argula von Grumbach, like Katherine Zell, had a share in the public controversies of the Reformation. Herself a daughter of the Bavarian nobility, in 1523 she wrote a trenchant letter of protest to the faculty of the University of Ingolstadt who had exacted a humiliating recantation of Wittenberg's theology from a young member of the teaching staff. She wrote:

"To the honorable, worthy, highborn, erudite, noble, stalwart Rector and all the Faculty of the University of Ingolstadt: When I heard what you had done to Arsacius Seehofer under terror of imprisonment and the stake, my heart trembled and my bones quaked. What have Luther and Melanchthon taught save the Word of God? You have condemned them. You have not refuted them. Where do you read in the Bible that Christ, the apostles, and the prophets imprisoned, banished, burned, or murdered anyone? You tell us that we must obey the magistrates. Correct. But neither the pope, nor the Kaiser, nor the princes have any authority over the Word of God. You need not think you can pull God, the prophets and the apostles out of heaven with papal decretals drawn from Aristotle, who was not a Christian at all. I am not unacquainted with the word of Paul that women should be silent in church (1 Tim. 1:2) but, when no man will or can speak, I am driven by the word of the Lord when he said, 'He who confesses me on earth, him will I confess and he who denies me, him will I deny,' [Matt. 10, Luke 9],

97

A medal of Argula von Grumbach

and I take comfort in the words of the prophet Isaiah [3:12, but not exact], 'I will send you children to be your princes and women to be your rulers.' You seek to destroy all of Luther's works. In that case you will have to destroy the New Testament, which he has translated. In the German writings of Luther and Melanchthon I have found nothing heretical, and there are a goodly number of Luther's works of which Spalatin has sent me a list. Even if Luther should recant, what he has said would still be the Word of God. I would be willing to come and dispute with you in German and you won't need to use Luther's translation of the Bible. You can use the one written 31 years ago [actually the Koburger of 1483]. You have the key of knowledge and you close the kingdom of heaven. But you are defeating

Woodcuts from the Koburger Bible of 1483

yourselves. The news of what has been done to this lad of 18 has reached us and other cities in so short a time that soon it will be known to all the world. The Lord will forgive Arsacius, as he forgave Peter, who denied his master, though not threatened by prison and fire. Great good will yet come from this young man. I send you not a woman's ranting, but the Word of God. I write as a member of the Church of Christ against which the gates of hell shall not prevail, as they will against the Church of Rome. God give us his grace that we may all be blessed. Amen."

The Arsacius Seehofer to whom she refers was, at the age of 18, an instructor at the University of Ingolstadt. He had previously studied at the University of Wittenberg, not under Luther who was at the time secreted at the castle of the Wartburg, but under Melanchthon from whom he imbibed the gospel of justification by faith. Apparently Seehofer was also influenced by the more radical Carlstadt, who called for the abolition of academic degrees as tokens of pride in wordly learning. The young man might have been diverted from his university career had not his family induced him to enroll at Ingolstadt, where, having taken his degree, he began to teach. Ingolstadt had a very different atmosphere from that of Wittenberg. Its most renowned professor was John Eck, Luther's most implacable prosecutor. Seehofer introduced into his lectures the doctrines learned from Melanchthon. This prompted an investigation. His quarters were searched and books came to light written by Melanchthon and by Luther. He was three times imprisoned and would assuredly have been burned if turned over to the court of the bishop. But through the intervention of his father he was granted the concession that his case would be handled only by the duke and the university. Seehofer, under terror of the stake, was induced to make a public recantation. His hand upon the gospel and weeping for shame, he abjured his errors and thanked the university for treating him with such lenience. He was then incarcerated in an isolated cloister pending further orders.

Argula von Grumbach, who took up the cudgels on his behalf, was of the noble Bavarian house of Hohenstaufen. She

signed herself *Stauffer von Adel*. Her family had been impoverished by wars between the nobles and the dukes. When she was
about ten they sent her to be reared as a maid-in-waiting to
Kunigunde, the mother of the duke, and the sister of the Emperor Maximillian. Under her tutelage Argula received a sufficient education to enable her to write a spirited German, but
Latin she never learned. As she was leaving home, her father
gave her a copy of the Koburger Bible of 1483, a German translation adequate as to the sense, though not captivating as to the
style. Argula did not at the time steep herself in its pages because she was warned by the Observant Franciscans that it might
lead her astray. But she may well have been impressed by the
woodcuts of the heroines of the Old Testament to such a degree
that in later life she disregarded the injunction of the Apostle
Paul that women should be silent in church. Shortly after her
arrival at court Argula lost both her father and mother within
five days, presumably through the plague. Duke William consoled her that he would be to her not only a prince but also a
father. In 1516, when she was 24, she was married to Friedrich
von Grumbach, also of the nobility, also impoverished and glad
of the stipend attached to the office of prefect of the Duke of
Bavaria in a local district. Argula bore him two sons and two
daughters.

In the 1520s the writings of Luther were circulating in Bavaria.
Argula read avidly all that she could obtain. A list mentioned in
the letter was sent to her by Spalatin, the chaplain of Frederick
the Wise and friend of Luther. She also started a correspondence
with Luther. Unhappily these letters are lost. Her concern, like
his, was for the salvation of the soul rather than for a role in
the reform of the Church.

The Seehofer affair brought her into the fray. When the news
of his enforced recantation reached her by way of Nürnberg
she promptly went to consult the evangelical minister, Andreas
Osiander. He reported that she was incredibly versed in Scripture and that's all he did. Argula considered that if a man prominent in the reformed ministry did not feel called upon to speak
out, she would. The letter quoted above followed. It was not her
only manifesto.

Ein Chuſtéliche ſchuifft
einer Erbaren frawen/vom adel
Daryn ſie alle Chriſtenliche ſtendt
vnd obuigkeyten ermant/Bey der
warßeit/vnd dem woit Gottes zu
bleibé/vnd ſolcßs auß Chriſtlich=
er pflicßt zum ernſtlicßſten zußand
ßaben.

Argula Staufferin

M.D.xxiiij.

Actuum.4.
Ricßtér jr ſelb/obs voi got recßt
ſey/das wir eucß meßi gehorſam
ſein ſollen den got.

Title page of Argula's tract
to the magistrates

A copy of this letter was sent to Duke William together with another of equal length addressed specifically to him, but also to magistrates in general. The scope was wider than that of the preceding, because Argula took off from the Seehofer affair to denounce the financial exploitation and immorality practiced by the clergy, whether secular or regular. At this point her strictures would meet with general approval in Germany. For half a century the *Gravamina,* or complaints of the German nation, had been submitted to successive diets by Catholics perfectly loyal to the popes.

Argula reminded the duke of his promose to be to her not only a prince, but also a father. She thanked him that by reason of his intervention, Seehofer had been saved from the clutches of the bishop and the flames of the stake. Then in general she reminded him and all magistrates that the authority which they receive from God does not allow them to encroach upon the authority of God. If they overstep the bounds, their lands will be plagued by hunger, pestilence, invasions, and death, and the dead will be food for birds and beasts. God has said this by the mouths of the prophets, not of Luther.

"Behold how the Turk rages. No wonder, when the pope follows the counsel of the devil in forbidding marriage to priests and monks, as if the gift of chastity were conferred by putting on a cowl, and the pope then collects taxes on bastards! No wonder, when a priest receives annually 800 florin and never preaches once a year! The Franciscans, vowed to poverty, devour widows' houses. Priests, monks and nuns are robbers. God says so. I say so. And even if Luther says so, it still is so. Have regard, gracious princes, to the flock of the Lord Jesus Christ, purchased not with silver and gold but with his rose red blood. Dated on the Sunday before the elevation of the Holy Cross, 1523."

> Humbly, Argula von Grumbach
> Born a Stauffer.

A contemporary hand in the Munich copy has written below these printed words:

> Born a Lutheran whore and gate of hell
> 13 December, 1523.

The University of Ingolstadt did not deign to reply to a woman. The duke did not reply. A student at the university, who gave his name merely as John, replied in rhyming couplets. The first lines contain a pun on the name Argula.

> Frau Argula is your name,
> And what's more ornery, without shame
> You forgot that you're a maid
> And are so fresh you're not afraid
> To assume the role of doctor
> And teach new faith to prince and proctor.
> By your stupidity inflated
> Ingolstadt is castigated.

Argula responded in kind:

> I answer in the name of God
> To shut the mouth of this bold snob.
> Reproaches me with lack of shame
> When he is scared to give his name.
> A "free student" at Ingolstadt,
> I will not give him tit for tat.
> If, as he boasts, he is so free
> Why not give his name to me?
> He tells me to mind my knitting.
> To obey my man indeed is fitting,
> But if he drives me from God's Word
> In Matthew ten it is declared
> Home and child we must forsake
> When God's honor is at stake.

Argula was right that the new teaching would not subside because of repressive measures. Possibly spurred by her example, another woman published a tract. Her name was Ursula Weyden. She dealt primarily with the question of clerical marriage.

The authorities were not inclined to let all of this pass in silence. The university reported the matter to the duke. He had a conference with his brother. Rumor had it that the two decided to leave Argula to the discipline of her husband with authority to chop off a few of her fingers, and if he strangled her he would not be brought to account. The report probably arose as a surmise based on what actually was done. She was left to her husband, but his ire was aroused because he was deposed from the office of prefect. With a wife and four children to support he was greatly embittered and maltreated her. In the meantime public abuse continued. A preacher at Ingolstadt on the day of the Virgin Mary referred to Argula as "an insolent daughter of Eve, a heretical bitch and confounded rogue." [1]

In the fall of 1523 the diet of the empire met at Nürnberg. The Count Palatine, perhaps out of curiosity, invited Argula to a conference with complete freedom to speak her mind. She spoke it and followed up with a letter rejoicing that the count was seeing the light, encouraging him to bear witness joyfully and without trembling before earthly powers. Another letter went to Frederick the Wise, expressing the hope that God would strengthen the hands of those at the diet concerned for the proclamation of the Word to the poor people, and that he would restrain the hands of the heathen priests who crucify Christ afresh. Despite the hearing Argula left the diet despondent because most of the princes cared only to guzzle and gorge.

Her own family was against her. She defended herself to them by a letter to her cousin, Adam von Törring. "I hear," she said, "that you have been disturbed over what I wrote to the University of Ingolstadt. I have suffered much reproach, shame, and spite because of it. In view of your friendship I am resolved to write, and I am sending you copies of what I have said. Be not surprised that I confess God, for he who does not confess God is no Christian, though he has been baptized a thousand times. Each man must answer for himself at the last day. No pope, no king, no prince or doctor can answer for me. Therefore, my dear cousin, take it not amiss if you hear that I confess Christ. I count it a great honor to be reviled for his sake. I am said to be a Lutheran. I am not. I was baptized into the name of Christ, not of Luther. But I confess that Luther is a true Christian. God grant that we may never deny this, not by reason of reproach, prison, stripes, or death. God help us. Amen. I hear you have heard that my husband has locked me up. Not that, but he does much to persecute Christ in me. At this point I cannot obey him. We are bound to forsake father, mother, brother, sister, child, body, and life. I am distressed that our princes take the Word of God no more seriously than a cow does a game of chess. They say, 'It is enough to believe what our parents believed.' I have even heard some say, 'If my father and mother were in hell, I wouldn't want to be in heaven.' Not me, not if all my friends were down there. Talk about the faith of parents. They send children to school to learn Ovid and Terence, that is the art of adultery. I am not very hopeful with regard to the meeting of another diet. I saw too much at the one in Nürnberg. I hope the princes won't suffer the fate of Pharaoh. I do hope you will read the Scriptures, at least the four Gospels, though preferably the whole. Luther said he didn't want people to believe his books. They were intended to lead them to the Word of God. You can do great good if you will install godly and learned ministers in your district. I understand that my husband will be deposed from his office. I can't help it. God will feed my children as he feeds the birds and will clothe them as the lilies of the field. My dearly beloved cousin, I commend you to God's grace that you may dwell with him now and forever."

Argula communicated more than once with Luther who reported to Spalatin, "I am sending you the letters of Argula von Grumbach, Christ's disciple, that you may see how the angels rejoice over a sinful daughter of Adam, converted and made into a daughter of God." [2] Again to a friend Luther wrote, "The Duke of Bavaria rages above measure, killing, crushing and persecuting the gospel with all his might. That most noble woman, Argula von Stauffer, is there making a valiant fight with great spirit, boldness of speech and knowledge of Christ. She deserves that all pray for Christ's victory in her. She has attacked the University of Ingolstadt for forcing the recantation of a certain youth, Arsacius Seehofer. Her husband, who treats her tyrannically, has been deposed from his prefecture. What he will do you can imagine. She alone, among these monsters, carries on with firm faith, though, she admits, not without inner trembling. She is a singular instrument of Christ. I commend her to you, that Christ through this infirm vessel may confound the mighty and those who glory in their strength." [3]

Luther himself then took up the cudgel in defense of the propositions which Seehofer had been driven to recant "by all the swine in Bavaria congregated at Ingolstadt." Argula apparently felt that Luther had not rendered the fullest witness and called upon him to get married. He replied that he was not insensitive to his sex. He was no log or stone, but he was of no mind to marry because he expected daily the death of a heretic. Two years later he did marry. On the occasion of the meeting of the diet at Augsburg in 1530 Luther was unable to attend because he was under the ban of the church and the empire. Instead he was secreted nearby at the castle of the Coburg. There Argula paid him a visit and they broke bread together. Luther passed on to Katie Argula's prescription for weaning the baby. He added that he might have to leave his hideout at the Coburg because it was becoming a place of pilgrimage, and if too many people came to see him, the Elector would take fright lest news of this should come to the ears of the Emperor.

The Seehofer affair elicited several further publications, among them a satire addressed ostensibly to a Catholic theologian named Schatzgeyer.[4] He was told that had he only been present at the examination of Seehofer, he would have been readily refuted, despite a fantastic knowledge of Scripture with which the professors at Ingolstadt could not deal. Then a satirical account is given of the proceedings. A theologian, an ornament of the university, argued that Seehofer must be a heretic because he had said that laymen and women could be theologians, whereas theology is a clerical and masculine science. Another admitted that for himself he placed more stock in the credit of the Fuggers than in the credo of the church. Still another reported the claim of Seehofer that many passages in Scotus cannot be proved from the Bible. The peasants should not be allowed to hear this because Argula von Stauffer, who knows the Bible from cover to cover, says that she is better versed in Holy Writ than all the professors at Ingolstadt, though she has never been to a university. The medical faculty is made to decline judgment until after receiving a report from the analysis of Seehofer's specimen. The jurisitic faculty insists that he should not be condemned in absentia. He is brought in and launches into such a lengthy exposition of his doctrine that the satire loses its punch.

In May of 1524 a diet met at Regensburg to consider the enforcement of the Edict of Worms against Luther. Argula sent a letter to the diet saying that their mandate, prompted by Satan against the Word of God, drove her to remonstrate though she had reason to believe that her word would be received with derision.

For the next 40 years Argula abstained from activities which came to public notice. Her husband died shortly after her visit to Luther in 1530. Two years later she married again to a man with estates in Bohemia. He lived thereafter only a year and a half. Argula was not deprived of her inheritance and found herself fully occupied with the management of estates and the care of four children. One son was to be a comfort to her, the other a trial and as to the daughters we do not know. Seehofer escaped from the monastery and became an evangelical preacher and teacher. He appears to have been somewhat unstable. At any rate he moved about a great deal. His wife is reported to have been tactless.

In May of the year 1563, just 40 years since her first outburst, the Duke of Bavaria communicated to the council of a town in his domain that for a second time he had imprisoned the "old Staufferin," who had incited the people to disobedience by circulating books contrary to the Catholic religion.[5] She had seduced them from the services of the church and had conducted private conventicles in her home. She had gone to the cemetery and had officiated at funerals without Christian ceremonies, though the Bible, the canon law, and the civil law forbid a woman to usurp this office. The council, in reply, pointed out to the duke that to play up this affair would be indiscreet at a time when Bavaria was seeking subventions (presumably from the Emperor). "Besides," said they, "the Staufferin is an enfeebled old lady. Better to have pity on her age and stupidity." She was released. One suspects that the description given by the council was meant for the duke, because the behavior ascribed to Argula indicates that she was neither enfeebled nor stupid. The flax had smouldered for 30 years, but it still smoked.

BIBLIOGRAPHY

The most fully documented account of Argula is that of Th. Kolde, "Arsacius Seehofer und Argula von Grumbach," *Beiträge zur bayerischen Kirchengeschichte* XI (1905), 49-77, 97-124, 148-88. He publishes documents relative to Seehofer and some having to do with Argula's son George, together with other correspondence. Of necessity Kolde gives references to Luther's letters in the Enders edition. In the Weimar edition they are *Briefwechsel* II, No. 509, IV, Nos. 706, 713, 800, V, 1581-4. Also in the *Beiträge* XXVIII (1922), 162-4 there is a notice by Theobold about "die alt Staufferin." He observes that the name Argula does not occur and opens the possibility that a sister might be meant, but Argula never mentions a sister. Felix Joseph Lipowsky, *Argula von Grumbach* (München, 1801), is still of value for documents on the Seehofer affair and all tracts of Argula in modern German. I have had to rely on this version for the address to the Magistracy at Ingolstadt (Lipowsky III) and her letter to her cousin, Adam von Töring (Lipowsky XII).

The following originals have been available to me:

Wie ain Christliche Fraw des Adels . . . Sendtbrieffe/ die Hohenschul zu Ingolstadt (1523). Xerox Staatsbibliothek Munich.

Ein Christeliche schrifft . . . Dem Durchleuchtigen . . . Wilhelmen/ Pfaltzgrauen bey Reyn (1523). Beinecke Library, Yale University. Xerox of another edition from the Staatsbibliothek, Munich.

Dem Durchleüchtigen . . . Johansen Pfaltzgrauen bey Reyn (1523). Beinecke Library, Yale University.

Dem Durchleüchtigen . . . Johannen Pfaltzgrauen bey Reyn (1523). Beinecke Library, Yale University.

Luther's defence of Seehofer in 1524 is in *W.A.* XV, 95 ff.

NOTES

1. Kolde, p. 101.
2. BR, 503.
3. BR, 706.
4. Kolde, p. 149 f.
5. Kolde, p. 164 f.

6.

Elisabeth of Brandenburg
(1485-1545)

Elisabeth of Brandenburg became involved by her marriage in a nexus of family relations which portended ill for harmony in religion. She was herself a Danish princess, the sister of Christian II, who introduced Lutheranism into Denmark. Her mother, Christine, was the sister of Frederick the Wise and John the Steadfast, who successively were the electors of Saxony and protectors of Luther. Her husband, Joachim I, the Elector of Brandenburg, was the brother of the Cardinal Archbishop of Mainz, Albert of Hohenzollern, against whom Luther directed his Ninety Five Theses. Joachim was a more intransigent Catholic than his brother. At the Diet of Worms he had been on the committee which sought to break Luther down after his dramatic stand. Joachim said to him, "If I understand you correctly, you are saying that you will not yield unless convinced out of Scripture." "That's right," answered Luther. When the emperor issued the edict which put Luther under the ban, although it had not been signed by all the princes, Joachim announced it "in the name and with the consent of all," and promptly enforced it in his own domain.[1] At the Diet of Augsburg in 1530 he blamed Luther for the peasants' war and spoke so hotly against the heretics that the pope believed the Holy Ghost to have spoken through his mouth.[2]

Yet religious differences did not develop between the elector and his wife until 25 years after their marriage. They were

Elisabeth of Brandenburg

united in April, 1502, when she was 17 and he 18. He then
conferred upon "his beloved wife" the castle of Spandau with
the village and lands adjoining and all the rights thereunto
appertaining. If widowed she should receive an annuity of 6,000
gulden a year. Excessive affection cannot be inferred from this
dower because it was a part of the wedding contract arranged by
the families. But four years later he added a codicil on his own
saying that he had inadvertently omitted the hunting rights.[3]
She bore him five children, two boys and three girls. The first
born, a son named Joachim, succeeded his father as the elector.
John, the last born, received the province of Küstrin. The three
daughters were Anna, to be the Duchess of Mecklenberg; Elisabeth, the Duchess of Braunschweig, to whom the next sketch
will be devoted; and Margaret, the Duchess of Anhalt.[4] All were
reared in the Catholic faith, and the Electress herself showed no
sign of deviation. When in 1513 her brother-in-law, the Cardinal
Archbishop of Mainz, sent her a fragment of the Holy Cross, she
replied with extreme gratitude and a promise to revere it with
the utmost devotion, adding in a postscript, "By the way, you
couldn't let us have a flask of Rhenish wine, could you?" [5]

After a quarter of a century of marriage Elisabeth was infect-
ed by the Lutheran heresy. By what bug she was bitten we can
only conjecture. Perhaps by her brother, King Christian II of
Denmark. He had been exiled from his kingdom and not without reason, for he was treacherous and brutal. He found a refuge
partly with his wife's uncle, the Elector of Saxony. We have
already noted that he gave a gold ring to Katherine von Bora
prior to her marriage. Naturally he was even more frequently
at the court of his sister and brother-in-law at Berlin. Joachim,
despite the religious difference, was ready for dynastic reasons
to assist Christian's return to his kingdom, and Elisabeth loaned
him nearly all her jewels to the value of 24,000 gulden (which
she never saw again).[6] Though neither an exemplary nor a
steadfast Lutheran, he would inevitably tell his sister about
Luther, whom he had lately visited. More impressive was his
own wife, Isabella, the sister of the Emperor Charles V, the great
leader of Catholic Europe. Yet Isabella was a staunch Lutheran.[7]
Then, too, Elisabeth may have been approached by itinerant

Elector
Joachim I
of Brandenburg

Christian II
of Denmark

evangelists, who, disguised as merchants, disseminated Luther's tracts and sang Luther's hymns. Joachim issued an edict forbidding under dire penalty the singing, reading, or teaching of Luther's heretical hymns.[8] She may also have read Luther's Bible. After it had been judged by a committee of theologians to contain a hundred errors, Joachim prohibited its circulation.[9]

Yet, despite all his precautions, his wife came somehow to be persuaded that Luther rightly interpreted the Word of God. Around Easter of the year 1527, during the absence of her husband, she received communion in both kinds at the hands of a Lutheran minister, both the bread and the wine. When Joachim returned, he discovered what she had done. An early tradition has it that she was betrayed by her daughter, Elisabeth. The Elector was enraged to have his will flouted in his very own household and gave his wife six months in which to submit. Then his confessor called upon her with a demand that on November 1, before the expiration of the six months, she should join her husband in receiving the Mass in one kind only. Thereupon the Elector received protests from his own two sons-in-law, Erich of Braunschweig and Albert of Mecklenberg. He retrenched, said that the confessor had exceeded his instructions and that his wife might have until Easter of 1528. In the meantime he summoned his councilors, who advised that her offense was not worthy of death, and that divorce was allowable but not expedient. Better to incarcerate her for life.

As Easter approached, her anxiety became intense. She took counsel with her uncle John of Saxony. He advised flight and offered an asylum. Let her destroy his letter. Instead she returned it and it is extant. On March 25, a few days before Easter, her husband went to visit their daughter in Braunschweig. The Electress enlisted the aid of a lady in waiting and a nobleman, the custodian of the castle, who opened the gate leading to the moat. Disguised as a peasant and carrying her remaining jewels, the Electress and the lady descended to the water, embarked, and were rowed past the last grave in God's acre. Here they scrambled ashore and clambered aboard a wagon arranged for them by King Christian, who awaited their arrival at the border of Sax-

Von der nyderlag vnd vngeluck Ku/
nig Criftiern etfchwa künig zů Denmarck Schweden vñ
Norwegen Hertzog zů Schleßwick zů Holftein Stor/
marn vñ der Dietmarifchen/ Graue zů oldenburg
vnnd Dalmanshorft/ Gegen denen von Hom
burck ꝛc newlych auf der ofter fee ergangē.
Mit angehenckter clag fo Fraw Ifa/
bella Künigin von Denmarckt.
Rayferlycher. Maieftat
fchwefter ꝛc zů jer le/
ften zeiten ge/
thon.

A tract describing the defeat at sea
of Christian II of Denmark

ony and thence wafted them to Torgau before the Elector had returned to Berlin.[10]

Joachim raged and hotly demanded that the Elector John send her back. She had been subject to no physical violence, he averred. The leaders of Europe encouraged him to insist on her return. Ferdinand of Austria declared that she had no right to leave her husband. The Cardinal Archbishop of Mainz, her brother-in-law, said that she should have referred the matter to him and he would have found a solution. Even Philip of Hesse, though a Lutheran, doubted whether she should have run away. But the Elector John proved even now that he deserved the title later conferred upon him—"John the Steadfast." At his request a committee of Wittenberg theologians drafted a reply to Joachim, telling him that he had no right to constrain the conscience of his wife by forcing her to receive communion in one kind only. In any case she had every reason to leave him because he had not been living with her for two years and had been disporting himself with a number of women, unmarried and married.[11]

They did not go into detail, but they must have had in mind a case which had become notorious. The Elector Joachim had seduced the wife of a certain Wolf Hornung, who forgave her when penitent but when the Elector prevailed again covered her with recriminations. This time she flared up. He struck her with a knife. She fled and told the Elector who banished Hornung on the charge of attempted assassination. The wife really wanted a reconciliation with her husband, but she was so closely guarded that word could be sent to him only surreptitiously through some confederate, and all attempts at a meeting were frustrated. She appealed to Luther. His reply was intercepted and returned unopened. He then sent two scathing reproofs to the Elector. Hornung appealed to the Diet of Speyer, which confronted Joachim with the accusations. Apparently mindful of Luther's word to him at Worms, he answered flippantly that if Luther could find a warrant in the Word of God, he would marry the woman. The chronicler of the diet adds, "and make a whore into an electress." [12] Broken in spirit and utterly impoverished, Hornung was given lumber by the Elector John to build a little dwelling in a Saxon village.[13]

Elisabeth, in justifying herself for not returning, made reference to all this only obliquely, when in two letters she said in addition to religion there were "other valid reasons." She did not refuse negotiations. Her husband's terms were that she must return to ancient Catholic usage. Her terms were that she should be guaranteed safety of body and goods, resumption of marital relations, permission to have a preacher of her own choice, and to receive the sacrament in both kinds as often as she chose.[14] Her conditions were rejected and she did not return. Adultery she could forgive. On religion she would not compromise.

There followed years of poverty, worry, and loneliness. Her husband would send her no money. Her sons could smuggle through only a little and were not permitted to visit her. We find her now at Torgau, now at Weimar, now at Wittenberg. In an undated letter she wrote to her sons that she suffered from arthritis, gout, cramps, and loss of teeth. She had not a gulden or a pfenning, no castle, no town, garden, or meadow. She ought to have oxen, calves, mutton, swine, geese, hens, butter, cheese, wine, and beer. But she had nothing, save only a bedroom and a sitting room and not enough money to buy an egg. For two years she nearly died of hunger.[15]

By such privations and infirmities her mental balance was affected. In 1537 she stayed for a time with the Luthers. Her daughter, Margaret of Anhalt, offered to come with servants to look after her and asked Luther to secure lodgings. He replied: "I am extremely sorry, but it is simply impossible to find quarters for you here. Everything is full, every last corner of Wittenberg. To have you come without accommodation would be very inconvenient. I can assure you that your mother is receiving the very best of care." [16] One suspects that Luther was not too unhappy over the congestion. He wanted to have the Electress transferred. But the daughter did come and no doubt the servants. Who doubled up on beds to make room for them we do not know.

The Luthers were finding the care for Elisabeth more than they could manage. Luther wrote to the Elector begging to be

Elector Joachim II of Brandenburg

relieved of the burden: "Every day there is some fresh annoyance. She barges into the room and even into the bedroom. I won't say that she is simply crazy, but she is childish. When some money did come from her sons, she gave it away lavishly and even to persons she hates when she is herself. She is a child, and a child must be kept away from the fire." [17] At the end of the week he addressed an even more emphatic plea: "I just don't see how we can carry on. She was steady till some money came from her sons. Then she began throwing it around and gave me two vessels and a hundred gulden. Of course I can't accept it, and now she is sulking. I do hope you can get her to Lichtenberg." [18]

The daughter Elisabeth also came, the very one who had betrayed her, but now of the same faith. She stayed with the Luthers for some six weeks and greatly embarrassed Luther by her indiscretion, for she confided to her brother Joachim the story, no doubt subsequently expanded, that in church Luther had prayed against her uncle the Cardinal Archbishop of Mainz and Duke George as possessed of the devil. Protests came to the Elector. Luther denied that he had mentioned them in public prayer, but at the table in Elisabeth's presence he had said that he would pray against them as possessed of the devil. He bore her no grudge and on a later occasion sent her sprouts of mulberry and figs.[19]

Luther's suggestion that she go to Lichtenberg has reference to a castle which the Elector had renovated for her residence. The Elector, by the way, was no longer John, but now his son John Frederick. He arranged the transfer. Luther visited her there and reported: "It is pitiable to see a woman of such noble birth and character so grievously afflicted. May the Lord Jesus make her well." [20] He was not too happy over his own plight. As they sat at meat she wished him another 40 years of life. "Good Lord, no," said he. "If God offered me paradise on condition that I stay down here for another 40 years, I'd turn it down and send for the executioner to chop off my head." [21]

As a matter of fact, Elisabeth need not have stayed at Lichtenberg. She might have gone home two years earlier when her husband died in 1535. The sons invited her back, promising the properties at Spandau and the annuity of 6,000 gulden stipulated in the wedding contract. "Yes," she answered, "but what about religion?" She would not return unless not only her sons but also the estates of Brandenburg agreed that in her area she might follow "the pure Word of God as set forth in the Augsburg Confession." This meant not only that she personally should enjoy this freedom, but that all the people in her little area should follow her practice. She would be imposing Lutheranism on a segment of the population. Her sons declined; they had sworn to their dying father that they would introduce no innovations. Joachim II had married the Polish princess Hedwig as his second wife and she was a Catholic. If there were any interference with her religion when she visited Spandau, her father, the King of Poland, might intervene,[22] and Ferdinand of Austria warned that conflicts might ensue.[23] Moreover, the two sons of Elisabeth had joined the Halle alliance of Catholic rulers. They would not accede to their mother's demands. She would not return.

And then in Spandau, on All Saints Day in 1539, Joachim II celebrated the Mass with communion in both kinds and without any popish embellishments. Very shortly thereafter a similar Mass was celebrated in Berlin, though not quite so devoid of popish embellishments. Joachim reiterated his urging that she now come home, for he could not see why she should hold out over such trifles. The younger son, John, paid her a visit. But she was not yet satisfied. A church ordinance had been instituted in Brandenburg which retained many of the Catholic ceremonies. Joachim explained that processions on Palm Sunday, on the day of the Martyrs at Easter, and Pentecost were indeed more observed at Berlin than at Wittenberg, but not to give offense, rather to educate the young. "We are not bound," said he, "to follow the lead of Wittenberg any more than that of Rome. In the early church there was diversity of practice without a breach of unity so long as there was agreement in essentials. Other people cannot understand nor can we, why you should take these points so seriously. There is nothing here contrary to the Word of God. You can have it your way at Spandau, but let us have it our way here and we shall be bound to you as loving sons." [24]

Luther was consulted. He answered: "Provided the gospel of Jesus Christ is preached purely with no human additions and the sacraments of Baptism and the Lord's Supper are observed, with no invocation of the saints, no carrying of the sacrament in procession, no daily masses and vigils for the dead, no holy water and salt, and provided that pure hymns are sung in Latin and German, then it does not matter if there be a cross of gold or silver, whether the cope be of saffron, silk, or linen; and if the Elector is not content to put on one gown, let him have three the way Aaron wore them, one on top of another; and if he doesn't find one procession enough, let him go around seven times like Joshua with the trumpets blowing; and if he wants to leap with harp, psaltry, and cymbals, let him dance like David before the ark. Conscience is not to be bound, and if we have given up these practices in Wittenberg, we may have reasons which are not valid in Berlin. Except where God has commanded let there be freedom." [25]

The Electress was not as broad as Luther. She was a precursor of those English Puritans who called the vestments of the clergy "the rags of Antichrist." She was still unwilling to return.

But in 1545 her son John appeared at Lichtenberg with 500 horses to bring her back.[26] She was impressed. He paid her debts and settled her at Spandau, agreed to support a minister of her choice, and to grant full freedom of conscience to her and to her household. She would be free to travel, and if she were not satisfied at Spandau, she could return to Saxony.

In her household she herself conducted family devotions. Her chaplain said that she made him into a genuine minister. But her spirit was not healed. Her long suffering had made her a trifle querulous and disposed to dwell on past miseries. To John she wrote: "I cannot conceal from you out of motherly love that the dear God, our heavenly Father, has laid upon me a heavy cross with sickness, poverty, misery, trouble, and terror, more than I can tell. I would not have believed that such trials could be on earth and would comfort myself with the words of Job, 'The Lord has given. The Lord has taken away. Blessed be the name of the Lord.' You should know how long I have lived in misery and great sickness and have had to suffer such shameful poverty in my old age as not to have a penny on earth, nor a bite of sausage in my mouth. If God in his especial grace had not upheld me, it would have been no wonder if my heart had broken in two for sheer misery." [27]

As she sensed the shortening of her days, she asked her son the Elector, to transfer her, though desperately sick, to Berlin. As soon as suitable quarters could be arranged she was moved. As she was dying, the moon was eclipsed. Friends wondered whether she might not view this as a bad omen. " 'Clipse, 'clipse," said she. "Who's afraid of a 'clipse? I believe in him who made the sun and the moon and all the stars and gave life to all creatures. He will uphold me. May he not tarry to fetch me. To him will I go. I am so weary of life." [28]

One wonders why she wanted to die and be buried in Berlin instead of Spandau. The clue is in her will. She requested that she be interred without ceremonies in a grave beside her husband,[29] whom she had abandoned 27 years ago for the sake of religion.

BIBLIOGRAPHY

Sketches of the life of Elisabeth of Brandenburg

Adolf Friedrich Riedel, "Die Kurfürstin Elisabeth von Brandenburg in Beziehung auf die Reformation," *Zeitschrift für Preussische Geschichte und Landeskunde* II (1865), 66-100, 354-5.

Ernst Dan. Mart. Kirchner, "Elisabeth von Dänmark" in *Die Churfürstinnen und Köninginnen auf dem Throne der Hohenzollern* I (1866, Berlin).

Wilhelm Bauer, "Elisabeth, Churfürstin von Brandenburg, die Bekennerin," *Deutsche Blätter* (1873), 521-40.

The Reformation in Brandenburg

Julius Heidemann, *Die Reformation in der Mark Brandenburg* (Berlin, 1889).

Paul Steinmüller, "Einfürung der Reformation in die Kurmark Brandenburg durch Joachim II," *SVRG* 26 (1903).

Cultural Background

Adolf W. Schmidt, "Hofleben und Hofsitten der Fürstinnen im sechzehnten Jahrhundert," *Zeitschrift für Geschichtswissenschaft* II (Berlin, 1844), pp. 220-65.

Peter Gerrit Thielen, "Die Kultur am Hofe Herzog Albrecht von Preussen (1525-1568)," *Göttinger Bausteine zur Geschichtswissenschaft* XII (1953).

Special Points

G. Berbig, "Ein Gutachten über die Flucht der Kurfürstin Elisabeth von Brandenburg aus dem Schlosse zu Berlin," *ARG* VIII (1910/11) 380-94.

Rudolf Jakobi, "Die Flucht der Kurfürstin Elisabeth von Brandenburg," *Hohenzollern Jahrbuch* XIII (1909), 155-96.

Friedrich Wagner, "Der Schatz der Kurfürstin Elisabeth von Brandenburg," *Hohenzollern Jahrbuch* I (1897), text and facsimiles.

Paul Zimmermann, "Der Streit Wolf Hornungs mit Kurfürst Joachim I von Brandenburg und Luthers Betheilung an demselben," *Zeitschrift für preussische Geschichte und Landeskunde* XX (Berlin, 1883), 310-43.

Documents

Adolf F. J. Riedel, *Codex Brandenburgensis*. An extensive series. Index volume (Berlin, 1867).

Abbreviations:

ARG	*Archiv für Reformationsgeschichte.*	
BR	*Briefwechsel,* Luther's in the Weimar edition.	
Codex	*Codex Brandenburgensis,* ed. Riedel.	
DRA	*Deutsche Reichstagsakten,* jüngere Reihe.	
SVRG	*Schriften des Vereins für Reformationsgeschichte.*	

NOTES

1. *DRA* II, pp. 597, 606, 654, 949.
2. Steinmüller *SVRG* 26 (1903), 21 ff.
3. *Codex* I, 11, No. 172, postscript No. 174. Cf. III, 3, No. 113.
4. Heidemann, p. 143.
5. *Codex* III, 3, No. 230.
6. Riedel, p. 83. Cf. Wagner.
7. Bauer, p. 527. Charles V told Christian II that he would support him only if his wife, Charles' sister, abandoned Lutheranism. Jakobi, p. 191. Luther testified to her stalwartness and that she had suffered in consequence. *W.A.* XXVI, 630. Carl Ferdinand Allen tells how at the Diet of Nürnberg she received communion in both kinds at the hands of Osiander, moved the diet to tears by her plea and stood up to her brother Ferdinand who told her he wished she had never been his sister. *De Rebus Christiani Secundi* (1844), 53-54.
8. Ludwig Frege, *Berlin unter Einflusse der Reformation* (Berlin, 1839), 217.
9. Steinmüller, *SVRG* 26 (1903), 21-24.
10. These events are related in Riedel and Kirchner. The account of the flight is fuller in Jakobi. Elisabeth's version is in *Codex* III, 3, 359-62.
11. Berbig, *ARG* 8 (1910/11), 380-94.
12. *DRA* VII, p. 714.
13. Zimmermann, *Der Streit.*
14. Riedel, pp. 80-81.
15. Schmidt, *Hofleben* . . . pp. 256-7.
16. *BR* VII, No. 3177, Sept. 26, 1537.
17. *BR* VIII, No. 3185, Nov. 7, 1537.
18. *BR* VIII, No. 3188, Nov. 16, 1537.
19. *BR* VII, Nos. 2160 and 2164, and *ARG* 25, p. 80. Also *BR* VIII, No. 3257.
20. *TR* III, 3644ba.
21. *TR* IV, 4647 f.
22. Riedel, p. 86 f. Kirchner, p. 254.
23. *Codex,* Supplement No. 123.
24. *Riedel,* pp. 94-95.
25. *BR* VIII, No. 3421, Dec. 4/5, 1539.
26. Jakobi, p. 181.
27. Riedel, p. 99.
28. Kirchner, p. 281.
29. Bauer, pp. 538-9.

7.

Elisabeth of Braunschweig
(1510-1558)

Elisabeth of Braunschweig was more influential in the politics of the Reformation than any of the women considered so far, even more than her mother, Elisabeth of Brandenburg, who hurt her own influence by her exile. The daughter was to be for five years the ruler of her land. She was married in 1525 at the age of 15 to Duke Erich of Braunschweig-Calenberg, 40 years her senior. After the death of his first wife he had a concubine.[1] Elisabeth required that he dismiss her with a pension of 1,000 gulden but when, after bearing four children, Elisabeth was for a time unequal to wifely relations, he returned to his discarded partner. Elisabeth charitably suggested that he had been bewitched. There followed a witch hunt and someone was burned, but not the concubine.[2] Elisabeth's four children were three daughters—Elisabeth, Anna Maria, and Katherine, and a son Erich.

For ten years after their marriage, there was no religious differences between husband and wife. Both were Catholic. In 1538 Elisabeth received a visit from her mother, and her brother John of Küstrin, who had already made public declaration of his adherence to the evangelical faith. At his request she invited a Lutheran pastor named Corvinus[3] from the domain of Philip of Hesse to preach to them. She was so deeply affected that before the expiration of the year she announced her adherence to the faith of the reformers. Duke Erich did not intervene. "If she does

Elisabeth of Braunschweig

not interfere with my religion, I will not interfere with hers." [4]
He had been present when Luther made his valiant stand at
Worms and had been so moved that he sent him a silver tankard
of beer.[5] But for himself, he said, "I'm too old to grub around to
find out what is true, what false. I will die in the faith in which
I was baptized and which is held by the emperor, whose vassel I
am and whom I am bound to obey." [6] Erich may not have realized that allowing Elisabeth to follow her own persuasion meant
more than tolerating an occasional reception of the Lord's body
in bread and wine. She was determined to evangelize the entire
land. A beginning had already been made. Two cities, Göttingen
and Hannover, by the payment of huge sums to the depleted
coffers of the duke, had bought religious freedom and had gone
Lutheran. Northeim shortly followed.[7] Elisabeth would go beyond the cities to convert the countryside.

Her endeavor threw her into a nexus of religious and political
forces, inextricably tangled. The conflict of confessions cut
across long-standing strains in German constitutional history.
Centralization and decentralization were in perpetual tension,
as they had been throughout the Middle Ages. Germany was
made up of a number of territories and the empire, headed by
Charles V, sought to achieve consolidation through diets and
an overall court of justice. The territories strove to maintain
their independence by engaging in petty but devastating wars.
Yet within the territories the princes were endeavoring to do in
miniature what the emperor envisaged on a larger scale. As they
resisted the emperor, so in turn they were resisted by the nobles
and the peasants.

While administrative power was being consolidated within
the units despite resistance, the number of units was being increased by the practice of dividing territories between brothers.
Thus Saxony had been split into the Ernestine and Albertine
branches. Joachim I had passed the electoral dignity to his elder
son Joachim II, but had given the district of Küstrin to the
younger, John. Similarly Braunschweig had suffered divisions.
The territory ruled by Erich was called Braunschweig-Calenberg.
Contiguous was Braunschweig-Wolfenbüttel, governed by Erich's
nephew Heinz, popularly called "the wolf" from the name of

his locality. The division was untenable because mining rights and other jurisdictions overlapped. Consequently, each ruler sought reunification, or at least dominant control at the expense of the other.

Then religion entered to accentuate the cleavages. So long as Erich and Heinz were Catholic, the issue did not arise, but Elisabeth's conversion was to turn Heinz into an implacable foe. The empire could not but be involved. Charles V was resolved to suppress Protestantism. If the Protestant princes refused to obey his behests, they were guilty of revolution. They tried to avoid this conclusion by pointing out that the emperor was an elective monarch and might be resisted by the electors. But then the electors were divided. Fredrick the Wise and his successors were Lutherans. Joachim II joined them, but Joachim I, Albert of Mainz, and Richard of Trier, among others, were Catholic. The theory became increasingly untenable, and the Protestant resistance assumed the aspect of an attempt to disrupt the very structure of the empire. Erich wanted to be neutral, but the times were not tolerant of neutrality.

Erich's position was constantly compromised by the activities of his wife. The passion of her life was the purification of religion according to the Word of God contained in the Bible translation of Martin Luther. She had also two other goals, which she hoped would reinforce the first. One was to maintain her widow's dower consisting of the town of Münden with its adjacent lands, and the town of Göttingen.[8] She was resolved that this endowment should never be alienated, partly for the sake of her own security, but partly that she might administer the area in her own name and introduce Lutheranism, even against the wishes of her lord. A further goal was to keep Braunschweig-Calenberg intact for her son Erich. All three concerns coalesced to make her a foe of Heinz the Wolf. Tough and crafty, he had kept his brother in prison for 11 years until he conceded the principle of primogeniture. Craftiness was also evident in his handling of complaints about his relations with his mistress. Having announced that she was very ill, he then proclaimed that she was dead. A great public funeral was held with vigils and masses for her departed soul, while in the meantime her body departed to a remote castle where she bore more children to her enamored lord.[9]

Contemporaries were less shocked by a romantic affair than by the wasting of masses for the dead when they could do no good. Plainly Heinz took his Catholicism lightly as to religion but seriously as to politics. For all his irreverence, he would not disrupt the social structure of bishoprics, dioceses, or abbacies within the framework of the Holy Roman Empire. He would not tolerate Lutheranism.

Elisabeth felt constrained to seek a counterpoise and turned to Philip of Hesse, the political leader of the Protestants. Young Erich should be married to Philip's daughter.[10] Philip was asked to *lend* one of his preachers to Elisabeth.[11]

Erich, the elder, was increasingly in a quandry. He did not wish to be dominated by the overbearing Heinz, and he did not wish to be allied with the all too ardent Philip. He knew that if he fostered Lutheranism, he would be in trouble with the emperor, whom he would soon have to meet at a diet meeting at Hagenau in 1540. Before going he made his will. If at the time of his death his son were not of age, there would have to be a regent. Heinz of Wolfenbüttel was quite ready to take over. Erich instead appointed Elisabeth, but she would need a guardian. Heinz was ready, and he could scarcely be altogether disregarded, but there might be a counterpoise in another guardian. Heinz and Philip of Hesse were appointed. This was like yoking the wolf with a lion's whelp. They had already been at war. Philip suspected Heinz of planning to subdue Protestantism by armed force. One of Heinz's messengers was intercepted, his bags rifled, and documents found which confirmed the suspicion. Philip then fell upon Heinz, captured him, and held him a prisoner for two years.[12] To keep these two from throttling each other a third guardian, Joachim II of Brandenberg, Elisabeth's brother, was appointed.[13]

Erich then went to Hagenau where death relieved him of his dilemma. So depleted was his treasury that there was not enough money to pay the expenses of returning his body for burial. It had to lie in state for one whole year pending the transfer.[14]

Erich, the son, was only 12 years old and would not reach his

Erich I of Braunschweig

majority for another five years. His mother was the regent and took over the administration with a vigorous hand. She had already had some experience in her dower at Münden and could count on a staff of trained officials and numerous servants. The number of mouths to be fed in her household is estimated at 200 by a modern work which publishes the records of her administration, listing in full all the data on finance, justice, jewels, edibles, and livestock: oxen, sheep, rabbits, hens, geese, bacon, cheese, butter, wine, and beer. Elisabeth of course delegated details, but kept watch over the whole.[15]

More important to her than all this was the dissemination of the Word of God. She had asked Philip of Hesse for the loan of a minister. He sent the very one who had dedicated a tract to her in 1538, Antonius Corvinus, ardent, able, and fearless. For Elisabeth he drew up a hymnbook and a church ordinance which required that concubinous priests should marry their mates on pain of dismissal. The ordinance for cloisters did not call for their discontinuance. The inmates who so chose might stay. Those who elected to remain should be free at any time to leave.[16] In the meantime they should discard their habits. wear ordinary dark clothes and "underwear like that of any other Christian." [17] Corvinus then undertook a visitation of all the churches and convents, accompanied at times by Elisabeth. His enterprise was perilous because in the country districts any religious innovation might endanger his life.[18]

Nothing was of greater importance to Elisabeth than the rearing of her son in the reformed faith. Corvinus recorded his pleasure at seeing the lad with others kneeling in the church and singing antiphonally with the congregation.[19] Young Erich was thoroughly grounded in the catechism. As he approached his majority the mother desired to have him married to a soundly Lutheran wife with some political influence.

At one time the thought had been to engage him to the daughter of Philip of Hesse, but Philip had crippled his political influence as the leader of militant Protestantism by his bigamy in 1540. He was not happy in his arranged marriage with the daughter of Duke George of Saxony and, like so many princes, found satisfaction on the outside. His conscience had not trou-

Bericht / ob man on die
Tauff vnd empfahunge des leibs
vnd blüts Christi / allein durch den
glauben / könne selig werden /
An die durchleuchtige
vnd hochgeporne Fürstinnen vnd
frawen / Fraw Elizabeth / geporne
Margreffinnen zü Brandenburg /
Hertzoginnē zü Braunschwig vñ
Lenneburg geschrieben / durch
M. An. Coruinum /

Gedruckt zü Marpurg
Anno 1 5 3 8

CLEOPATRA

A tract of Antonius Corvinus dedicated
to Elisabeth of Braunschweig

bled him while he was a Catholic, but after becoming a Lutheran he felt unworthy to go to the Lord's Table. He informed the Lutheran theologians that if he had a wife for whom he really cared, he could restrict himself to her. They told him that bigamy was not prohibited in the Bible and in the forum of conscience was preferable to promiscuity. But since it was contrary to the law of the land, the second marriage should be kept secret. Had this been done the new wife would have been regarded as a concubine, and he would have had no trouble. But Philip would have no subterfuge and announced the marriage. Then, to avoid being put under the ban of the empire, he had to withdraw from the leadership of the Schmalkald League of Protestant princes. Philip's daughter would not now do for Erich.[20]

Elisabeth looked to a region more remote, to ducal Saxony. This was the area once ruled by Duke George, the doughty Catholic. On his death in 1539, through the complacence of his successor and the fervor of his successor's wife, the region became Lutheran. The children of this couple were Moritz, now the duke, and his sister Sidonia. She was the choice. Elizabeth took Erich to Saxony to make the arrangements and on the way called on Luther, who examined Erich as to the faith and found him entirely sound. But to Corvinus Luther reported, "I hope he will not succumb to the pressures to which princes are subject." [21]

As the time of Erich's majority approached, Elisabeth prepared for him a treatise on government, and no mean document it was, with sound counsel on all matters of administration, concluding with an exhortation "to obey God, the emperor, and your mother." [22] She could not conceive of any conflict between the first and the third of these loyalties. She was to discover that the second might not comport in her eyes either with the first or the third.

When her son became Erich II, she acted in one respect as if she meant to turn the administration over to him and withdraw. She remarried, taking as her second husband Duke Poppo of Henneberg, a solidly Lutheran prince whose elder brother was already married to her own daughter Elisabeth. At the same time she desired to retain her widow's dower at Münden, presumably because she did not yet know whether her son would prove to be an efficient administrator, or if he was capable of warding off the encroachments of Heinz the Wolf. But even while retaining Münden she asked her new husband for a second dower in his domain. He suggested that she provide the funds by disposing of her dower at Münden for a monetary consideration. This she would not do, but the dispute did not chill their affection.[23]

Elisabeth also undertook to make an advantageous marriage for her daughter Anna Maria with some powerful Lutheran prince. None was more suitable than Albert of Prussia, though he was 40 years her senior. Having lost his beloved Dorothea he was not inclined to marry at all, but because he needed a son for his succession and had only a daughter, he agreed.[24] Erich said to his sister, "Why are you going to marry that old duffer? He is not as handsome as the paintings make him out to be." She answered, "I'd rather marry a wise old man than a young fool. He is so Christian and honorable and faithful to me, as you are not to your wife." [25] Elisabeth then composed for her daughter a treatise on marriage and domestic life in which she said that the wife should be obedient to her husband and "should rule him by love and reason without bitterness." [26]

Elisabeth would have liked to accompany her daughter to Königsberg, the Prussian capital, but felt needed at home. Her husband Poppo was willing to serve as the chaperon, and Elisabeth resigned herself to the sacrifice of a long separation. Little did she surmise that it would be a full four years. Consequently he was not at hand when she needed him most.[27]

For Erich behaved quite contrary to his mother's expectation. In 1546 he received an invitation to attend the diet of the empire meeting at Regensburg. He was undoubtedly flattered that at the age of 18 he should assume a place among the princes of the realm. He may have thought to get help from the emperor to curb the encroachments of Heinz the Wolf. Elisabeth may have hoped so, too, but she was lacking in insight if she did not perceive that the emperor granted concessions to Lutherans only if they were in a position to exert political pressure. Elisabeth took umbrage at the expense of Erich's proposed journey. When he did go, he was accompanied by 400 horsemen. If they were not to eat off the land and alienate every place through which they passed, Braunschweig would have to foot the bill. Her greatest fear was at the point of religion. Might not Erich be sucked into the vortex of the anti-Lutheran imperial policy? Before his departure she partook with him of the body and blood of the Lord, the bread and the wine, and received from him an oath that he would not desert the faith. In conversation with Corvinus Erich declared that "whatever he had in his breast he would stake for the reformed religion." When this was repeated to another he commented, "Perhaps my lord had a snot rag in his vest." [28]

The fears of Elisabeth were abundantly realized. Erich was seduced by imperial blandishments and lined up with the Emperor's policy—a few concessions to the Lutherans in the Augsburg *Interim,* and a promise of force to those who refused to comply. Göttingen, Hannover, and Braunschweig refused to comply.[29] Magdeburg was obdurate. John Frederick of Saxony would not submit. Philip of Hesse, though his wings had been clipped, sprouted new feathers and joined his old colleagues in resistance. The Protestant princes had become revolutionary and were ready to wreck the structure of the empire rather than compromise on religion.

There were, however, a few who were not so clear-cut in their stand, chief among them Erich's brother-in-law, Moritz of Saxony.[30] Fellow Lutherans called him a Judas, and modern historians have dubbed him a Machiavelli, concerned only for aggrandizement and power. His policy was complicated because he wanted both to support Lutheranism and reunite the administration of Saxony by divesting John Frederick of the electoral dignity in favor of himself. This goal could be achieved only in alliance with the emperor. Without renouncing Lutheranism for himself, Moritz joined the forces of the Catholic emperor and fell upon the other Saxony. At the battle of Mühlberg in April of 1547 the Protestants were defeated. John Frederick was made a prisoner. Moritz became the elector. The emperor then set out to enforce the *Interim* and subdue the rebels.

Erich returned to Braunschweig not merely to enforce the *Interim,* but to restore Catholicism in full. His wife Sidonia

opposed him. He threatened to cast her off if she did not renounce Lutheranism. She refused and he did cast her off.[31]
Corvinus groaned that Christ seemed to be asleep in the boat.[32]
Corvinus was apprehended by Spanish soldiers, imprisoned, and
his library burned. The very archbishop of Bremen, seeing this,
protested that the books were not to blame. Corvinus was placed
in solitary confinement. Not even his wife could communicate
with him. A fellow minister repeatedly walked five miles to
converse with the captive through the window.[33] Then the window was boarded up.[34] The minister Mörlin at Göttingen was
expelled.

"O Lord God," cried Elisabeth, "to whom have I given birth?
Whom have I reared? To deny the plain truth is a sin which
cannot be forgiven on earth or in heaven. To persecute, maltreat, and abuse the servants of the Word of God is to persecute,
maltreat, and abuse Christ Jesus, our only Savior, mediator, and
intercessor, who has borne our sins. My son has brought me to
bed. If he keeps on, he will bring me to the grave." [35]

She addressed Erich: "How have you fallen into such insane
raving and raging against God, against his Word, his servants,
his churches and against me, your dear mother, against the whole
country and the poor oppressed subjects? Did you learn all this
in foreign parts? God have mercy on you. If you do not turn
about, God will smite you as he has always smitten those who
would pull Christ from his throne. . . . Woe, woe, woe and
again woe to you if you do not change. You have made me so sick
and weak from weeping that I have not strength to write and
have had to dictate. I must say this or my heart will break. If I
do not speak the very stones will cry out." [36]

"If you have a single drop of blood that believes in God, consider what he does to those who set themselves against him." [37]

"I beg you as your mother that you desist from your godless
abuses and abominations invented by men and not commanded
in Holy Scripture . . . but rather forbidden on pain of damnation. Stop. Release the prisoners." [38]

Erich answered: "My very dear Mother, the matter of Corvinus is not in my hands. I would not have expected from you
such denunciation. I beg you to desist. If your words should

become public they would create a very bad impression. I will act as answerable to Almighty God and the emperor." [39] And again: "As for Mörlin, I hear that he has reviled the emperor and other leaders of the Holy Roman Empire and uses the most injurious, offensive, stinking, slanderous abuse. I have written to the council to expel this rebellious ass. His language can create riots and civil war. These scamps are guilty of *lese majesty*. . . . I have not failed my father, and there is none I hold in greater love than yourself. You should not revile me. I would restore the ancient Catholic religion of our fathers and my father, which you have brought to naught. I would build it up again. You would stir up rebellion among my subjects, as if they were your subjects and not mine. I will answer before God, the emperor, the Holy Roman Empire, and all Christendom. If you will not leave off your denunciations, I shall have to take measures, which will give me very great pain." [40]

Erich was right that the ministers did not hesitate to fling at him all the epithets of abuse culled from the Bible and the barnyard. He was right that disobedience, even though non-violent, was a form of rebellion and disrupted the constitution of the empire. He was right that he was returning to the religion of his father, and he could not understand why his mother had been able to live in amity with him, though a Catholic, and could not do the same with her son. Erich could not understand, because he had never been a mother. He did not grasp that he was the fruit of her womb. She had grounded him in the catechism, had beamed when he sang the antiphons in the church, had glowed when Luther found him sound in the faith. She had looked to him to crown her labors, and now he had restored the abomination of desolation and had even made friendly gestures to Heinz the Wolf, just as Pilate and Herod drew together against Jesus. [41] Then Erich went to Spain with instructions to his officials not to relax his orders.

Elisabeth secured a pastorate for Mörlin in the territory of her son-in-law, Albert of Prussia. To Mörlin she wrote: "I don't know whether I can stay or must leave. My son is in Spain. There is a rumor that he will return with Spanish troops. Alas to God that I should have borne such a son! May God convert him.

Otherwise deliver me from his tyranny, for the natural knowledge of God and the love of a mother are darkened in him. He has become brutal, merciless. I see his damnation before my eyes and my grief is crushing. I am resigned to God's will. I have not lost faith in my God, nor in Albert of Prussia and my brother John. All else is dark. I am glad Albert has been able to provide for you. Hold on." [42] She held on and was indefatigable in her appeals to rulers, officials, town councils, and even to Heinz the Wolf, to take measures for the release of Corvinus. She was told that the orders of her son must be obeyed. [43]

Thereupon came another shift of the kaleidoscope. After the battle of Mühlberg the emperor overplayed his advantage by allowing the treacherous arrest and imprisonment of Philip of Hesse. Philip was the father-in-law of Moritz, who was greatly attached to him and had often sought his judgment. Moritz now resolved, like William of Orange at a later date, "to drive these Spanish vermin from the land." Employing the chicanery in which the Spanish chancellery was versed, he utterly deceived the emperor, asking of him troops with which to subdue the recalcitrant city of Magdeburg, rebelling against the *Interim*. Moritz secured the submission of the city by promising that it would not have to adopt the *Interim* and then with his army swooped upon the emperor and sent him packing over the Alps. His person might even have been seized had not Moritz sensed that a captive emperor is of no more use than a captive pope. Moritz then undertook to pacify Germany by resolving the religious issue. He brought about the Peace of Passau in 1552 which led to the Peace of Augsburg in 1555 and gave the Lutherans a legal status at last. [44]

After Moritz' successful coup John Frederick and Philip of Hesse were released. At once Elisabeth turned to Philip, reminding him that Corvinus had only been loaned. Let Philip reclaim him. [45] There was no need. With the turn of events Erich, returning from Spain, veered like a weathercock, was reconciled with his ever forgiving mother, restored Lutheranism and released the prisoners. Corvinus had so suffered that he lived only two more months.

This reversal did not fully satisfy Elisabeth. There was still

IN · TABVLA · HAC · PICTVS
QVIS · SIT · SI · FORTE · REQVIRIS
CORVINI · FATIEM & LINIA
MENTA · VIDES ANNO · 1546

Antonius Corvinus

Heinz the Wolf, ever ready to encroach upon her and subvert her efforts. Let Erich send him packing like the emperor. Erich could scarcely succeed unaided. Elisabeth appears to have been the one who engineered an alliance with Albert Alcibiades,[46], duke of one of the divisions of Brandenburg, called Alcibiades to distinguish him from all the other Alberts. Elisabeth now gave her jewels to finance the stroke against Heinz.[47]

When Erich and Alcibiades were ready to spring, they found themselves confronted by an amazing coalition. At the side of Heinz was Philip of Hesse, who once had made him a prisoner, and together with this pair stood Moritz, Erich's own brother-in-law. The reason for this alliance was not religious, but inspired by German national feeling.[48]

Albert Alcibiades was an unprincipled, mercenary adventurer, always ready to join or foment disturbance. He had assisted Moritz against the Schmalkald League and against the emperor. But unlike Moritz he did not then seek pacification, but hired himself first to France, then switched to the emperor on the promise of lands to be wrested from the bishops of Würzburg and Bamberg.[49] The German princes, Protestant and Catholic alike, would not suffer this meteor to ignite conflagrations throughout Germany. It was one thing to resist the emperor for religion, another to disrupt the empire for adventure.

The battle of Sievershausen decided the issue in 1553. Alcibiades with plumed helmet charged with all the gusto of a Black Prince or a Henry of Navarre. Moritz fell. He was only 32. Heinz the Wolf lost two sons. Nevertheless the day was his. Alcibiades withdrew to eke out a desultory four more years. Erich had to submit to Heinz. The price of clemency was the expulsion of Elisabeth. She had to leave Münden and with her young daughter Katherine went to Hannover. Her husband Poppo might now have come to her but thought it better to keep his own domain intact. When the topaz fell out of her wedding ring, she suspected him of infidelity. Heinz cut off all her income. In dire poverty she eked out a bare existence for three years. Katherine had to go begging at the convents which had not been suppressed. The abundant letters of Elisabeth to Albert of Prussia are a constant dirge. She has no wood, she tells him, and not a pfenning. Her one time household which she numbered conservatively at 238 [a modern estimate gives 200] had vanished. Her mother at Spandau sent her a cook, but of what use was a cook if there was nothing to cook? Albert sent ten oxen. She reported that they were not very lean from the journey and could readily be fattened. Diseases afflicted her. A leg gave way. Friends were indifferent. Her son reviled her for getting him into this mess, and her brother Joachim said her fate was her fault.[50]

But although her letters are a book of lamentations, her hymns are a book of psalms. Here breathe constancy, love, and joy. They are not great poetry. The metre is halting and the rhymes inexact, but there pulses through them a resolute spirit. Here is a hymn composed on leaving Braunschweig:

> Braunschweig I now must leave you.
> It is the Lord God's will.
> But though I must bereave you,
> May you be constant still.
>
> It is my will to leave you.
> Better be hurt than to hurt,
> And though I grieve to grieve you,
> You are by love begirt.
>
> The dear God, I know, will lead me
> And the Three in One,
> The chosen angels feed me
> Until the guerdon's won.

This hymn voices joy in the Lord.

> Joyful will I be
> And bless his holy name.
> He is my help and stay
> And comfort in my shame.
>
> Joyful will I be
> If he is but near.
> The cross has overcome,
> And nothing need I fear.

The chief respite in exile was the presence of Katherine, of whom she writes,

To Thee O God alone be praise
And thanks to Thee for grace,
That Thou hast vouchsafed to me
To look on Katherine's face.

The jewels she wears are godliness.
She helps me bear my cross.
She will have reward of thee.
She counts the world but dross.[51]

After three years of exile Albert of Prussia and Joachim II of Brandenburg obtained from the emperor permission for her restoration to Münden.[52] Together with Katherine she came back. Erich then, without telling his mother, arranged a marriage for Katherine with a Catholic nobleman who had estates in Bohemia. Profoundly chagrined, Elisabeth resolved nevertheless to attend the wedding. But Erich deceived her as to the time and when she arrived, Katherine was already married and on her way. "O what sin have I committed," cried Elisabeth, "that I should be so treated? Even a cowherd or a swineherd would invite a father and mother to a wedding." [53] Her mind gave way. She was taken to the estate of her husband in Henneberg. Even though her faculties revived, she was perhaps more difficult than if they had not. Duke Poppo cared for her with great tenderness until her death on May 25, 1558, at the age of 48.[54]

Little did she perceive that her failure was her success. Not with Erich, to be sure! He went off to serve the emperor in Holland, Spain, and Italy. He died and was buried at Pavia. Shortly before her collapse Elisabeth wrote a book of consolation for widows in which she said, "No one without the experience knows the anguish which children can cause and yet be loved." [55] Elisabeth's victory lay not with Erich, but in the triumph of her cause. The old Wolf, chastened by the death of his two sons and no longer needled by the aggressive Elisabeth, grew mellow even to the point of allowing Lutheranism in his domains. All of Braunschweig embraced the Confession of Augsburg, not as a result of princely coercion but through conviction engendered by the labors and sufferings of the evangelical ministers and their preceptress, Elisabeth of Braunschweig.

BIBLIOGRAPHY

Karl Schottenloher, *Bibliographie der deutschen Geschichte*. See Braunschweig bibliography.

There are many articles in the *Zeitschrift der Gesellschaft für niedersächische Kirchengeschichte*. Abb. ZGNKG.

The best sketch of the life of Elisabeth is that by Paul Tschackert, "Herzogin Elisabeth von Münden," *Hohenzollern Jahrbuch* III (1899), 49-65. This also appeared separately with an appendix giving the full text of the *Regierungshandbuch* and the *Ehestandsbuch* (Leipzig, 1899).

The two above mentioned works of Elisabeth are fully analyzed by Regula in ZGNKG XVI (1911), 280-94 and XVIII (1913), 28-43.

There is a brief sketch of her life without documentation by A. Kurs, *Elisabeth, Herzogin von Braunschweig-Calenberg* (Halle, 1891).

The fullest and best treatment of her hymns is that by Freiherr von der Goltz-Greifswald, "Lieder der Herzogin Elisabeth . . . " *ZGNKG* XIX (1914) 147-208.

Her letters to Albert of Prussia are edited by Ingeborg Mangel, "Elisabeth von Braunschweig-Lüneburg und Albert von Preussen . . . " *Veröffentlichung der historischen Kommission für Niedersachsen*, 13/14 (1954).

The correspondence with Mörlin is edited by Franz Koch, "Briefe der Herzogin Elisabeth von Braunschweig-Lüneberg . . . ," *ZGNKG* X (1905), 231-66 and XI (1906), 89-146.

The correspondence with Corvinus is edited by Paul Tschackert, "Briefwechsel des Antonius Corvinus," *Quellen und Darstellungen zur Geschichte Niedersachsens* IV (Hannover, Leipzig, 1900).

There are many references to her in his "Antoninus Corvinus Leben und Schriften," in the above series III (1900).

There are two studies dealing primarily with her political activities by Adolf Brennecke, "Die politischen Einflüsse auf das Reformationswerk der Herzogin Elisabeth . . . ," *Niedersächisches Jahrbuch* 1 (1904), 104-45. And "Herzogin Elisabeth von Braunschweig-Lüneberg, die hannoverische Reformationsfürstin, als Persönlichkeit, ZGNKG 38 (1933), 140-70.

On her administration the documents are given by Albert Brauch, "Die Verwaltung des Territoriums Calenberg-Göttingen während der Regentenschaft der Herzogin Elisabeth 1540-46," *Quellen und Darstellungen zur Geschichte Niedersachsens* 38 (1930).

Her relations with Poppo are covered in detail by Hilde Liederwald, "Die Ehe des Grafen Poppo von Henneberg mit der Herzogin Elisabeth von Braunschweig," *Neue Beiträge zur Geschichte deutschen Altertums*, Heft 23 (Schmalkalden, 1931), 37-88.

NOTES

1. Mengel, No. 35, p. 52.
2. Brennecke, *Persönlichkeit*, p. 151.
3. Tschackert, *Corvinus Leben*, p. 83.
4. Kurs, p. 11.
5. *Ibid.*, p. 9.
6. *Ibid.*, p. 8.
7. Tschackert, *Corvinus Leben*, p. 107; *Herzogin*, p. 7.
8. Brennecke, *Persönlichkeit*, p. 152.
9. Friedrich Koldewey, *Heinz von Wolfenbüttel* (Halle, 1863).
10. Brennecke, *Politische Einflüsse*, p. 26. Cf. Tschackert, *Corvinus Leben*, p. 96.
11. Tschackert, *Corvinus Leben*, pp. 85, 96.

12. *Ibid.*, p. 56.
13. Brennecke, *Persönlichkeit*, p. 154.
14. Tschackert, *Herzogin*, p. 8.
15. Brauch, *Die Verwaltung*.
16. Tschackert, *Corvinus Leben*, pp. 99 ff.
17. Tschackert, *Herzogin*, p. 9.
18. Tschackert, *Corvinus Leben*, p. 136. *Briefwechsel, passim.*
19. Tschackert, *Corvinus Leben*, p. 150, note 2.
20. *Brenneke*, p. 162.
21. Luther *Weimarer Ausgabe, Briefwechsel*, No. 4059.
22. Tschackert, *Herzogin*, p. 33.
23. Details in Liederwald.
24. Mengel, No. 14a.
25. *Ibid.*, No. 54, p. 74.
26. Tschackert, *Herzogin*, p. 48.
27. The separation was from Sept. 2, 1553 to Dec. 10, 1549. Mengel, Nos. 57, p. 80; 216, p. 228. Cf. Koch, p. 143. Fuller details in Liederwald.
28. Kurs, p. 20.
29. Tschacket, *Corvinus Leben*, p. 166.
30. Heinrich Bornkamm, "Kurfürst Moritz von Sachsen zwischen Reformation und Staatsräson," *Zeitschrift für Geisteswissenschaft* 1 (1938-9), 398-412.
31. Tschackert, *Corvinus Leben*, pp. 165-6.
32. *Ibid.*, p. 162.
33. *Ibid.*, pp. 182, 184.
34. Koch, No. 59, p. 112.
35. Tschackert, *Corvinus Leben*, pp. 178-9.
36. Tschackert, *Corvinus Briefwechsel*, No. 297.
37. Tschackert, *Corvinus Leben*, p. 179.
38. Koch, No. 45, p. 93.
39. *Ibid.*, No. 50.
40. *Ibid.*, No. 52. Both mother and son used the official prural of the first person. Since I think it was merely a habit I have used the singular in the translation.
41. *Ibid*, No. 55, p. 107.
42. *Ibid.*, No. 81, p. 139.
43. *Ibid.*, No. 44 and Tschackert, *Corvinus Leben*, p. 184.
44. Bornkamm listed in note 29.
45. Tschackert, *Corvinus Leben*, p. 187.
46. On Albert Alcibiades see the ADB.
47. Von der Goltz, p. 157.
48. Brennecke, *Politische Einflüsse*.
49. Enc. Brit. on Albert Alcibiades.
50. Expressions of distress: Mengel, Nos. 213, 216, 227, 228, 255. Von der Goltz, p. 198; Kurs, p. 32.
51. Von der Goltz, Nos. 3, 6, 8.
52. *Ibid.*, under July 7, 1555.
53. Tschackert, *Herzogin*, p. 13.
54. Brennecke, *Persönlichkeit*, p. 168. Liederwald in great detail.
55. Tschackert, *Herzogin*, p. 21. But incomplete.

8.

Women of the Anabaptists

In the case of the women of the Anabaptists we have not sufficient information about any one to write a sketch as full as the preceding. The records of trials and the letters of husbands and wives give us many glimpses. Here is a verbatim account of the examination of Elizabeth Dirks in Holland. This territory was at the time under Catholic control.[1]

Elizabeth was arrested on January 15, 1549. When the captors came to her home they found a Latin Testament. As she was apprehended, one called out, "We've got the right one. We've caught the teacher." They asked her, "Where is your husband, Menno Simons?" She was then taken to the city hall and afterwards between two Premonstratian monks to prison. They brought her before the examiners who asked her on oath whether she had a husband. She answered, "We are not allowed to take an oath. Christ said, 'Swear not at all, but let your speech be yea, yea, nay, nay.' I have no husband."

EXAMINERS: We understand that you are a teacher and have led many astray. We want to know who your friends are.

ELIZABETH: I am commanded to love the Lord my God and honor my parents. Therefore I will not tell you who my parents are. That I suffer for Christ is damaging to my friends.

EXAMINERS: We will let that rest for the present, but we want to know whom you have taught.

ELIZABETH: No, my Lords, do not press me on this point. Ask me about my faith and I will answer you gladly.

EXAMINERS: We will make it so tough that you will tell us.

ELIZABETH: I hope through the grace of God to guard my tongue that I shall not be a traitor and deliver my brother to death.

EXAMINERS: What persons were with you when you were baptized?

ELIZABETH: Christ said, "Ask those who were present" (John 18:21).

EXAMINERS: Now we see that you are a teacher because you make yourself equal to Christ.

ELIZABETH: No indeed. Far be it from me, for I count myself no better than the offscouring from the house of the Lord.

EXAMINERS: What do you mean by the house of the Lord? Don't you consider our church to be the house of the Lord?

ELIZABETH: I do not, my Lords. For it is written, "You are the temple of the living God" (2 Cor. 6:16). As God said, "I will dwell with you" (Lev. 26:11).

EXAMINERS: What do you think of our Mass?

ELIZABETH: My Lords, I have no faith in your Mass but only in that which is in the Word of God.

EXAMINERS: What do you believe about the Holy Sacrament?

ELIZABETH: I have never in my life read in Scripture about a Holy Sacrament, but only of the Supper of the Lord.

EXAMINERS: Shut your mouth. The devil speaks through it.

ELIZABETH: Yes, my Lords, this is a little matter, for the servant is not greater than his Lord (Matt. 10:24).

EXAMINERS: You speak with a haughty tongue.

ELIZABETH: No, my Lords, I speak with a free tongue.

EXAMINERS: What did the Lord say when he gave the supper to his disciples?

ELIZABETH: What did he give them, flesh or bread?

EXAMINERS: He gave them bread.

ELIZABETH: Did not the Lord continue to sit there? How then could they eat his flesh?

EXAMINERS: What do you believe about the baptism of children, seeing that you have had yourself baptized again?

ELIZABETH: No, my Lords, I have not had myself baptized again.

Interrogation of an Anabaptist

I have been baptized once on my faith, because it is written, "Baptism belongs to believers." [She deduces this from Peter's confession, Matt. 16:15-16.]

EXAMINERS: Are our children then damned because they are baptized?

ELIZABETH: No, my Lords. Far be it from me to judge the children.

EXAMINERS: Do you not think that you are saved by baptism?

ELIZABETH: No, my Lords. All the water in the sea cannot save me. All my salvation is in Christ, who has commanded me to love the Lord, my God, and my neighbor as myself.

EXAMINERS: Do priests have the power to forgive sins?

ELIZABETH: No, my Lords. How should I believe that? I say that Christ is the only priest through whom sins are forgiven.

EXAMINERS: You say that you accept everything in accord with Holy Scripture. Do you not then hold to the word of James?

ELIZABETH: How can I not hold to it?

EXAMINERS: Did he not say, "Go to the elders of the congregation that they should anoint you and pray for you"? (James 5:13).

ELIZABETH: Yes, but would you say, my Lords, that you are such a congregation?

EXAMINERS: The Holy Ghost has made you so holy that you don't need penance or the sacrament.

ELIZABETH: No, my Lords. I freely confess that I have transgressed the ordinances of the pope which the emperor has confirmed with placards. But if you can show me that in any articles I have transgressed against the Lord, my God, I will wail over myself as a miserable sinner.

This was her first hearing.

Then they took her again before the council and brought her to the torture room. Hans, the executioner, was there. The Lords said, "So far we have treated you gently. Since you won't confess we will put you to the torture." The Procurator General said, "Mr. Hans, take hold of her." Mr. Hans answered, "Oh no, my Lords, she will confess voluntarily." But since she would not, he put screws on her thumbs and on two forefingers till the blood spurted from the nails.

EXAMINERS: Confess and we will ease your pain. We told you to confess and not to call upon the Lord, your God!

But she held steadfastly to the Lord, her God, as above related. Then they eased her pain and she said, "Ask me. I will answer, for I feel no pain any more at all as I did."

EXAMINERS: Then won't you confess?

ELIZABETH: No, my Lords.

Then they put two screws on her legs and she said, "Oh my Lords, do not put me to shame. No man has ever touched my bare body." The Procurator General said, "Miss Elizabeth, we will not treat you dishonorably." Then she fainted and one said, "Maybe she's dead." Reviving she said, "I'm alive. I'm not dead." Then they took off the screws and tried to bend her by blandishments.

ELIZABETH: Why do you try me with candied speech as one does with children?

So they could get from her not a word against her brothers in the faith, nor against any one.

EXAMINERS: Will you recant everything you have said?

ELIZABETH: No, my Lords. I will not, but I will seal it with my blood.

EXAMINERS: We will not torture you any more. Will you now tell us in good faith who baptized you?

ELIZABETH: Oh no, my Lords. I have told you all along that I will not do it.

Then, on March 27, 1549, Elizabeth was condemned to death and drowned in a sack. And thus she offered up her life to God.

Beyond this examination we have only the scantiest information about Elizabeth.[2] We do know that she came from a good family. Her parents placed her in a convent in East Friesland. Here she learned Latin and came into possession of a Latin Bible. Steeped in its teaching she came to doubt whether the monastic life was the Christian life and resolved to flee, relying on the Lord to help her. In making her escape she was aided by the milkmaids. Her first asylum was with a Mennonite family at Lier. But they feared that she would be traced and transferred her to Leeuwarden. Here she was arrested. This is as much as we know, and we may well be surprised to know this much.

Was her examination taken down verbatim and if so, how did the record ever come into the hands of a Mennonite martyrologist? On the first score we need have no qualms. Both the ecclesiastical and civil courts preserved detailed accounts of examinations. As for the accessibility of the record, we are to remember that the martyrology in which this recital is found was not published until 1660 and by that time Holland was under a Protestant government and the files of the criminal court of Friesland might be disclosed. Besides we have letters written by those under sentence of death and preserved by the recipients.[3]

The most essential point about Elizabeth is that she was an Anabaptist, meaning a repeater of baptism. The term was de-

Drowning of an Anabaptist

vised by opponents who said that to baptize adults who had already been baptized as infants was to repeat baptism. But those to whom the name was applied rejected it on the ground that infant baptism was no baptism at all but only a "dipping in the Romish bath." They called themselves simply Baptists. At the Diet of Speyer in 1529 they were placed under the penalty of death by Catholics and Protestants alike. The Catholics usually burned, the Protestants drowned the victims. Elizabeth was drowned by the Catholics, however. One reason for such severity was the revival of Roman law, that is to say the code of the Emperor Justinian, which inflicted the penalty of death upon repeaters of Holy Baptism.

But more was involved in the case of the Anabaptists than an antiquarian revival. They threatened the very structure of late medieval society in which church and state were united and every one in the community belonged to both by reason of baptism in infancy. The Anabaptists did not believe in the possibility of a Christian society. Men, said they, are divided into the once born and the twice born. Only those born again in the Spirit should be baptized, and they alone should constitute the church, which should be "gathered" out of the world. But since the state embraces the entire community, whereas the church does not, the two cannot be conjoined. The church, moreover, must be a voluntary society. No one should be forced to enter or remain because the new birth cannot be constrained. Force has no place in religion. Here are three points which have come to be axiomatic in the United States: separation of church and state, the voluntary church, and religious liberty.

Other points of social subversiveness were involved. The Anabaptists sought to put into practice the precepts of the Sermon on the Mount and would therefore take no oath, by which at that time all contractual agreements were sealed. Only centuries later did the Quakers acquire the right simply to affirm. The Anabaptists also took literally the injunctions not to resist evil, love the enemy, and turn the other cheek. They acknowledged that civil government is ordained of God, as the Apostle Paul said (Romans 13), and the ruler bears the sword to protect the good and punish the bad. But the use of the sword, the Anabaptists said, was ordained because of sin and should be wielded only by sinners to restrain other sinners. The saints should not vindicate themselves, but should suffer. The Christian, therefore, cannot be a soldier or a magistrate, charged with the infliction of death.

Because of their doctrinal views, the Anabaptists were condemned by the Catholics and by many Protestants as heretics. Because of their social views Luther regarded them as seditious, saying that if all Christians were pacifists and refused to wield the sword, the coercive power of the state would be subverted.

This whole situation explains why we know so little about the women of the Anabaptists. They were not able to settle down in parsonages as ministers' wives. The men who led the movement wandered as outlaws, and one by one in the late 20's and early 30's of the 16th century were burned, drowned, or beheaded. The wives frequently shared their fate, or if left alive, had the task of bringing up a brood in the midst of a suspicious society. There were also fewer educated women among the

Anabaptists than among other Protestants, for when the learned leaders were plucked, literacy declined.

Our information comes largely from the records of trials as well as from the martyrologies. The trials sometimes yield no more than the lists of names of those examined, as for example in the case of these women in Bavaria: Getraut Heisesin, Afra Schleichin, Anna Berchtoldmairin, Magdalena Seitzin, Anna Kochin, Elizabeth Wollschlagerin, Margareth Berchtoldin, Martha Beckin, Maxencia Wisingerin, Elizabeth Leitlin, Anna Malchingerin, Anna Butzin, and Regina Weisshaubtin.[4] Names, names, names! Of such is the stuff of history, thousands who have left no other memorial, millions who have passed into oblivion.

The records do reveal incredible persistence on the part of many women and incredible patience on the part of the authorities given their assumptions. The records about to be cited come, however, from the end of the century when the death penalty was becoming infrequent, and the punishment then might be imprisonment or banishment with confiscation of goods.

Here is the two-year record of a man and his wife:[5]

1573 Melcher Staib and his wife Anna say they would rather have their goods confiscated than go to church and to go once is as bad as to go regularly.

1574 Melcher Staib refuses to pay the fine for not going to church. He and his wife Anna are arrested. Then he goes to church, but she refuses. She's a real Anabaptist. She won't go to church or to the Lord's Table and all persuasion is useless.

Here are entries spread over 38 years.[6]

1574 Maria, the wife of Alexander Weber, is still around. She goes seldom to church and never to communion, does nobody any harm and has no following.

1575 *Spring.* Maria Weber will not go to church, much less to communion. She's hard to restrain from controversy.

1575 *Fall.* Maria Weber has not been to church for two years and, when summoned by the superintendent, excuses herself on the ground that she has to cook for the family.

1576   *Spring.* Maria Weber goes neither to church, nor to communion. Her husband goes to church, but not to communion.

1576   *Fall.* Maria Weber has not appeared at the command of the prince.

1577   *Spring.* Does not go to church or communion.

1577   *November.* Still obstinate.

1583   She has often been dealt with but to no avail.

1586   *February.* Maria Weber has been an Anabaptist for 20 years. She was to have appeared, but has disappeared.

1608   *September.* The obstinate Maria Weber, who was rebaptized 40 years ago has been imprisoned.

1609   She is just as bad. [Marginal note: Such people should be banished or put in prison in chains.]

1610   The same story.

1612   Alexander Weber's wife has accepted the confession of our church. [Marginal note: Praise the Lord.]

Here is an isolated note from the year 1608. Apollonia is now 80. She has attended an Anabaptist assembly in the woods.[7]

The entire Protestant movement was bound to have significant consequences for marital relations. Any revolution, any civil war may unite and divide. We have noticed already that Katherine von Bora, Katherine Zell, and Wibrandis Rosenblatt were drawn to their husbands by a community of faith, while Elizabeth of Brandenburg and Argula Grumbach were alienated. Even more was this the case for the Anabaptists, when the penalties for adherence to the sect were so severe and so universal. Toward the latter part of the century an asylum was found in Moravia, but only a few could avail themselves of it. Those who suffer together for the faith are cemented. Those on opposite sides often find it hard to achieve an affectionate intolerance.

We have in the Anabaptist martyrologies devoted letters between husbands and wives when one or both were in prison. Though separated, they were not deprived of communication, and their letters following executions would not be denied to friends. Here is the farewell of Hendrick Verstralen to his wife as he awaited execution.[8]

"Oh my Janneken, my lamb, how hard it is to be separated

from you and from the children. How deeply you are graven into my heart. Therefore I am in sore trial. May the Lord help me to be victorious. My dear wife, my lamb, my life, I thank you from the depths of my soul for your letter, which has done more to lift the heaviness from my heart than any treasure on earth. Do the best for my little children. The Lord will take care of you. He who gives fodder to the wild ass in the wilderness and feeds the ravens when they cry will feed you also. And now my dear wife, my flesh and blood, I will say goodbye, my faithful helper, my loyal friend. I praise God that he gave you to me, you who have sustained me in all my trial. Goodbye, Susanneken, my Abraham, my little Isaac. Goodbye Janneken, dearest love on earth. You have borne me six children. Three are at rest. May the almighty God uphold my elect wife and the three innocent bairns to eternal life."

An exchange of letters has been preserved between Jeronimus Segerzoon and his wife Liskin.[9] They were imprisoned separately at Antwerp in 1551. Both were tortured, and both suffered death.

The husband wrote: "My beloved lamb, I have seen from afar the promised land. I hope soon to come into the city which lies four square, whose foundations are precious stones and her streets are of pure gold. . . . I thank the Lord that you have lived with me so faultlessly. I wish I might lie in prison for you on bread and water for a year, that I might die for you ten deaths. If only I could help you with my tears. Be at peace. I have written this letter with tears when I learned how you have been afflicted. I hope you will write me how you are."

The wife responded: "My dearest in the Lord, I hope that we two through the crucified Christ may enter into eternal joy."

The husband: "When I received your letter and learned how you stand my soul leapt for joy. I could not read to the end but fell upon my knees to thank God. I have never known such joy, nor would I have thought it possible in prison. I can scarcely sleep for joy. If only I could help with my blood. Oh my beloved wife in the Lord, let us look unto Jesus the author and finisher of our faith (Heb. 12:1), who before us gave himself unto death that we might sit with him on thrones and be clad in white raiment."

The wife: "I wish for my dear husband in the Lord and for myself an imperishable joy in Christ, the crucified. My dear, beloved husband in the Lord, I hear how steadfast you have been. I pray the Lord to give me strength to suffer for his name."

The husband: "I was deeply moved by your letter in which you besought the Lord with tears to give you strength to endure. Fear not. He will not suffer us to be tempted above our strength."

His last letter before execution: "My darling lamb, fear not the torments. Not a hair of your head shall perish without the Father's will. My dear wife, I take leave of you, for I do not expect to see you again, but after not many days we shall be united before the altar of Christ."

Whereas a common faith cemented marriages, a divergent faith might dissolve a marriage. Some Anabaptists said that marriage no longer exists when there is not agreement between husband and wife as to the Word of God. In Switzerland in 1531 a husband complained to the council that his wife, though twice imprisoned for Anabaptism, had broken her oath and had reverted to the sect, abandoning him with seven children. He asked for a divorce. The decision was to summon her in order to hear both sides. She stubbornly resisted a summons from an earthly power. The decision then was not to grant a divorce, which might induce many separations, but to punish her severely for desertion.[10]

In come cases the couples were quite willing to continue in marriage though divided in faith, but the law banished or imprisoned one partner and fear of the law drove some to the road. We have the record of an Anabaptist whose wife and four children came to his hiding place and warned him of danger. He continued to hide for two days and then took to horse and went to the house of his brother-in-law, who, seeing the sheriff passing by, advised him to flee again before the house was searched. By foot he made his way to a group of Anabaptists, who received him with joy. His wife and children again sought him out. He warned them not to do so again, because all would be caught and drowned. All wept. They stayed with him for two days. Then he took again to the road.[11]

In the Palatinate area we have a petition to the ruling count from the wife of an Anabaptist, who disagreed with her husband. He had been banished and burdened with a heavy fine. Because of inability to pay, the stock of wine which they marketed was to be confiscated. She could not make the vineyard productive because she was unequal to the hard manual labor with a brood of little children about her. Would not the count, in Christian charity, permit her husband to come back for a few weeks to give them a hand? [12]

Ten years later we have a petition addressed by the husband to the count. In the interim the wife had joined him with three of the five children. The other two had been taken into families. The husband had received permission to sell his goods and take the money with him, but he had not been able to find a purchaser. He could not support his family. Might he not be allowed some income from his property? As for the children left behind, he had been assured that they would receive better care than could be provided by the parents. They would like to see for themselves. Could they not be allowed a visit? [13]

In Bavaria in 1539 we have the petition to the government of Ursula Weinbergin: "Most noble lords, I beg you to look upon my petition with favor. Gabriel Weinberger was arrested for heresy. His case has dragged on for a long time. I am left with my little children without the help of their father, and I find it very difficult to provide daily bread. We would like to live together again, and I believe that if I could be permitted to speak to my husband, I could persuade him for my sake and the children's to give up these ideas, because he was never a leader and never induced any one to take up these errors, but simply listened to others. That my children may be supported, I beg you to let me talk with him, and I will not cease to pray God that your government may have long life and good fortune."

Petition granted.[14]

Some of the above-mentioned trials took place before Catholic and some before Protestant tribunals. Before leaving the women of the Anabaptists, let us record the letter of a mother to her son and of a son to his mother.

A widowed Anabaptist mother to her son in the year 1587: "My dear son, I beg you to be mindful of the difference between us and the world. No one can hope for salvation except in the right and true congregation of Christ, which truly is built by God through the Word on the foundation laid by the apostles. I am convinced by God's grace in my heart, I am sure and certain that this is the true people of God and the way to eternal life. I beg you to think of your salvation. I hope you will follow the council of the brothers that before my end I may rejoice in you. Have you not the heart and courage? Your sisters have come in. You alone walk in the unrighteous way of the world. This troubles me deeply. If you do not come soon I think you will not find me alive." [15]

The son who wrote to his mother was Philip the Landgrave of Hesse, the only prince of the 16th century who would put no man to death for his faith.[16] He wrote in April, 1525:

"I assure you that I will not compel any one to leave or to stay in the cloister. Here I will exercise no constraint. This is a matter for the conscience of each. But I will not forbid saying the Mass in German with the omission of the canon. You tell me that I shall be in trouble with the emperor on that account. I reply that I must obey God rather than man. If I am to be constrained because of the Word of God, I will gladly suffer persecution and pray God daily that he will give me the grace to stand. You remind me that God wishes us to do good works. Quite right, but we must know what is a good work. We are to keep God's commandments. But if we think by our works to be justified or to acquire grace, then they are not good and you need not take my word for it. See what the Apostle Paul has written. As for the property of monks and nuns, I am not disposed to take anything away from them. But when it comes to sending out preachers, that I do gladly. I beg you not to take it amiss if I do not obey you, for I must rather obey God. But in all matters which do not touch God I am your obedient son." [17]

NOTES

1. Tilleman van Braght, *Het Bloedig Tooneel (The Bloody Theatre)*, commonly known in English as *The Martyrs' Mirror*. The first edition was published in 1660, the second at Amsterdam in 1685. Copy in the Beinecke Library at Yale University. The record here translated is in II, 911-94. It is reprinted in the *Bibliotheca Neerlandica* II, 91-92 with notes.
2. Van Braght as above, pp. 156-8.
3. Samuel Cramer, "De Geloofwardigheid van Van Braght," *Doopsgezinde Bijdragen* XXXI (1899), pp. 65-164.
4. *Quellen zur Geschichte der Täufer* V, *Bayern* II. Abteilung. ed. Karl Schornbaum (1951), pp. 19-20.
5. *Quellen zur Geschichte der Täufer*, I. *Herzogtum Württemberg*, ed. Gustav Bossert (1930), p. 381.
6. *Ibid.*, by date.
7. *Ibid.*, pp. 804-5.
8. First published in 1577. See note 3 above, pp. 79-80.
9. See note 1, pp. 121-26.
10. *Quellen zur Geschichte der Täufer in der Schweiz*, Bd. 1 *Zürich*, ed. Leonhard von Muralt und Walter Schmid (1952), No. 357, p. 338.
11. *Urkundliche Quellen zur hessischen Reformationsgeschichte* IV *Wiedertäuferakten 1527-1626*, ed. Walter Köhler, Walter Sohm, Theodor Sippell, Günther Franz (1951), No. 130, pp. 313-5. Feb. 1, 1546.
12. *Quellen zur Geschichte der Täufer* IV. *Baden und Pfalz*, ed. Manfred Krebs (1951). No. 300, pp. 318-9 before May, 1601.
13. *Ibid.*, No. 312, pp. 335-6, before June 1611.
14. See note 4, No. 59, pp. 82-3, Nov.-Dec., 1539.
15. See note 11, No. 211, pp. 498-9.
16. *Ibid.*, No. 150 B, p. 348.
17. *Urkundlichen Quellen zur Hessischen Reformationsgeschichte* II, 1525-47 (1954), No. 4, p. 7.

9.

Minor Sketches
Katherine Melanchthon and Anna Zwingli

Before leaving this section on the women of the Reformation in the Germanic lands, very brief sketches may be appended on two wives who might easily have been accorded as much space as the others.

The first is the wife of Philip Melanchthon, Katherine Krapp, the daughter of a magistrate at Wittenberg. In 1520 when Melanchthon was 23 he was advised by Luther, a full five years before his own marriage, to enter upon the holy estate. Philip feared that in such case he would be guilty of bigamy, for he was already wedded to scholarship. But urged by friends he became engaged to Katherine Krapp. "I am not cool toward her," he said, "and she has all the qualities that I could wish in a wife at the hands of the immortal gods. Some of my friends think that this will mean for me the end of scholarship. Rather than give that up I would renounce the light of life." He did succeed in keeping harmony between his two brides. When in later years a visitor from France came to see the famous man, he found him with one hand rocking a cradle, with the other holding a book. He and Katherine were well mated for 37 years. She cared assiduously for his never robust health. "She always thinks," said he, "that I am dying of hunger unless I am stuffed like a sausage." There were four children, two boys and two girls.

One source of friction with Katherine was her love of rollicking company. When she and her guests were in a state of uproarious hilarity the master of the house would temper the coviviality with seemly decorum. There was no conflict over

Zwingli's daughter

unbridled generosity, far exceeding even that of Luther. Melanchthon would sell presents to relieve the indigent. He was proud of a collection of coins from which he offered a guest any he might choose. The importunate ass said he would accept them all. Melanchthon winced and let him. But Katherine could not complain. She was just as bad. Who paid the bills would be a fine subject for a doctoral dissertation.

While at Heidelberg on business for the churches in the year 1557, Melanchthon received the news of the death of his wife. "I am glad," said he, "that she did not suffer further. I shall not be long in joining her. I am shattered."

The subject of the second sketch is the wife of Ulrich Zwingli, Anna Reinhart. He belongs not to Germany proper but to German-speaking Switzerland. She was already a widow with three children. Hans, her first husband, was of the illustrious family of Meyer von Knonau. Gerold, his father, did not approve of his son's infatuation with an innkeeper's daughter and arranged instead a union with a noble house. The son defied the father, married Anna, was disowned, and to support her and the growing number of children, took service with the Swiss mercenaries. Thirteen years after his marriage he came home broken in health to die in 1517.

Despite the alienation Hans christened his only son Gerold, after his father. When the son was three the nurse was taking him for a stroll through the fish market. The grandfather was sipping in front of what we call a café When a fleeting glance at the face of the lad evoked a memory, the old man had him brought in. Learning that the boy was Gerold, his grandson and namesake, he took the child on his lap and sobbed. The boy was taken to live with the grandparents until both were dead in 1520. Anna married Zwingli in 1522. She was glad to renounce the silks of her first marriage for the plain garb befitting a minister's wife.

Zwingli became a father to her children quite as much as to his own. Of these, there were several daughters deceased in infancy, a boy who reached only student age, a son Ulrich who attained maturity, and the daughter whose picture is here shown.

Of Zwingli's family life we know but little. There is a letter to his wife congratulating her on the birth of a son and sending greetings to the other children. Zwingli would not allow music in church but he found his skill on the lute and the fiddle of great use in quieting the children.

In 1531 came the second war of religion between the cantons. After the inconclusive peace that followed the first Kappell war with the Catholics in 1529, Zwingli favored a stroke by the Protestant cantons to vindicate their right to noninterference. His counsel was rejected. The Catholics then took the initiative and marched on Zürich. Taken by surprise the Zürichers went out to battle. Zwingli was with them not merely as a chaplain, but as a combatant with helmet and sword.

On that day Anna lost her husband, her son Gerold, a brother, a cousin, and a son-in-law. Capito consoled her that the memory of her husband was cherished in a thousand hearts and would never be forgotten. Butzer wrote, "Dear wife and sister, I beg you let us know if we can do anything for you and the orphans." Help was given mainly by Heinrich Bullinger, Zwingli's successor, who took the wife and the two children still at home into his own household, increasing its number to 15.

To conclude this section on the women of the Reformation in the Germanic lands at this point is arbitrary. One could readily continue with sketches of other wives in the Wittenberg circle and also for Strasbourg, Basel, Constance, Bern, Stuttgart, Augsburg, Marburg and others.

The day came in fact when a Protestant minister almost had to marry to demonstrate the genuineness of his conviction. The jibe of Kierkegaard at Luther was not so far amiss with respect to Lutherans and all Protestants. Kenneth Scott Latourette, when once twitted about his single estate, retorted that he did not know what was worse, the enforced celibacy of the Catholic clergy or the enforced matrimony of the Protestants.

BIBLIOGRAPHICAL NOTE

These two sketches are abbreviated from Paul Melhorn, "Die Frauen unserer Reformatoren," *Religionsgeschichtliche Volksbücher*, IV, 27 (Tübingen, 1917) and Oskar Farner's abundantly documented article: "Anna Reinhart," *Zwingliana* III (1920), 229-245.

Part II

WOMEN OF THE REFORMATION IN ITALY

The Reformation in Italy

The Reformation in Italy, being less well known and less successful than that in Germany, calls for a more complete introduction. In Italy the Reformation failed, and much of its energy fed ultimately into the Catholic Counter-Reformation. In the beginning the reformatory impulse was ambiguous. It was a phase of the upsurge of European religious vitality. The movement may be called evangelical Catholicism. Representatives were to be found in all countries. The most outstanding example was Erasmus of Rotterdam. The movement stressed piety and ethics with a return to the simplicity of the New Testament. The leaders studied Saint Paul and found the doctrine of justification by faith congenial.

The sources of the Italian Reformation were partly European and partly indigenous. From Italy emanated the Florentine revival of Neoplatonism with its depreciation of the sensory and consequent disparagement of the external manifestations of religion in the cult of relics, pilgrimages, and the like. There was a tendency to spiritualize outward aids to religion, such as the Sacrament of the Altar. The resurrection of the body was doubted. This tendency was reinforced by the skepticism of the University of Padua which, in the wake of the Arabic scholar Averroes, believed in immortality only in the sense of absorption into the world soul.

Franciscan piety was also very influential, with rapturous adoration of Christ the crucified and the disparagement of theology in favor of ethics, partly because the first Franciscans, being theologically untrained, were enjoined to confine their preaching to morals. A new branch of the Franciscans, the Capuchins, was in this tradition. Two of the women about to be discussed were active in defending this order against suppression.

Other influences on the Italian Reformation came from abroad. The Spanish leader, Juan Valdés, settled in Naples. He exhibited in himself the impact of Spanish mysticism, an Erasmian scorn for the external, and Calvinist theology. The works of northern reformers like Luther, Calvin, Butzer, Zwingli, and Bullinger, in Italian translation and often with false names and places, were smuggled into Italy. Perhaps because of the diversity of these sources no distinctively Italian theology emerged. Nevertheless, as the Italians found themselves indifferent to the disputes between the branches of Protestantism to the north, they moved in the direction of rationalism and pietism. Anabaptism gained many adherents, especially in the area around Venice.

The geographical distribution of the reform movements in Italy is not precise. Naples was the great center of the Valdesian circle, but Valdés, though he accepted the doctrine of justification by faith, cannot be called a Protestant. His followers were to go in diverse directions. Lucca had a considerable congregation, many of whom migrated to Geneva. This does not mean that they were more sympathetic to Calvin's theology than to Luther's, but only that Geneva was much closer than Wittenberg. Venice at first had a strong Lutheran cast because of the presence of a subsidiary of the German banking house of Fugger. The young German apprentices learned Italian and brought their faith with them. In the later period many Anabaptists flourished around Venice. There were also heretical groups at Piacenza and Ferrara.

Some historians have stressed that the reform in Italy was the work of laymen and especially of laymen trained in humanist studies. But not all were laymen. Vergerio was a bishop, Vermigli was an Augustinian monk, and Ochino the general of the Capuchins. Busale, the Antitrinitarian, was a monk. There were, to be sure, some lay humanist scholars, notably Curione and Morato. The women with whom we deal were not of the clergy. Neither were they nuns, though Giulia Gonzaga and Vittoria Colonna lived in convents. The observation of Erasmus was correct that the seed plot of heresy and sectarianism was not classical literature but scholasticism. This is notably true with respect to the Italian Antitrinitarians. They all drew from the scholastic treatments of the doctrine of the Trinity first brought together by the Spaniard Michael Servetus.

The social stratification of the Italian reformers reflects wide diversity. Even if the claim that Naples had 3,000 heretics be grossly exaggerated, we may be sure that all of them were not aristocrats. The same applies to the many exiles from Lucca and the whole village of Locarno in the Rhaetian Alps which migrated en masse to Zürich. The new gospel found adherents among armorers, tanners, furriers, painters, weavers, and others. Lelio Sozzini died in the house of an Anabaptist weaver at Zürich, and the humanist Giovanni Bauto, in exile at Cracow, was aghast to find himself among rag pickers, masons, and chimney sweeps.

The chronology of the Italian movement may be divided into three periods: 1) from the Fifth Lateran Council in 1513-17 to the establishment of the Roman Inquisition in 1542, the period of the efflorescence in the evangelical Catholic reform; 2) from 1542 to 1560; by which time the evangelic movement had lost all hope of converting Italy; 3) a period in which some irenic spirits sought reconciliation and tolerance. By the end of the century there was no further hope in this regard.

When the blow fell in 1542 the reformers of the earlier period were divided into three groups. Some went to the stake, some went into exile, both men and women, and others lapsed into silence and made cloisters of their own hearts. This they could scarcely do without some conformity to the external practices of the Church of Rome. Calvin dubbed these temporizers as Nicodemites, after Nicodemus who visited Jesus only by night. Renée of Ferrara in a measure fits this picture. Vittoria Colonna remained with the church and would have nothing to do with those outside it. Giulia Gonzaga refused to leave Italy and refused to condemn those who did.

There is no obvious explanation for the failure of the Reformation in Italy. Despite papal encroachments, the Italian city states were still ready to kiss the pope's toe in spiritual matters, even while stabbing him in the back or belly in temporal affairs. One possibility is that the Italian clergy were dependent on the papacy and did not form an independent national block. Another may well be weariness. From the 12th century on, Italy swarmed with sectarian movements, all of them extinguished by the Inquisition. How futile to start another! A further reason may lie in the realm of ideas. Luther said that his reformation differed from earlier movements because they stressed the life, and he stressed the doctrine. The Franciscan preachers, as observed, inveighed against vices rather than questioning the teachings of the church.

More significant than all was the wisdom of the papacy, especially after the sack of Rome, in sanctioning the founding of new monastic orders committed to cleansing the Augean stables. The Capuchins, the Theatines, and the Jesuits became the great arms of the papacy. Had the popes not been sagacious enough to grant them recognition, they could easily have become schismatic, if not heretical.

One must further bear in mind that the local rulers sided with the church. Caught as they were between the rival interests of France and the Hapsburg empire, they frequently sought a counterpoise in the papacy to save them from disastrous involvements. The Reformation never took hold in opposition to the will of the rulers.

The Italian Reformation was not without its influence. For one thing it affected the Counter-Reformation. The direct and enduring impact was made by the Italians in exile. Some, to be sure, managed to accommodate themselves to the theologies of the areas in which they took refuge to the north, but others were never at home and moved in the direction of rationalism and social radicalism. The one organized movement to emerge under their impact was Socinianism.

BIBLIOGRAPHY

Frederick C. Church, *The Italian Reformers* 1534-64 (New York, 1932). This is not a systematic history but a collection of essays on aspects of the reform with use of archival material. This work has been translated into Italian and expanded into two volumes by Delio Cantimori.

G. K. Brown, *Italy and the Reformation to 1550* (Oxford, 1933). Divided according to geographical divisions, based on secondary material and printed sources.

Delio Cantimori, *Eretici Italiani del Cinquecento* (Florence, 1939). This is a history of heretics rather than of the reformatory movements in their entirety. Particular attention is given to philosophical and theological ideas. Cantimori was a master of the literature and has published many articles of which the following may be cited for their over-all coverage.
"Recenti studi intorno alla Riforma in Italia e ai Riformatori all'estero 1924-34," *Rivista Storica Italiana* I, I (1936), 1-28.
"Attegiamenti della vita culturale italiana nel secolo XVI di fronte alla Riforma," *Rivista Storica Italiana* 53 (1936), 41-69.
Prospettive di Storia ereticale italiana del Cinquecento (Bari, 1960).

Antonio Rotondò offers a survey of heresy throughout Europe including Italy in "I Movimenti Ereticali nell'Europa del Cinquecento," *Rivista Storica Italiana* 78, I (1966), 103-139.
He deals with the heretical underground in
"Attegiamenti della Vita Morale Italiana del Cinquecento, La Pratica Nicodemitica," *Ibid.*, 79,4 (1967), 991-1030.

Documents relating to Trials of Heretics

Carlo Ginzburg, "Appunti e Documenti, Due Noti suo profetismo Cinquecentesco," *Ibid.*, 78,I (1966), 184-227.

Benedetto Nicolini has a number of articles which will be noted in course.

The sources for the Italian Reformation are in process of publication in critical editions in the series *Corpus Reformatorum Italicorum,* of which the first volume has appeared, the works of Camillo Renatò, edited by Antonio Rotondò (Chicago and Florence, 1968).

Dissemination of the Protestant Literature in Italy

Edouard Pommier, "Notes sur la Propagande Protestante dans la République de Venise au Milieu du XVIe Siècle," *Aspects de la Propagande Religeuse,* ed. Henri Meylan (Geneva, 1957), 240-46.

Facoltà Valdese di Teologia di Roma, *Ginevra e l'Italia* (Florence, 1959).

Carlo de Frede, "Per la Storia della Stampa nel Cinquecento in Rapporto con la Diffusione della Riforma in Italia," *Gutenburg Jahrbuch,* 39 (1964), 175-84.

Elizabeth G. Gleason, "Sixteenth Century Interpretations of Luther," *Archiv für Reformationsgeschichte* 60,2 (1969), 160-73.

J. B. Ross, "Gasparo Contarini and His Friends," *Studies in the Renaissance* XXII (1970), 192-232.

10.

Giulia Gonzaga
(1512/13 - 1566)

Giulia Gonzaga was a princess of northern Italy with some Germanic blood, whence her blonde hair. At the age of 14 she was married to a prince of southern Italy, Vespasiano Colonna, 27 years her senior, a widower with a daughter Isabella. Distinguished in arms, he survived his marriage by only two years. His will left all of his property to Giulia unless she remarried, in which case it would revert to Isabella, who looked without disfavor on the prospect of a second marriage for her stepmother. Giulia did not oblige and dissension ensued. Isabella married, had a son, lost her husband in two years, remarried, and the care of the child devolved upon Giulia.

She established her residence, or should one say her court, at Fondi in a charming villa, halfway between Rome and Naples and only two miles from the sea. Here Giulia became the center of a literary and artistic circle. The poets of the day were effusive in rhapsodies on her beauty, for she was reputed to be the fairest in the land. The poet Bernardo Tasso chanted her praises in lines which may be roughly rendered:

Her blond, undulating locks, mischievously straying with the breeze
Crown a forehead lofty and serene, beneath whose eyebrows dark
Lucid lights permit her from this terrestrial prison to behold the wonders of the Lord.

Her lips are rubies, her slender neck white as the driven
    snow,
Her angelic voice and words more fit for God than man.
In her the spirits of the blest rejoice as if the gates of heaven
    were ajar.[1]

Her hand was much sought, and none was more enamored of
her charms than Ippolito dei Medici, an illegitimate son of the
house of Medici and a nephew of Pope Clement VII. The family
accepted Ippolito and groomed him in all of the skills coun-
selled in the *Cortegiano* of Castiglione. His uncle, the pope,
thought he might better advance the fortunes of the Medici
were he a cardinal and forced upon him the dignity which pre-
cluded marriage. To Giulia he dedicated his Italian translation
of Virgil's *Aeneid* with the words: "One downcast is often solaced
by the sight of greater woe. So I, finding for my wound no healing, have looked upon the flames devouring Troy, since every
woe that fell upon her walls found in my breast a counterpart.
Therefore I send you these lines that may suggest what sighs,
tears and grief cannot convey." [2]

The fame of her beauty spread beyond Italy. Barbarossa, the
Turkish pirate, made a raid upon the Italian coast with intent
to capture her and, some surmised, present Italy's loveliest to
the seraglio of the Sultan. By a stealthy march through a wood
the raider was able to invade the sleeping town of Fondi and
enter her castle. Giulia, warned by a servant, escaped lightly
clad through a window and thence by way of a secret draw-
bridge reached another fortification where, by luck, horses were
at hand. Cardinal Ippolito, hearing of her plight, at once sent
troops. There was no longer need, for Barbarossa, having pillaged, slaughtered, and enslaved, had retreated to his galleys.[3]

In 1534, a year after this episode, Giulia moved to Naples,
perhaps for greater security, perhaps to be nearer the estates of
her husband, subject to vexatious litigation with Isabella. There
Giulia attended a sermon by the Savonarola of her generation,
the general of the Capuchins, Bernardino Ochino. The Capuchins were an offshoot of the Observant Franciscans, who were
deemed to have deteriorated from obedience to the rule of St.
Francis "without a gloss." The secessionists would follow with

Giulia Gonzaga

exactitude the saint's devotion to Lady Poverty. Like him they would beg, travel barefoot, sleep in the open or in the crudest shelters, devote themselves to the care of lepers, preach with denunciation of vice and warnings of impending doom, and burst into lyrical rhapsodies on the wounds of Christ. Ochino, having defected from the Observants, whom he had come to regard as hopeless, joined the Capuchins and was made their general when he was 50 years old.

He had already been preaching for 25 years, but only now began his phenomenal career. He was the perfect exemplification of the medieval saint: austere, emaciated, frail, and venerable, with the rapt and ethereal look of a Moses descending from the mount, the glory still haloing his countenance. With a white beard flowing over his coarse brown cowl, and his feet bare, the general tramped the thoroughfares of Italy from the foothills of the Alps to the shores of Sicily. His sermons were marked by chaste diction and vibrant emotion. There was no blatant striving for effect but the artistry of melodious words culminating in musical crescendos. His ravishing voice and Sienese pronunciation melted his hearers. *Dolcezza* was the word describing his speech.

So great was his popularity that the pope had to regulate his engagements. Huge throngs assembled hours in advance of his coming. On one occasion he requested the sacristan not to ring the bell because he was too ill to preach. The sacristan replied that he had already rung it, but in any case the bell made no difference because the church had been crowded since midnight, with some people even perched upon the roof. At Naples the emperor Charles "particularly delighted to hear Fra Bernardino of Siena, the Capuchin who preached in the church of San Giovanni Maggiore with such spirit and devotion as to make the stones weep." In Venice Cardinal Bembo declared that so saintly a man had never been seen. The power of Ochino's word in Naples unloosed purses and collected a huge sum for charity. At Perugia, in response to his appeal, a society was founded to care for orphans. At Faenza feuding factions were reconciled. At Rome an assembly gathered at two in the morning, including twelve cardinals. When the service ended at six, the preacher was scarcely able to finish his sermon because of the tears of his audience.

The popularity of Ochino was not due to flattery, for he denounced the sins of Venice and of Rome alike, declaring that penitential preaching would receive a better response in England or in Germany or even among the Turks and the Jews. If his hearers would not be as Nineveh then they would be as Sodom. Denunciation and exhortation were not, however, the staple of his preaching so much as the delineation of the way whereby the creature might be lifted to the vision of the Creator and the Christian dissolved in the adoration of the crucified.

"Let us consider the creatures," he appealed, "how in them as in a mirror are reflected all the divine goodness, wisdom, power and beauty, love and every perfection. Let us make of the creatures a ladder by which to ascend to the divine beauty. Behold the exquisite loveliness of flowers and fruits; rise to the contemplation of the light of the stars and the celestial bodies; look upon the beauty of the soul when clothed with virtue and adorned with spiritual gifts of light and grace; gaze with the eyes of the mind on the blessed and angelic spirits commencing with the angels, ascending to the archangels, from choir to choir up to the seraphim. And if one can glimpse the Mother of God in her beauty, this will reward every effort. Lift yourselves in loving thought, I will not say to the divinity of Christ but only to his gracious humanity, and behold his sacred wounds and his great love, for although God in creating and conserving the world has disclosed a drop of his power, goodness, justice, mercy, and wisdom, yet by joining himself to man and dwelling among us for thirty and three years in profound humility, conversing in love, teaching the way of salvation, dying for us a shameful death, behold in this not a drop merely of his goodness and mercy but an infinite sea.

"Let us, then, contemplate Christ upon the cross and put away all vanities and hold converse only with persons steeped in the divine love, whose words, when they speak of Christ, are flames of fire which deeply kindle. If, then, there enter into you some harmonious sweet and gracious sound, some melodic voice or angelic song, your spirit will lift you up to contemplate the harmony of the celestial hierarchy of the three divine Persons."

Such passages are redolent of Franciscan mysticism touched conceivably by the revived currents of Neoplatonism which celebrate the ascent of the soul beyond the trammel of the senses to union with the Ineffable.[4]

One would have supposed that such preaching would have been balm for Giulia, but quite the contrary. She came out of the church in great turmoil of spirit, torn, as she said, between the love of paradise and the fear of hell. The emotional impact of his preaching may have led her to cast her distress into the traditional conflict of heaven and hell. Ochino certainly did not fling around brimstone. Giulia was already disturbed, partly no doubt by the death of her husband, the Turkish raid, the friction with Isabella, but even more by a doubt with respect to her entire manner of life as a beautiful princess surrounded by obsequious flatterers.

She walked out of the church with a Spanish gentleman with whom she was already acquainted and to him she unburdened her disquiet. His name was Juan Valdés. In 1531 he had left Spain to extricate himself from the toils of the Inquisition. After some three years of service to the emperor in Italy, he had settled in Naples as the agent of Cardinal Gonzaga, the viceroy of Sicily and the cousin of Giulia. Valdés' duties were not onorous and left abundant time for conducting spiritual retreats at his villa on an island in the Bay of Naples. He is described as a man of singular saintliness and charm. The choicest spirits among the aristocracy, men and women, frequented his ashram. After his death one of them wrote: "Monsignor, I confess that Florence is lovely within and without. Yet the amenity of Naples, the shores, the eternal spring afford a higher degree of excellence: the entrancing gardens, the laughing sea, a thousand vital spirits that well up within the heart! I well know that you have often invited me to return, but, after all, where should we go now that Señor Valdés is dead?" [5]

While still in Spain Valdés had written a tract, *On Christian Doctrine*,[6] conceived in an Erasmian vein, though with cushioned barbs. There is a bare suggestion of satire in the assertion that the difference between Moors and Christians is that the latter abstain on certain occasions from meat. The entire stress is on inwardness in religion with disparagement of all outward acts and rites. All extremes af asceticism are to be avoided. Fasting should not undermine health, and the eating of fish Valdés found nauseating, as did Erasmus. The only valid vow is that taken in baptism, of which any other vow should be only a reminder. The counsels as well as the precepts of the gospel apply to all Christians and not simply to monastics. The distinction between monks, clergy, and laity largely disappears. Frequent attendance at Mass is desirable but nothing beyond an annual observance is obligatory. Confession may be said once a year to satisfy the requirement of the church but is really unnecessary because only mortal sins must be confessed, and the Christian is quite able not to commit them. One need not confess before going to Mass unless one feels impelled.

The tract which Valdés wrote to assuage the disquiet of Giulia, entitled *The Christian Alphabet,* was different in tone.[7] The form was the same, the dialogue, and considerable space was allotted to Giulia, for Valdés attenuated the injunction of St. Paul that women should be silent in church. This rule, said Valdés, applies only to women with husbands, only to those whose husbands are Christian, and only to those whose husbands are competent to instruct their wives at home.[8] All other women may speak up. Since Giulia was a widow, her freedom was unhampered.

Her crisis centered on the conflict of the love of heaven and the fear of hell. Valdés told her that both feelings were unworthy because both arose out of selfish concern for her own destiny. She should place herself wholly in the hands of God. Let her not be troubled by her doubt, for doubt is a mark of the wish to believe.[9] She should find her solace in the deed of God in Christ as expounded by the Apostle Paul. In approaching the Bible it were better to start with Paul than with the Gospels, because, for all their apparent simplicity, they do not so clearly set forth the drama of redemption.[10] God had to lay on Christ the chastisement for all the sins of men, whose hatred for God could not otherwise be overcome. As the proverb had it, "The offender never forgives." This does not mean simply that only the one offended can forgive an offense, but rather that the offender resents the offended. Thus man hates God. To overcome this impediment in man, God laid on Christ the penalty for all, that the offender, knowing that the penalty had been paid once and for all, might accept God's pardon without fear, in gratitude and love through an act of faith.[11] This faith is not a mere belief that God has done this [12]—it is a heartfelt, profound, continuous religious experience of response and commitment. This faith is not the cause of man's justification before God, but the result.[13] It is an aspect of incorporation into Christ.

The level is deeper than that of the mind. Valdés eschews rationalization, idle curiosity, theological speculation. The heart, not the head, is the organ of religion.[14] Experience is communicated by the Spirit, and the Spirit is superior to any written document, including the Bible. First one is illumined by the Spirit, then one turns to the Scripture for confirmation. The Bible is like a candle, useful in the darkness, but able to be blown out. Then, if there is no inner light, the darkness is complete. When the sun breaks, the candle is superfluous.[15]

In this work and in a number which followed, several of them dedicated to Giulia, one finds as in the earlier dialogue composed in Spain the disparagement of the external, rejection of austerities, fasting, gaing naked or barefoot, poverty, hairshirts and vigils—all are vain.[16] One might have supposed that such rejections would lead to a break with the Church, but Valdés did not deny its authority. He did say that Christ is its only head, but did not deny that the pope is Christ's vicar.[17] There is in Valdéz no spirit of rebellion.

Nevertheless there are tendencies which could be considered subversive. This is more true of the Italian works than of the one written earlier in Spain.[18] As a matter of fact the later productions are reminiscent of the Spanish "spirituals" with whom Valdés had been familiar while in his native land. Did he agree all along with their stress on spiritual illumination, and did he mute this note in his Spanish tract in order to elude the Inquisition already on their track? Did he follow an Erasmian line because at that moment Erasmus had not yet fallen into disrepute? Perhaps!

But maybe Valdés came under a new influence in Italy which prompted a change of direction. A recent discovery makes plausible the assumption that this new influence was John Calvin. A booklet very popular among the followers of Valdés was called the *Benefit of Christ's Death, Del Benefizio di Giesu Christo Crocifisso.* Only recently a scholar has observed that the last three chapters are based, with even verbal borrowings, on the *Institutes* of Calvin.[19] The author was Benedetto of Mantua, a Benedictine monk who frequented the seances of Valdés at Naples. A further observation has been made that Valdés' doctrine of justification by faith alone without regard to any merit is nearly identical with that of the *Benefizio.*[20]

Another point is that Ochino, who often received from Valdés the titles for his sermons, also came close to reproducing Calvin.[21] Calvin himself told a friend that his works were circulating in Naples.[22] Flaminio, who had been in Naples, later showed a copy of the *Institutes* to Carnesecchi.[23] One is tempted to believe that Valdés, perhaps unwittingly, was indoctrinating Giulia in the gospels as preached in Geneva.

How fully Giulia agreed with Valdés we cannot say. She never disagreed with him according to our knowledge. She sent a copy of his commentary on Romans to Vittoria Colonna [24] and to the very end unreservedly accepted Valdés' doctrine of justification by faith.[25] But she recognized the authority of the church and, if commanded, would give up the works of Valdés. She believed herself to be a good *cattolica.*[26]

The question of how to deal with heresy led to a division in the ranks of the Catholic reformers. One group was in favor of conciliation and sought a formula of accommodation with the Protestants. This was notably true of Cardinal Contarini, who devised a theory of double justification [27] which he trusted would satisfy both Rome and Wittenberg. Other cardinals of this school were Pole, Morone, and Seripando. The alternate method was to suppress heresy and reform morals with Puritan rigor. The leader of this party was Caraffa. He had long been on friendly terms with the others and was, therefore, well acquainted with their liberal views—views he was resolved to stamp out. Largely because of his drive the Roman Inquisition was established by Pope Paul III through the bull *Licet ab initio* in 1542. There had long been inquisitorial proceedings at Rome conducted by local tribunals, but now the Roman Inquisition was organized along the lines of the Spanish with Dominicans in charge.

Caraffa was a Neapolitan and desired to extend his implacable arm to his native territory. He had good reason to expect opposition: Naples was occupied by the Spaniards and an effort had been made in 1510 to introduce the Inquisition from Spain. The attempt met with overwhelming opposition. The citizens, 7,000 strong — nobles, commoners, clergy, the signory, the friars — marched in procession, carrying lighted candles to protest to the Viceroy. He gave in and agreed that there should be no Spanish Inquisition. Local tribunals continued to operate, and the Viceroy said he had hanged 18,000.[28] He did not see what more he could do.

But Caraffa thought more could be done by superseding the local authorities. The attempt was renewed in 1547 in an effort to bring in a Roman Inquisition. It was not Spanish, but it was modelled after Spanish methods. There was little difference. This time the protest ignited a war of 15 days. Spanish soldiers were murdered, and other Spanish soldiers massacred citizens, including women and children. The Roman Inquisition was kept out, but it did little good. Suspects were taken to Rome for trial, and the local tribunal became equally ferocious when Caraffa was made the Archbishop of Naples.[29]

Valdés would undoubtedly have fallen into his toils had he not died in 1541. Caraffa set himself persistently to ferret out Giulia's heresies. She was living now in a convent, though without having taken vows. Our information from this time on is derived chiefly from the testimony of Pietro Carnesecchi during a much later examination before the Roman Inquisition. He had been secretary to Clement VII. Handsome and brilliant, he had met Giulia when she was 22 and he 27. By her "angelic leading" he had been brought from darkness into light, and his religious concerns were profoundly deepened. He became a disciple of Valdés and later was in the service of Cardinal Pole. Brought before the Inquisition he was on that occasion exonerated, spent some six years in France, then returned to Italy only to find himself again in trouble with the heresy hunters.[30]

Giulia became aware that she too was the subject of incriminations circulating against her in Naples. "I perceive," she said, "that those who testify before the Inquisition tell not what they know, but what they imagine. My words may have been garbled." [31] She insisted that she recognized the authority of the church and would surrender the works of Valdés. At the same time, when Cardinal Pole came under suspicion and would have been brought back to Italy for an inquest had he not died in England, Giulia was indefatigable in her efforts to have his works published.[32]

In 1555 Caraffa became Pope Paul IV. Giulia by 1558 had come to realize that he was against her. Carnesecchi advised her to flee but she declined.[33] Cardinal Seripando, in order to put her above suspicion, sought to persuade her to leave the heretical sirens of the Neapolitan circle, and threatened to have the pope issue an edict that only nuns could live in convents in order to force her out.[34] She stayed.

The rigors were all the more intensified because of conspicuous defections. Immediately after the establishment of the Roman Inquisition, the most notorious to escape over the Alps was her old friend Bernadino Ochino, who had so excited and ministered to her distress. He had been disillusioned as to the validity of his ascetic deportment by the spiritualizing emphases of Valdés. But Ochino did not go so far with spiritualizing as to despair of any concretion of the divine society. Geneva appeared to him to be the perfect exemplification of the kingdom of God. To Geneva he fled. Another member of the Valdésian circle, the highly respected theologian Vermigli, joined Ochino in flight. Consternation struck Italy. Ochino was denounced with utter execration. The Capuchin order, of which he was the general, was in danger of suppression. Efforts at the extermination of heresy were renewed.

Giulia would not condemn Ochino. To her cousin she wrote that she would follow the command of Christ to judge not. She had heard that Ochino was confronted with a choice between martyrdom, if he answered the summons of Rome, and exile. She had always been devoted to him and had regarded him as a *bon cristiano*. She did not know why he was called to Rome.[35]

She was accused of harboring heretics and abbetting the flight of others. To a degree this was true. She gave funds to two of her servants to assist their escape, and when Isabella Bresegna fled to Switzerland, Giulia sent her an annual stipend. This was not because she agreed with her opinions or would have advised her flight, but because Isabella had followed her conscience, Giulia felt that she should be supported in her stand. When Carnesecchi considered flight to Geneva, Giulia advised against it. He was moved by the consideration that his defection would throw greater suspicion on his friends Pole and Morone. Constrained by the love of Giulia, he followed her counsel and paid for it with his life.[36]

Even the highest in the church were struck. Cardinal Morone, during the entire pontificate of Paul IV, lay in the inquisitorial prison beneath the Castellio di Sant Angelo. Giulia received with distress the news from Carnesecchi of this arrest and of others to follow.[37] Then Paul IV died in 1559. The mob broke into the chambers of the Holy Office, released the prisoners, and burned the records. Carnesecchi reported with glee that the Inquisition had been destroyed by the very medium it employed —by fire.[38]

The respite was not for long. The chief inquisitor, Ghislieri, became pope in January 1566 as Pius V. He exonerated Morone, but Carnesecchi was again brought to trial. After a close examination of his confiscated papers and a gruelling examination, the pope commanded every cardinal to assemble in solemn conclave. The only one who succeeded in having himself excused was Morone. Carnesecchi was condemned to be beheaded and burned. The execution was set earlier than the usual hour so the cardinals would not have to witness the spectacle as they assembled past the place of execution in the morning. Carnesecchi went to his death dressed for a fiesta. The fire which should have consumed his remains was dampened by rain, and as the cardinals filed over the bridge to a meeting of the consistory, they beheld the naked charred body dangling over the reluctant flames.[39]

Among his papers were found many letters from Giulia. When the pope was apprized of their content he said, "Had I known this, she would have been burned alive." [40] She cheated him by death on the 19th of April, 1566.

BIBLIOGRAPHY

Giulia Gonzaga

Amante, Brutto, *Giulia Gonzaga* (Bologna, 1896), detailed with many of her letters in an appendix.

Benrath, Karl, "Julia Gonzaga," *Schriften des Vereins für Reformationsgeschichte* LXV (1900), compact and informative.

Hare, Christopher, (pseudonym of Marian Andrews), *A Princess of the Italian Renaissance* (London, 1912), with accounts of her friends.

Nicolini, Benedetto, "Giulia Gonzaga," in *Studi Cinquecenteschi* I (Bologna, 1968), pp. 119-53, a character sketch and excellent bibliography.

Paladino, Giuseppe, *Giulia Gonzaga* (Naples, 1909), especially useful for the analysis of the testimony of Carnesecchi.

Associates of Giulia

Benedetto of Mantua, author of *The Benefit of Christ's Death*, edited in English, Italian and French by Edward Courtenay (London, 1855).

Pietro Carnesecchi

Ortolani, Oddone, *Pietro Carnesecchi* (Florence, 1963), with extensive excerpts from his testimony before the Inquisition.

Documentation of the trial:

Manzoni, Giacomo, "Estratto del Processo de Pietro Carnesecchi," *Miscellanea di Storia Italiana* X (Torino, 1870).

Bernardino Ochino

Bainton, Roland H., *Bernardino Ochino, Esule e Riformatore Senese* . . . (Florence, 1940).

Nicolini, Benedetto, *Il Pensiero di Bernardino Ochino* (Naples, 1939).

Ochino's *Dialoghi Sette* in *Biblioteca della Riforma Italiana* . . . (Rome, 1884).

Girolamo Seripando

Jedin, Hubert, *Girolamo Seripando*, 2 vols. (Würzburg, 1937), English tr. (London, 1947).

Juan Valdés

Literature

Cione, Edmondo, *Juan de Valdés* (Bari, 1938).

For the more recent:

Mergal, Angel M., in the *Library of Christian Classics*, Vol. XXV *Spiritual and Anabaptist Writers* (Philadelphia, 1957).

Studies:

Bakhuizen Van der Brink, J. N., "Juan de Valdés," *Mededelingen der koninklijke Nederlandsche Akademie van Wetenschappen*, Afd. Letterkunde, Niewe Reeks, Deel XXV, No. 3 (Amsterdam, 1962) brief, acute.

Heep, J., *Juan de Valdés*, Quellen und Darstellungen aus der Geschichte des Reformationsjahrhunderts (Leipzig, 1909).

Nieto, José C., *Juan de Valdés, Travaux d'Humanisme et Renaissance*, CXIII (1970).

Teresa, F. Domingo de Sta., "Juan de Valdès," *Analecta Gregoriana* LXXXV Ser. Hist. Eccl. Sec. B (n. 13), (Rome, 1957). Detailed, defends Valdes' orthodoxy.

Works

De Doctora Cristiana. Facsimile with introduction, ed. Marcel Bataillon (Coimbra, 1925).

In modern script in *Obras Clasicas de la Reforma* (Buenos Aires, 1946).

Excellent analysis by Marcel Bataillon in *Erasmo y España,* an enlargement of the earlier French version (Mexico City, 1966).

Alfabeto Cristiano in Italian ed. B. Croce (Bari, 1938). In Spanish in *Obras Clasicas de la Reforma* XIII (Buenos Aires, 1948).

Hundred and Ten Considerations, tr. Benjamin Wiffen and John T. Betts (London, 1865).

Cento e Dieci Divine Consideratione, reprint (Halle, 1860, in Cione's bibliography No. 58).

Translations by John T. Betts of the commentaries on Romans, I Cor., Matthew, Sermon on the Mount and Psalms and minor works entitled *Opuscules* in Cione's bibliography Nos. 48, 69, 70, 72, 73, 77.

Pietro Martire Vermigli

McNair, Philip, *Peter Martyr in Italy* (Oxford, 1967).

Background

Amabile, Luigi, *Il Santo Officio della Inquisitione in Napoli,* 2 vols. (Citta di Castello, 1892).

NOTES

1. Hare, pp. 101 and 276.
2. *Ibid.,* 100-110, 278.
3. *Ibid.,* 113-7, Benrath 28.
4. On Ochino see my biography and the briefer English version in *The Travail of Religious Liberty* (Philadelphia, 1951). The passages translated are from the *Dialoghi Sette,* pp. 21-23, 48-49.
5. Giuseppe Paladino, *Opuscoli e Lettere di Riformatori Italiani del Cinquecento,* 2 vols. (Bari, 1913 and 1927), I, pp. 95-96.
6. See the bibliography.
7. See the bibliography.
8. *Juan de Valdés' Commentary upon St. Paul's Epistle to the Church at Corinth,* tr. John T. Betts (London, 1882), p. 43.
9. *Considerations,* No. CIII, English, p. 540.
10. *Opuscules de Juan de Valdés,* tr. John T. Betts (London, 1882), p. 43.
11. *Considerations,* No. XXIV, English, pp. 270-1 and XI, p. 234. *Opuscules,* pp. 107-08, 128, cf. 181. On *Matthew,* p. 393.
12. *Opuscules,* p. 154. *Alfabeto,* ed. Croce, p. 49.
13. *Opuscules,* pp. 159-60.
14. *Considerations,* No. LXXVII, English, p. 443.
15. *Ibid.,* LXIII, pp. 393-4.
16. *Alfabeto,* ed. Croce, pp. 109-116.
17. *Considerations,* No. CIX, pp. 573-75. On *Matthew,* p. 286.
18. Note that whereas in the *De Doctrina* the list of recommended readings includes Erasmus' *Enchiridion, Colloquies* and the *De Contemptu,* but in the *Alfabeto* these drop out.

19. The scholar is Bozza. For a review of the entire problem see Valdo Vinay, "Die Schrift 'Il Benefizio . . . ,'" *Archiv für Reformationsgeschichte* LVIII (1967), Heft 1, pp. 29-72.
20. Teresa, pp. 211 ff.
21. Erich Hassinger, excursus on Ochino in *Studien zu Jacobus Acontius* (Berlin, 1934).
22. McNair, p. 149. *Cal. Op.* XI, 419. For McNair's view which I endorse, p. 47.
23. Manzoni, *Estratto,* p. 556. Cf. Amante, p. 400.
24. Vittoria Colonna, *Carteggio,* ed. D. Tordi (Torino, 1892), No. CXLII, p. 240.
25. Manzoni, *Estratto,* p. 296.
26. Amante, p. 449.
27. P. Pas, "La doctrine de la double justice au Concile de Trente," *Ephemerides Theol. Lovanienses* XXX (1954), pp. 5-53.
28. McNair, p. 165.
29. Amabile, on the attempt in 1510, pp. 108-120; on that in 1547, pp. 195-200.
30. Details in Ortolani.
31. Amante, p. 449.
32. Paladino, *Giulia,* p. 113; Amabile, p. 154; Benrath, p. 92.
33. Manzoni, *Estratto,* p. 529. Paladino, *Opuscoli,* p. 97.
34. Paladino, *Giulia,* p. 121; Amabile, p. 155. Hubert Jedin, "Girolamo Seripando," *Cassiacum* II, (Würzburg, 1937), Bd. II, p. 309.
35. Amante, pp. 434-5.
36. Manzoni, *Estratto,* 215, 231-33, 279, 284, 303, 324, 327, 568, especially 313-5 and cf. 558. Paladino, *Opuscoli,* 98, 102, 103, 104. See *infra,* pp. 221-223.
37. Paladino, *Giulia* and Ortolani.
38. Manzoni, *Estratto,* p. 374. Paladino, *Opuscoli,* 105.
39. Ortolani.
40. Benrath, p. 99.

11.

Caterina Cibo
(1501 - 1557)

Caterina Cibo, the Duchess of Camerino, was another of
those princesses of the Renaissance deeply concerned and ac-
tively involved in the movements for the reform of the church.
Unfortunately, as in the case of Giulia, most of what we know
about her comes from the testimony of men. We are informed
that she was more learned than the other women of Italy in our
survey because she knew not only Latin, but also Greek and
Hebrew. She was no less adulated than the others in literary
circles and had greater influence than most because she was the
niece of Medicean Pope Clement VII, and the house of Medici
gave support to the duchy of Camerino. Her reformatory efforts
in her earlier period were all within the framework of the Catholic stucture.

By reason of her connection with the pope she was able to
save the Capuchins [1] from suppression. That they should have
been in danger of suppression may come as a surprise after what
has been said about the immense popularity of their general,
Ochino. But his meteoric career would scarcely have been possible had there been no order of which to be general. The reason
why fellow Franciscans sought to extinguish the order goes back
to the time of St. Francis himself in the early 13th century. He
was resolved to inaugurate a new type of monasticism to accommodate the new urban culture. The monasteries of the agrarian
Middle Ages were themselves communities withdrawn from the

centers of population. The monks had to stay in residence. The friars, as the followers of St. Francis were called, were mobile, seeking out men whether in field or mart. They had no fixed abodes and slept in huts, haystacks or on cathedral steps. Drastic poverty was accentuated as a rebuke to the spirit of rising commercialism. Not only were individuals to have no private possessions, as in the monasteries, but the order itself must have no corporate wealth. St. Francis was resolved that his order should not go the way of the monasteries which throughout the Middle Ages had fought a losing battle to stay poor. They were repeatedly undone either by donations from others or by their own industry and thrift. St. Francis ruled that the friars might accept as alms or wages only what they could wear or eat. Nothing should be saved. The friars should devote themselves to preaching, caring for the lepers, and reconciling feuds.

The program was feasible so long as there were not more than a dozen or so of these troubadors of God with their jubilant improvidence. When there were 500 begging for only a day at a time, some days were bound to be lean. The temptation to accept money was irresistible. The problem emerged in a new form after St. Francis' death, when the erection of a church was commenced in his honor. Church building requires skilled masons, and skilled masons have to be paid. A money box was set up. One of the brothers smashed it. Then came a rift in the order. One party, called the Conventuals, accepted a compromise. The church could own property and grant them the use of it. The radical party, called the Spirituals, spurned the subterfuge and insisted on following the rule of St. Francis "without a gloss." Not even the pope could grant a dispensation from the rule which had been given to St. Francis by the Holy Ghost. If the pope relaxed the rule, he should be disobeyed.

Revival of the early church's belief in the imminent end of the age increased the ferment. Prior to the time of St. Francis, a Calabrian monk named Joachim of Fiore, had predicted the coming of a new age when the papal church would be superseded by the church of the Spirit. Primitive Christianity would be restored and humanity reborn. The new dispensation would be heralded by the emergence of a messianic figure who would be resisted by Antichrist. In 1241 when the Spiritual Franciscans discovered these prophecies, they promptly identified the messianic figure with St. Francis, now dead. Antichrist signified emperors and popes, present and to come, who impeded the advent of the Spirit.

Intense strife ensued, especially in the period when the papacy removed from Rome to Avignon, in what is now southern France. The transfer meant the loss of revenues from the estates of the church in Italy. Pope John XXII sought by every device to replenish the papal coffers. The Spirituals scathed his avarice, and he burned some of them. Then he made a move which alienated all of the Franciscans. He declared that Christ owned property. Even the Conventuals, though they compromised for themselves, would not concede that Christ had ever compromised. The upshot was a new alignment. The Conventuals continued, but the Spirituals disappeared to be replaced by two parties, the one less, the other more rigorous. The Observants agreed to observe the rule of the saint in so far as the church allowed. The radical party, the Fraticelli, insisted on the rule "without a gloss," even in defiance of the church's rulings. They were branded as schismatics and heretics, and by the end of the 15th century the Fraticelli had been wiped out by the Inquisition.

By the 16th century the Observants had fallen away even from their compromise. The Capuchins arose as a protest, cherishing the writings and revering the memory of the martyred Spirituals. The Observants feared the disruption of their branch through defections to the Capuchins, and the popes feared the outbreak of another schismatical and heretical sect. The founder of the Capuchins was Matteo da Bascio, distinguished for the unstintedness of his sacrifice and the austerity of his preaching.

When in 1523 a plague devastated the city of Camerino, of which Caterina was the Duchess, Matteo left the Observant house to which he belonged to care for the stricken. As the need diminished, he fled from the plaudits of the crowd as he had not fled from the plague itself. He was disturbed when some of the Observants passed by a starving beggar on their way home to a good dinner. Thereupon he went to Rome to ask Pope

Clement VII for permission for himself alone to follow the exact
teachings of St. Francis. The pope approved of his resolve but
gave only a verbal assurance. The Minister Provincial of the
Observants, himself a reformer, was disturbed by the prospect
that the more ardent spirits would defect in the wake of this
pestilential vagabond. Matteo da Bascio was locked up.

At this point Caterina, the Duchess of Camerino, intervened.
A glimpse at her manner of life enables one to understand why
she should have concerned herself for the Capuchins, Born in
1501, she was early betrothed to Giovanni Maria Varano, the
lord of Camerino, 20 years her senior. By him she had a daughter Giulia, born in 1523. The mother's life was fraught with
strife. Camerino and the neighboring Urbino were feudatories
of the popes and bitter rivals. After the death of her husband
she thought to put an end to the strife by marrying her daughter Giulia to the Duke of Urbino. Her uncle, Pope Clement VII,
feared that his vassals might be more intractable if united. The
next pope, Paul III, wanted to give Giulia to a Farnese, his own
relative, and forbade the marriage to the Duke of Urbino. Caterina defied him, and the marriage went through. The squabbles
which followed, the wars, and the brief imprisonment of Caterina herself fed her disgust with it all and her admiration for
the sons of St. Francis and the followers of Lady Poverty.

When Matteo was imprisoned, she intervened. In the meantime the situation had grown more serious. Other Observants
wanted to join Matteo and found a new order. The provincial of
the Observants constrained them by arms, but they escaped. The
Duchess of Camerino and the Duke (who was at that time still
alive) arranged a conference, and the case was taken to the pope.
Caterina's plea for the radicals prevailed. In June 1528, Clement
VII granted permission for the formation of a new order with
a superior of its own and with permission to receive converts
from other orders without the consent of their superiors. Thus
was founded the order of the Capuchins. The name came from
their pointed hoods.

But there was more opposition. A compromise was arranged
in November of 1532 whereby if the Capuchins returned to the
Observants, four or five houses would be alloted for strict ob-

Bernardino Ochino

servance of the primitive rule. The next year this bull of authorization was suspended. Then came a crisis: the same provincial who had imprisoned Matteo da Bascio seceded to the Capuchins. So also did Ochino.

Then on April 15, 1534, Clement VII ordered all of the Capuchins to go back to the Observants. Those in Rome were to leave the city within the burning of a candle. They arose at once from the table, 150 of them, and carrying only their breviaries, marched behind a red wooden cross to the Basilica of San Lorenzo beyond the walls. Caterina bolted to Rome [2] and the order was revoked. Then the pope died, and her influence at the papal court ceased. The defense of the Capuchins passed to Vittoria Colonna, the subject of a later sketch.

All of these proceedings naturally brought Caterina into contact with Ochino, the new general of the Capuchins. What Valdés was for Giulia Gonzaga, Ochino was for Caterina. She knew him at Naples and was to know him also later at Florence. As Valdés composed his *Alfabeto Cristiano* as a dialog between himself and Giulia, so Ochino wrote seven dialogs chiefly between himself and Caterina. They have the air of authentic conversations. Here are brief summaries of the first and the seventh.[3]
"CATERINA: According to the Scripture everything depends on the love of God. How am I to love him?
BERNARDINO: Some people even hate him.
CATERINA: I know. Some seem incapable of loving him. And yet we receive all good gifts from God and all creatures are flames of love. . . . In this present life the love of God is above all else sweet and precious. He should be loved not for good or for ill, not for convenience or inconvenience, not for pleasure or displeasure, not for honor or dishonor.
BERNARDINO: Right! Strange that whereas God is loved by the saints, angels and by the creatures, in so far as they can, yet man, endowed with reason, despises God as if he were the vilest creature!
CATERINA: That is because we cannot love God above ourselves. . . . The eagle cannot fly on top of himself, and we cannot rise above ourselves.
BERNARDINO: I am not talking about natural love, but about the

love which is free and rational. On the wings of love the soul can fly above itself. Does not the natural man put the love of country above the love of self, and shall we not give the highest place to the heavenly country? The martyrs and the saints love God above themselves. With the aid of grace it can be done, and without grace what sinner can be saved?

CATERINA: I love the creatures right enough, but God not so much.

BERNARDINO: Those who love God for his gifts are really loving themselves. We must love God solely for his honor and glory. This goes contrary to the natural man, but it is possible through divine grace which is denied to none.

CATERINA: But is love in our power?

BERNARDINO: Yes, spiritual love. It is possible to love even enemies.

CATERINA: What shall I do to give God my love? I perceive that I cannot love God and the world.

BERNARDINO: Despising the world arises in us from the love of God and not the other way around.

CATERINA: We read of the philosophers that they despised the world without loving God.

BERNARDINO: Yes, but why did they despise the world? Was it not that they might be praised for it? They were not philosophers unless moved by the love of virtue.

CATERINA: Some of them were.

BERNARDINO: Yes, but they were still concerned for human glory. The true Christian must so love God that he despises himself, for hate arises from love.

CATERINA: Another problem. How can we love what we do not know? Must we not be like the cherubim and seraphim with direct knowledge of God in order to love him? We have but a little knowledge of God. We see through a glass darkly. We are like bats who cannot look upon the light of the sun. God is infinite, immense, uncircumscribed, but our intellect is finite, limited, imprisoned in this body of darkness, tainted with primal sin. The best way, then, to know God is to contemplate him. [At this point she introduces a creed including belief in the Trinity, in human freedom, but at the same time divine determination.] If we know all this we can love God.

BERNARDINO: You sound as if only scholars can love God, but I would say that the simplest old woman can love God above all the scholars in the world. Speculative knowledge is arid and cold. Practical knowledge serves God. Those who would love God must avoid useless and curious doctrine.

CATERINA: What then is the knowledge which lifts us to the love of God?"

At this point Ochino bursts into the rhapsody already cited for its impact on Giulia Gonzaga. He concludes that the best way is to meditate on the life and words of Christ.

"CATERINA: I am still bothered because we cannot love God unless we know him, and we cannot know him unless we love him. Must we, then, just concentrate on loving the way a blind man concentrates on the taste of honey? Does tasting the sweetness of God help love?

BERNARDINO: No, it does not. We do not love God for his sweetness, but in the midst of persecution, poverty, and the cross.

CATERINA: I understand, and just talking this over with you kindles my spirit.

BERNARDINO: Yes, the Holy Spirit descended in tongues of flames and the disciples after the walk to Emmaus said, 'Did not our hearts burn within us?'

CATERINA: I want to love God supremely. Isn't it enough that I want to?

BERNARDINO: Yes, if your desire is intense. The love of God is like the burning bush of Moses, like the fiery chariot of Elijah. In the love of God alone is our peace, the blessed goal of our desires, the true repose from our labors, the certain remedy for our woes, the healing for all our ills. May your Ladyship engage in such exercises, annihilating self, being transformed into God, who for our love gave his Son to suffer on the cross. Alleluia.

CATERINA: I place myself in your hands.

BERNARDINO: You should place yourself in God's hands.

CATERINA: Well, what would you have me do?

BERNARDINO: Become a nun.

CATERINA: I had not thought of that, for a number of reasons.

For one thing I have not found an order that suits me.

BERNARDINO: I know one that would suit you. It is the order of perfection.

CATERINA: Oh no, I am not up to that.

BERNARDINO: Yes, you are. Every one should strive for perfection. You don't have to change your place, but only your behavior; not your costume, but your customs. Tonsure not your hair, but your desires. Supplicate God with your heart and not your mouth. Be pure in heart and mind without reserve and take for your companions all the virtues. In this religion there is no novitiate. You simply join right away.

CATERINA: Very well, I will make my will. I, Caterina Cibo, Duchess of Camerino, testify that I now take the three vows. The first is poverty. I will live without love of any created thing. The second is obedience to all the laws of the spirit. The third is chastity, that my mind may be immaculate and free from whatever is displeasing to God. I will regard him as my father, Christ as my brother and the Holy Spirit as my spouse. I will hold myself ready to endure martyrdoms, pangs, infamy, exiles, imprisonments, persecutions, crosses, and deaths insofar as I am able. I will cast myself wholly into the arms of the crucified, through whom alone I hope for the pardon of my transgressions. I will place my reliance on the merits and glory of all the angels, the saints in paradise, the Madonna in glory, and above all in the merits of Christ, his triumph, his victory, and his blessedness. I will rejoice in the divine perfections, in the infinite blessedness of the three divine persons. I will flee evil and seek good and, even though I should suffer an infinite number of indignities, every instant I will forgive them all in Christ into whom I am transformed. Knowing that all good comes from God, I will recognize in all his works the highest good, infinite power, wisdom, love, mercy, beauty, justice and all perfections, and I will never cease with all my heart, my works, my life, my words, and all that in me is to laud, exalt, magnify, glorify, and honor God. I will have him ever in my thoughts and will recognize in every creature and even my own conscience that in good faith I, Caterina, Duchess of Camerino, have signed this with my own hand in the year 1539."

One senses the influence of the Florentine revival of Neoplatonism in the discussion of the nature of love in relation to knowledge and especially in the rhapsodies of Ochino on the ascent of the soul from the creatures to the blessed Virgin and her divine son.

In 1542 when Ochino defected to Geneva, he is alleged to have exchanged his monastic habit for lay clothes in the house of Caterina, then in Florence. Further, Carnesecchi at his trial testified that Caterina had been in touch with Ochino both before and *after* his departure. But communication thereafter would necessarily be limited. Carnesecchi, though in Italy, saw little of her,[4] and with respect to the last 15 years of her life till her death in 1557 we know almost nothing.

But it is plain that in the latter period of her life she found another spiritual adviser in Marc Antonio Flaminio.[5] It was he who polished the Italian style of the tract, *The Benefit of Christ's Death,* which reworked portions of Calvin's *Institutes.* Flaminio was a person of no little distinction, a poet whose ode on the accession of Pope Paul III is regarded as one of the finest examples of Neo-Latin poetry. He had been in the service of popes Leo X and Clement VII and had spent 14 years with Giberti, the reforming bishop of Verona. He stayed for six months with Carnesecchi, and showed him a copy of Calvin's *Institutes.* In his earlier days he had been associated with Valdés and Giulia Gonzaga in Naples, and in his latter period was a secretary to Cardinal Pole at Viterbo, Flaminio was able to subscribe doctrinally to what Rome required of him. Caraffa, who attended his deathbed, was satisfied when he subscribed to transubstantiation, but after his death, having learned more of his opinions, said that he would like to dig him up and burn his remains.

We have two letters written by Flaminio to Caterina.[6] The first, dated February 25, 1547, was to console her on the death of her daughter:

"You have already suffered so many afflictions that you are in a measure prepared for this bereavement. From a worldly point of view you are of all most unfortunate, but if I regard you in Christ, then the most blessed and favored of God, for when tribulations increase then are we the more made like to Christ, the crucified. I am assured that you are among those whom God has foreknown and predestined to be conformed to the image of his son, who bore the cross in this world and declared that he who would be his disciple must bear it daily. . . . You may be comforted that your daughter has been transferred from this vale of tears to the light of God's blessed kingdom. If there are those who are at pains to marry their daughters in Poland or distant lands, that they may be queens, though never seen again, ought you not the more to rejoice that your daughter has been called to her celestial spouse in paradise to receive the crown of righteousness which God has prepared for those who love him?"

The second letter was written two years later in 1549. He begins by relating the circumstances of his own sickness:

"At times I was in my senses but at others not altogether rational. I seemed then to repose wholly in God and Christ. With the eyes of the mind I saw God who caressed me as a mother her sick child. I saw Christ who took my soul to paradise. This vision gave me such delight that I began to taste the joy of eternal life. While the doctors were despairing of me, I experienced such sweetness of spirit, as if I were already in paradise prior to the separation of body and spirit. The joy of dying was so multiplied in body and in spirit that I fell into a grievous temptation which lasted more than three hours. Having arrived at the gate of paradise, I was sent back to this vale of misery and sins. Then I saw how self love had beguiled me and I said, 'Oh, you ingrate! Is this your thankfulness to God who has done so much for you? When he takes you to heaven you are jubilant. When he sends you back to earth you are downcast. Is this the obedience which you give to God? You love yourself more than you love God.' By such thoughts I was delivered from this dreadful temptation and by grace was made content to live or die as shall please his Divine Majesty. In my sickness I felt that I had touched the fatherly healing granted to those who by grace have a live faith in Jesus Christ, our Lord, and suffer themselves to receive with joy from our most gracious Heavenly Father sickness and health, life, and death.

"Do not let this letter get out of your hands, and don't show it to any one.—Rome, May, 1549."

Why the secrecy? The doctrine of justification by faith is present only by implication. Was it that the vision would stamp him as an Illuminist? The church was very wary of those who claimed immediate divine revelations eluding ecclesiastical control. Carnesecchi thanked Giulia for reminding him of the prohibition of "ecstasies." He hoped that the Inquisition would not interpret anything of his in that sense.[7]

One may assume that Caterina would have been sympathetic toward all that Flaminio said. When Carnesecchi was questioned as to her orthodoxy, he said that he and Flaminio visited in her home at Florence and discussed with her the doctrine of justification by faith. "I don't know whether she went further than this. She may have. I haven't seen her for many years." [8]

BIBLIOGRAPHY

B. Feliciangeli, *Notizie e Documenti sulla vita di Caterina Cibo-Varano Duchessa di Camerino* (Camerino, 1891).

NOTES

1. Father Cuthbert, *The Capuchins*, 2 vols. (New York, 1929).
   Bainton, Roland H., *Bernardino Ochino*, Biblioteca Storica Sansoni N. S. IV (Florence, 1940).
2. Feliciangeli. p. 164.
3. Ochino, "Dialoghi Sette," *Biblioteca della Riforma Italiana* (Rome, 1884).
4. "Estratto del Processo di Pietro Carnesecchi," ed. Giacomo Manzoni, *Miscellanea di Storia Italiana* X (Torino, 1870), p. 201.
   "Compendio dei processi dal Santo Ufficio di Roma," ed. C. Corvisieri, *Archivio Societa Romana* III (Rome, 1880), p. 272.
5. Cuccoli, Ercole, *M. Antonio Flaminio* (Bologna, 1897).
   Maddison, Carol, *Marcantonio Flaminio* (Chapel Hill, 1965).
   Some of his letters are in Giuseppe Paladino, *Opuscoli e Lettere di Riformatori Italiani del Cinquecento* (Bari, 1913), vol. 1.
6. Feliciangeli, pp. 231-34 and 235-40.
7. Paladino, *op. cit.* I, p. 101.
8. Manzoni, *Processo*, pp. 201-202.

Michelangelo's drawing of a woman
believed to be Vittoria Colonna

12.

Vittoria Colonna
(1490-1547)

Vittoria Colonna is best known of all the Italian women treated here because of the inspiration which she afforded to Michelangelo. That inspiration was religious, and her religion must be understood before the subject can be approached. She was another of the high born ladies of the Renaissance, educated in Latin as well as in Italian.[1] A daughter of the house of Colonna, she was married at 17 to the Spanish *hidalgo* D'Avalos, the Marchese of Pescara. The marriage of 18 years was but briefly romantic, for he was often absent in the wars and faithless to his vows. After his death she poured forth sonnets adulating his memory. Was this a love that would not let him go or a literary affectation? At any rate her verses as well as her station made her an admired figure among the *literati*. The great stylist in Latin and Italian, Pietro Bembo, highly regarded her skill, while she acknowledged her inability to emulate his own.[2] Castiglione submitted to her judgment a manuscript of his *Cortegione*.[3]

Vittoria had as much reason to be disquieted over her role as a feted Marchesa in the world of genteel courtesy and brutal strife as did Caterina Cibo. The Colonnas were traditionally at war with the Orsini and were embroiled in the wars of the papacy and the empire, with a leaning to the latter. Vittoria's brother Ascanio had a feud with the pope because of Ascanio's refusal to allow his peasants to abide by a papal monopoly on the sale of salt. The Colonnas made a raid on Rome and Ascanio was repulsed and restricted to Naples. Vittoria told him that war could not be justified over a matter of 30 cows.[4] Her sonnets complain bitterly alike of war and papal corruption. For example:

> When the breath of God that moved above the tide
> Fans the embers of my smouldering state,
> And the winds of God begin to dissipate
> The fetid stench of the church, his bride,
> Then the swaggering knights prepare to ride.
> The war begins. They gloat and cannot wait.
> They think they are the masters of their fate
> And would display their valor far and wide.
> Then within they hear God's trumpet blow,
> And they, whose gods were goblets and a crest,
> Appalled by death, their headlong charge arrest.
> They cannot lift the vizier to the rays
> Which penetrate the heart beneath the vest.
> Would they but discard their gear and ways! [5]

For the depravity of her age she foresees another and more frightful flood:

> Father Noah, from whose good seed God graced
> To populate the ancient world anew,
> When the inundating deluge grew
> Till they were drowned who had the world defaced.
> If our age, no less impure, were faced
> By the holy eye of him who knew,
> With what holy ire would he then spew
> A second flood, from blood of men disgraced.
> Pray that in such fury I may be
> Humble, pure in mind, and standing stark,
> Nor swerving from the task imposed on me.
> But dwelling inwardly inside the ark,
> For the dear wounds of blood have set me free
> And my live faith released me from the dark.[6]

Yet, for all her strictures on the times and the church, she did not impugn the spiritual authority of the popes nor refrain from using her influence to determine their decisions. She was responsible for the elevation of Bembo to the cardinalate.[7] All this she might have done without any change in her religious stance, but a change did take place. The one responsible appears not to have been Valdés, whom she almost certainly knew in Naples,[8] but Ochino, whom she heard preach in Rome. Giulia Gonzaga sent Valdés' commentary on Romans to Vittoria as a gift,[9] but otherwise his name is not mentioned in her correspondence. She heard Ochino when he preached from two to six in the morning before a congregation including empurpled cardinals, and she, with the rest of the audience, was moved to tears.[10]

Two letters of indeterminate date from her pen are reminiscent of Ochino. Writing to another highborn dame of the Renaissance she announces:

"This morning my thoughts were directed to our Lady and in utter joy to embrace her Son. In the purest light I discerned a thousand knots binding them in the most ardent love. In her person creature and creator are united. Through her immaculate conception and true redemption, she is able on the wings of her great merit, to rise above the celestial choirs. The glorious Lady is above the angels, who served her on the way to Egypt; above the archangels, who govern but a single kingdom, whereas she is the queen of all; above the power to work miracles and cast out demons, for she has conquered hell; above the principalities, which are but inferior lights, while she is the true light which illumines all the blessed; above the dominions, above the thrones, above the cherubim, above the seraphim. She rises to the light which is one and three. In this clear and pure crystal one beholds the light invisible, supreme. The Father is pleased to have shown in her his power. The Son rejoices in her wisdom and the Spirit is consoled to see relucent in this most perfect bride his perfect goodness." [11]

The style reminds one of Ochino's rhapsody, already cited for its impact on Giulia Gonzaga. But Vittoria changes the emphasis. Ochino was concerned to show how one can rise from the knowledge of the creatures to the knowledge of God. Vittoria chose rather to exalt the queen of heaven above all the celestial hierarchy. One suspects also a touch of feminism, seeing that the next letter lauds another woman, Mary Magdalene, identified as was then common with the Mary who met the risen Lord in the garden. "Consider," writes Vittoria, "how Christ made this beloved woman the first to witness the resurrection and commissioned her to bear the news to the disciples. Was it not this redeemed woman who followed him with burning love to the foot of the cross? When others fled she stood with the queen of heaven and the Holy Spirit. She became the perfect herald of the word divine, and on the mount of penitence was visited by the radiant star with the highest love.[12] One of the sonnets carries the same theme.

> The damsel fair as she sat weighed by woe
> Felt the great yearning which dispels all fear.
> Alone by night, disdaining sword and spear
> In ardent hope she essayed to go,
> Entered the sepulchre by grief bent low,
> Saw not angels, cast not for self a tear,
> Fell where she thought the Saviour's feet were near,
> Aflame with love no tremor could she know.
> The men elected to enjoy such grace,
> Strong, though they were, together crouched from fright.
> The light became a naked sprite or shade.
> If then the true is not to error made
> Credit to the women goes by right.
> They have the open heart and unaffrighted face.[13]

Vittoria Colonna, like Caterina Cibo, repelled by the society about her and aflame with a passion for the divine, took up the cause of the Capuchins after the influence of Caterina had waned at the papal court. No doubt the enthusiasm for the preaching of Ochino, their general, was the immediate incentive. On their behalf she wrote to Cardinal Contarini:

"The Capuchins are accused of being Lutherans. If St. Francis was a heretic, then call them Lutherans. If to preach the liberty of the Spirit is a vice, when subject to the rule of the church, what will you make of the text, 'The Spirit gives life?' If those who trouble these friars had seen their humility, poverty, obedience, and charity they would be ashamed. As for obedience, they wish to restore the rule of St. Francis. They are not rebellious against the clergy. The charge is made that they do not obey their own general, but he does not reform. The pope should support them. They want freedom simply to follow the rule of their founder, and I do not see why St. Francis should not receive as much favor at Rome as St. Benedict. Francis did not enforce his rule by prisons and death, but by humility, poverty and love. I do not see why human arguments should supersede the divine, that new laws should break the sacred constitution of the church. We should not follow our own judgment, but that of Christ and Paul. These Capuchins are not asking for greatness or riches. They ask in the name of the stigmata of St. Francis and the wounds of Christ to be left in peace to observe their rule. A cardinal inspired by God well said, 'If your holiness does not approve of this rule, you will have to deny the gospel of Christ on which it is founded. There are orders which display on their banners the ensigns of the Guelfs and the Ghibellines, and shall not these brothers be allowed to renew the habit of their glorious father?' " [14]

One observes in all that has been cited the warm piety of evangelical Catholicism with never a hint of any deviation from the standards of orthodoxy. But there are strains in her devotional poetry which could lead either to the Reformation or the Counter-Reformation. Neoplatonic influence is discernible in the frequent contrasts of light and darkness, brilliance and shadow, fire and frost, fervor and aridity, as well as in the desire to mount with wings to the true light and the true love.[15] There is a depreciation of *prudenza humana* which does not mean exactly the prudential so much as reliance on the human intellect rather than upon spiritual illumination. This anti-intellectualism might lead to an uncritical acceptance of the dogmas of the church or to a complete indifference to any dogmas at all. All of this is in line with Franciscan piety, itself often anti-intellectual and centered upon the example of the wounds of Christ. Such themes may be further illustrated from her sonnets. The following one deals with the dangers of learning.

> If the sun bestows his rays benign,
> May we, not robed in virtue, nor in vice,
> Through his sweet mercy, not our own device,
> Lift up our heads to meet the grace divine.
> Not sipping human lore, as it were wine,
> And reading learned tomes, not once but twice,

> For when the soul essays too great a rise
> The more does it from faith and truth decline.
> Shut then the eye to left, open to right,
> On wings of faith and love essay to soar.
> They lift the soul above the mortal view.
> By true humility we reach the light
> And know the sacred writings to be true.
> Read little, then, and believe the more.[16]

The following sonnet voices the doctrine of justification by faith. But different levels of faith are distinguished. The faith "which light and joy endow" is not sufficient, but only that faith "kindled by heaven's fires."

> One cannot have a lively faith I trow
> Of God's eternal promises if fear
> Has left the warm heart chilled and seer
> And placed a veil between the I and Thou.
> Nor faith, which light and joy endow
> And works, which in the course of love appear,
> If oft some vile, deep dolor drear
> Injects itself into the here and now.
> These human virtues, works and these desires
> All operate the same, are but a shade,
> Cast as a shadow, moving or at rest,
> But when the light descends from heaven's fires
> Kindling hope and faith within the breast
> Then doubt and fear and dolor, these all fade.[17]

At the same time good works receive some sort of recognition since Noah was saved because his good deeds were pleasing in God's sight:

> You, Noah, were delivered in the ark, but why?
> And you became the father of the race.
> Why God should have conferred on you such grace
> Is something you cannot explain, nor I.
> You and yours alone were not to die,
> For heaven looked with favor in your case.
> You only by your deeds were no disgrace
> But ground for love or envy by and by.
> When all the world looked on you with despite
> And gnashed their teeth from their imbedded hate,
> Sweet love and peace relieved you in your plight.
> And when the waters heaved their mighty weight

Since your good deeds were pleasing in God's sight
The waves of grace delivered you from fate.[18]

The Christ-centeredness of Vittoria Colonna's piety can be
illustrated by her sonnets on the annunciation, the star at the
nativity, and the cross.

The Annunciation

Blessed angel with whom the Father swore
The ancient covenant now sealed anew,
Which gives us peace and shows the pathway true
To contemplate his gifts for evermore.
For this holy office held in store
With soul inclined and mind in constant view
By his high embassy he did imbue
The virgin's heart, which joyful I adore.
I beg you now behold the face and hands,
Humble response, tingéd with chaste dread,
The ardent love and faith with pulsing beat
Of her, who come from out no earthly lands,
With humble heartfelt yearning, sweet desire replete,
Greets, adores, embraces all God said.[19]

The Star

What joy, oh star and blessed sign
Twinkling on the cattle stall,
From the fabled east you call
Wise men to the birth divine!
Behold the King amid the kine
Swaddled in no lordly hall.
Above, what love surpassing all
Lifts our hearts and makes them thine!
The place, the beasts, the cold, the hay,
The lowly coverlet and bed
Of thy love what more could say?
Then, for the star which hither led
And gave such proof of thy design
To joyful praise our hearts incline.[20]

The Cross

When writhe the Saviour's shoulders on the tree
And droops the holy body from the weight,
Is there then no key to fit the gate
That heaven should not open for to see?
What grievous pangs he bore from sheer pity
And for our sakes endured so cruel a fate
Thus by his guiltless blood to recreate
Our spirits laved of all impurity!
Our surcease from war, within, wherever,
Comes from him, the author of our peace.
He is the sun whose brilliance blinds our eyes.
The Father's, secrets how he will release
To whom and where and when none can surmize.
Enough for us to know he cannot err.[21]

The friendship between Vittoria Colonna and Michelangelo may have begun as early as 1538 and certainly endured until her death in 1547. His feeling of indebtedness to her in his advancing years is evident in these lines:

You had no need, my love, of any chain
To take me vanquished and make me your thrall,
For I am sure—I very well recall—
One glance sufficed to make of me your slave.
Perhaps it was that I had known such pain
That in my weakness I should so behave.
Who would believe—though I do credence crave—
That your two lovely eyes so very soon
Should cause a withered tree to burgeon and to bloom? [22]

Whether her ideas of religious art directly affected his style is difficult to say. She arranged an interview between him and a Portuguese man named Ollanda, in the course of which Michelangelo set forth his theories of art. When he was asked what is needful in order to portray the Lord, he answered, "One needs almost to be a saint." [23] With that judgment she would assuredly have concurred.

Michelangelo painted three pieces especially for Vittoria Colonna. One is a drawing of the Samaritan woman at the well. Perhaps he undertook it in order to illustrate her sonnet where she celebrates, as does the gospel, the universality of the Spirit.

The Woman at the Well

The Woman at the Well

Oh blessed dame, to whom beside the fount
Where you had come to fill your jar he spake,
At whose word the sea and mountains quake,
No more of old nor on the sacred mount,
With hearty faith we now our wants recount,
With sweet tears or bitter supplicate
The Father, who will inward wishes take,
And silent prayers, as they were spoken, count.
But then was thy deep yearning met
When on thee fell that burning vibrant ray
Illumining Samaria and mankind.
In haste you ran thereat in each byway
That none this festive day should e'er forget
But honor him with heart and soul and mind.[24]

Michelangelo's depiction of the woman at the well offers nothing strikingly novel. She is pointing to the water in the well, while Jesus is evidently discoursing on the water of life. The next two drawings done for Vittoria are quite different. The pietà is markedly divergent from the pietà done in Michelangelo's youth, now in the Vatican. There the mother looks upon her son with the pensive melancholy of Neoplatonic composure. Here she is not looking at him at all, but in ecstasy her gaze is upward and her arms outstretched as the mediator and intercessor, a concept not alien to Michelangelo or Vittoria. The center of attention is held by her son. Beneath his feet we see the crown of thorns. Almost emerging from his body the cross ascends with the inscription, "One cannot grasp what blood it cost." The very form of this cross makes it the more a symbol of redemption because it is the cross conserved at Santa Croce, which was carried in procession to stay the great plague of the Black Death in 1348. The supports of the arms of the cross form a triangle with the crossbeam. Since this is reproduced from an actual cross, one would not suspect symbolism until observing that the head of the mother and the hands of the son form another triangle suggestive of the Trinity. The composition is thus determined by considerations of theology.[25]

The greatest innovation of all is evident in the depiction of the crucifixion. From the twelfth century on, under the impact

Michelangelo's *Pietà* for Vittoria Colonna

of Bernardine and Franciscan piety, the emphasis was upon the intense suffering and utter lassitude of the dead Christ. His head was made to fall upon the right shoulder. The arms sagged. The legs were crossed and held by only one nail so that the body assumed the shape of an S, exhibiting the utter collapse after the agony of death. This crucifix of Michelangelo is alive. The head is upright. The eyes are open. The body is the *bel corpo ignudo* of the David. This is the Christ triumphant over death. Beneath the arms of Christ on each side are little angels, not for the purpose of holding a chalice to catch the blood but rather to point to the wound and give comfort to Christ.[26] In this treatment Michelangelo was returning to the style of early portrayals of the crucifixion in the fifth century. Whether he had actually seen the picture herewith reproduced is doubtful, but he was in line with a general tendency of the Catholic liberal reform to restore primitive Christianity.[27]

Vittoria, in thanking him, said she had entertained the greatest faith that God would confer upon him the supernatural grace to execute this work, but now she found it marvelous beyond all expectation. She believed that the Archangel Michael would set Michelangelo at the right hand of the Lord at the last day.[28]

The greatest crisis in the life of Vittoria Colonna, as for many others, came with the establishment of the Roman Inquisition in 1542. She was disturbed when some of her friends came under suspicion and even more when some were guilty of defection. The severest blow was the flight of Ochino. He sent her a letter explaining his reasons for scaling the Alps. She refused to open the letter and turned it over to Cardinal Pole, who forwarded it to the Inquisition at Rome. Ochino was for her outside the pale because no longer in the ark. "The more he excuses himself," said she, "the more he accuses." [29] How did she know if she did not open the letter?

Making life even more bitter for her was her brother's conflict with the pope. As a result of this conflict, the Colonnas were expelled from the papal patrimony and her brother exiled to Naples. Vittoria sorely needed a new spiritual counsellor. She found one in a man equally in need of her.

A 13th century Crucifixion

Cardinal Reginald Pole [30] was of the house of the Plantagenets, a relative of Henry VIII of England and a possible claimant to the throne. Henry sought to win him for his cause in the matter of his divorce, but Pole refused to be swayed and came out with a public declaration in condemnation of the king. Henry could not touch his person since he was abroad, but the royal ire fell upon his family. Two brothers were executed and, after a time, also his mother. Pole told Vittoria he had never believed he would be the son not only of a saint but also of a martyr.

In his grief he found a second mother in the Marchesa, ten years his senior. At the same time he became her spiritual director and dissuaded her from the rigorous asceticism with which she sought to assuage her disquiet. Carnesecchi testified that before the encounter with Pole Vittoria afflicted herself with fasts, hairshirts, and other mortifications and nearly reduced herself to skin and bones.[31] That Vittoria should have had recourse to such a discipline shows plainly that she had not grasped the gospel of Valdés but was closer to the Ochino of the Capuchins before his disillusionment with outward macerations. Pole persuaded her to temper her austerities.

Had she lived longer, she would almost certainly have been suspected of heresy, as was Pole himself. Nearly ten years after her death he had to defend himself vigorously to Paul IV, saying that he did not complain of being deprived of his legation to England—this was under the restoration of Catholicism in England by Mary Tudor—but the insinuation of heresy he could not stand. He besought the pope to be like that Abraham whose hand was stayed from the slaying of his son.[32] Pole was certainly no heretic. Neither was Vittoria. Both accepted the doctrine of justification by faith, but this was not heretical prior to Trent. When the subject was up for a pronouncement by Trent, Vittoria said that Pole was mercifully delivered from attendance by a severe case of catarrh,[33] but when against his dissent the doctrine was promulgated, he submitted. Vittoria would undoubtedly have done the same. Carnesecchi did report that she was pleased with Luther's commentary on Psalm 45.[34] It must have been in an anonymous and truncated translation, because the

Michelangelo's *Crucifixion*
for Vittoria Colonna

full version contains blasts against the Roman church which she could never have countenanced.[35]

She died in 1547. Michelangelo confessed in the following lines that with her passing his creative power was paralyzed.

> The sculptor's hammer according to his will
> Gives to the rugged stone a human form.
> The hammer of itself knows not the norm
> And must be guided by the sculptor's skill.
> The hammer forged remains a hammer still.
> There is a power that rides above the storm,
> Beauty alone creates, invests with form,
> Able to recreate and also kill.
> The hammer, if the hand be lifted high,
> Descends with greater force upon the stone.
> Mine upraised was snatched with her away.
> Untouched about me now my carvings lie.
> I know not what to do. I am alone,
> Unless the great Artificer will show the way.[36]

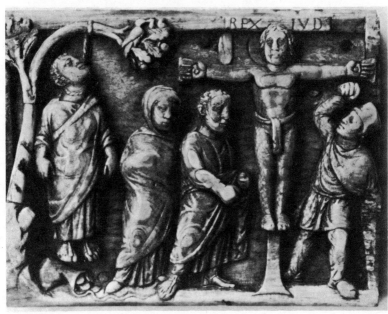

A fourth century Syrian depiction
of the Crucifixion

BIBLIOGRAPHY

Biographies

Alfred von Reumont
Vittoria Colonna (Freiburg im Breisgau, 1881). The standard treatment.

Benedetto Nicolini
"Sulla Religiosità di Vittoria Colonna," *Ideali e Passioni nell'Italia Religiosa del Cinquecento* (Bologna, 1962), an interpretation with up-to-date bibliography.

Eva Maria Jung
"Vittoria Colonna: between Reformation and Counter-Reformation," *Review of Religion* XV (1951), 144-59.

Sources

Vittoria Colonna . . . Carteggio, ed. E. Ferrero and G. Müller (Turin, 1892). Abbreviation, *Carteggio*.

Le Rime di Vittoria Colonna, ed. Pietro Ercole Visconti (Rome, 1840). Abbreviation, *Rime*.

"Estratto del Processo di Pietro Carnesecchi," ed. Giacomo Manzoni, *Miscellanea di Storia Italiana* X (Turin, 1870), 187-573. Abbreviation, *Carnesecchi*.

NOTES

1. Testimony of Ollanda in English translation as an appendix to Charles Holroyd, *Michel Angelo Buonarroti* (London, 1903), p. 271. There is no certainty that Ollanda reports an actual conversation.
2. *Carteggio*, XL, p. 61; XLI, p. 62.
3. *Ibid.*, XXXIV, p. 38.
4. *Carteggio*, CXXIX, p. 218.
5. *Rime* II, CXXXIV, p. 294.
6. *Ibid.*, II, XCVI, p. 256.
7. *Carteggio*, CIV, p. 174.
8. Bibliography on this point in Nicolini.
9. *Carteggio*, CXLII, p. 240.
10. Roland H. Bainton, *Bernardino Ochino* (Florence, 1940), p. 33.
11. *Carteggio*, CLXIX and CLXX, pp. 205 and 302. Jedin sees here the influence of Pole. I would say rather that of Ochino.
    Hubert Jedin, "Kardinal Pole und Vittoria Colonna," *Kirche des Glaubens, Kirche der Geschichte* I (Herder, 1966), p. 189.
12. *Carteggio*, CLXX, pp. 300-301.
13. *Rime*, II, CLXII, p. 317.
14. *Carteggio*, LXXI, 111 f.
15. *Rime*, II, CVI, p. 266.
16. *Ibid.*, II, XXXIV, p. 194.
17. *Ibid.*, II, CXLV, p. 305, Cf. II, XXI, p. 191 *solo per fede* and CLVIII, p. 318; CXCI, p. 351.
18. *Ibid.*, II, XCVII, p. 257.
19. *Ibid.*, II, CIV, p. 264.
20. *Ibid.*, II, CIX, p. 269.
21. *Ibid.*, II, LXV, p. 225.
22. Italian text in William Wells Newhall, *Sonnets & Madrigals of Michelangelo Buonarroti* (London, 1900), No. XXIV, p. 54. Opening line: *Mestier non era all'alma tuo beltate*.

23. English translation in Holyrod, p. 319. See note 1 above.
24. Johann J. Wyss, *Vittoria Colonna* (Frauenfeld, 1916), p. 87.
25. See the discussion in Alexander Perrig, *"Michelangelo Buonarrotis."* Letze Pietà-Idee, : *Basler Studien zur Kunstgeschichte* N. F., Bd. I, pp. 21-35. On the state of the drawing consult Rollin N. Hadley, *Drawings. The Isabella Stuart Gardner Museum* (Boston, 1968). This drawing has manifestly been clipped because the last word of the inscription on the cross has been removed. The full inscription is from Dante's *Paradiso* XIX, line 91 *No vi si pensa quanto sangue costa.* The full form of the original can be seen only in the engraving made from it in 1546.
26. See the discussion in Charles de Tolnay, *Werk und Weltbild des Michelangelo* (Zürich, 1949), p. 70. The following work deals mainly with the influence of this crucifixion of Michelangelo on subsequent portrayals: Guido Cimino, *Il Crucifisso di Michelangelo per Vittoria Colonna* (Rome, 1967).
27. See the illustrations.
28. *Carteggio*, CXXIV, p. 209. Cf. CXXIII, p. 208.
29. *Ibid.*, CXLIX, p. 257.
30. W. Shenck, *Reginald Pole* (London, 1950).
31. *Carnesecchi*, p. 499.
32. Ludwig Pastor, *History of the Popes*, XIV, pp. 308-11.
33. *Carteggio*, p. 342.
34. *Ibid.*
35. *Luthers Werke, Weimarer Ausgabe* 40, II, 472-610.
36. Italian text in William Wells Newall. See above note 22. No. LXI, p. 150. The first line reads: *Se'l mio rozzo martello i' duri sassi.*

13.

Isabella Bresegna
(1510-1567)

In 1557, when Isabella Bresegna was a fugitive from the Inquisition in northern Italy living in Grisons, the Italian-speaking portion of Switzerland, she received letters from her husband, brother, and sons imploring her to return to *la patria*. Then two of the sons, with authorization from the father, visited her repeatedly in the hope that continued importunity would break down her resolve. She replied that gladly would she follow her husband and family to any spot where liberty of conscience was assured. But nowhere in Italy was that any longer the case. She was adamant.[1] One son joined her in exile.

She was another of the Neapolitans, reared at any rate in Naples, though born in Spain in 1510. She loved gaiety and the chase, but was far from frivolous and, in the light of the sequel, one may regard as more than flattery the description of her in her youthful days as "beautiful, gracious, unassuming, devout, upright, and unflinching." [2] At the age of 16 or 17 she was married to Garcia Manriquez, a Spanish captain. From her father she received a considerable fortune, far exceeded by that of her husband, so that she was able to live in high state. No doubt she was lavish in maintaining her station, but her taste ran more to administration than to display, and she started several industries near Naples. When her husband was made the governor of Piacenza in 1547, she was unable to accompany him immediately because her financial obligations in the Neapolitan area had to be regulated.

While still in Naples she could not well have been untouched by the religious ferment which led shopkeepers, artisans, and loafers to discuss theology. During Lent in 1536 she sat under the divine eloquence of Ochino. In 1539 she was involved with Juan Valdés in matters financial and, no doubt, spiritual. Her intimacy with Giulia Gonzaga is witnessed by a letter which Giulia sent to her agent when Isabella finally departed to join her husband on July 10, 1548. "I am sending two horses," she wrote, "for so-and-so on the boat which takes Signóra Donna Isabella Manriquez to Piacenza. . . . You know that she is the dearest friend I have. Please give her every possible service and wait upon her as if she were myself." [3]

Once in Piacenza she became again so involved in administration that she was addressed as the *governatrice di Piacenza*. Her husband, frequently absent because of his military career, was entirely willing to turn over to her such cares. We have a number of her letters on such subjects to Ferrante Gonzaga (a relative of Giulia's), the governor of Milan to which Piacenza was subject.

During these years she was successful in establishing her children. Georgio went into a military career. Pietro became a civil servant. Two daughters were married, one to a gentleman in the service of the Emperor Maximillian II at Vienna. Yet in 1555 we find Isabella in Milan and in 1557 in Germany. The first move to Milan may well have been for political reasons, because Piacenza passed from the Spanish to the French domination when Ottaviano Farnese, the nephew of the pope, took over the city.[4] But the flight to Germany was for religion.

What had happened? One factor was certainly the intensified activity of the Inquisition. Her husband, the governor, wrote to Ferrante Gonzaga at Milan, saying, "My wife has made me aware of the impertinence of the officials of the Inquisition who are proceeding against many citizens and throwing their minds into confusion and disorder. This innovation appears to me highly inexpedient at this time [the status of Piacenza was precarious because of the rivalry of the French and the Spanish interests]. I leave the remedy to your prudence." Gonzaga replied, "This behavior of the Inquisition is indeed impertinent and altogether intolerable and must be curbed for the entire welfare of this city. It is decidedly inexpedient to bring charges of heresy against any one without the participation of the *podestá,* for this is an encroachment on the temporal power and the service of the emperor." [5]

Whether or not Manriquez knew the degree to which his wife might herself be subject to the inquisitorial procedures is not certain. We do know that she harbored at her court persons of liberal and even heretical opinions. Villafranca died in her home,[6] Tizzano was in her employ for two years,[7] and Girolamo Busale was her secretary for less than a year.[8] Tizzano said that he had conversed with her and others at Naples "as with those who were of his religion and persuasion." [9] Two of these men, Tizzano and Giovanni Laureto, eventually gave themselves to the Inquisition and made long depositions with many details about their confederates. A brief review of their testimonies is in order.

Tizzano said that he had been a friar of the order of Monte Oliveto at Naples. He had been permitted to leave the monastery and to function as a secular priest. For nine years he had been a chaplain to a noble lady. While in Naples he heard of the fame of Juan Valdés, who was highly commended by many, including the Lady Giulia. He conversed with Valdés and read his books, supplied to him together with some of Luther's by another Spaniard, Villafranca. Through these works he became convinced of the deception practiced by the Roman Church. He had discussed Lutheran and Anabaptist ideas with a number of the noble women including Giulia Gonzaga and "Isabella Manriquez, wife of the governor of Piacenza."

His own heresies were of three kinds, embraced consecutively at intervals of about two years. The first was Lutheran, the second Anabaptist, and the third diabolical. The name of Villafranca, the seducer, appears in all three connections.

The Lutheran tenets included justification by faith; denial of the power of the pope; denial of purgatory; denial of the invo-

cation of the saints or the Virgin; dismissal of dietary rules; and
a belief that confession was necessary only to God.

In 1550 Tizzano went to study medicine at Padua and there
remained for five or six years. Here he came into contact with
Girolamo Busale, a Calabrian abbot and his brother Matteo
who was even more radical. From them he imbibed the Anabaptist and diabolical doctrines. Curiously in the case of the
Anabaptists he made no mention of the repetition of baptism
and the rejection of the sword of the magistrate. The heretical
views included denial of the Virgin birth and of the real presence of the body of Christ on the altar. The Mass was declared
to be idolatry (this was equally Lutheran). The diabolical tenets
were that the true Messiah is yet to come and was not Christ.
He was the greatest of the prophets, but not God. The soul dies
with the body to be brought to life again at the time of the
general resurrection. After some wanderings Tizzano gave himself up to the Inquisition at Padua requesting that he might
be given a secret absolution and allowed to live, without damage
to his reputation in Venice. He went to Padua in 1553 expecting
to be free but was again imprisoned and made there the full
deposition which has just been reviewed. What became of him
thereafter we do not know.

Giovanni Laureto, who also gave himself up at Venice in 1553,
tells us that he had been a chaplain in Naples to the Sisters of
St. Francis (with whom Giulia Gonzaga resided). From Valdés
he learned the doctrines of justification by faith and the denial
of purgatory. To be more fully informed on such points he set
out for Germany. Being unable to complete the journey, he
stopped at the court of Isabella Bresegna at Piacenza and spent
two years in her employ. Here he lived as a Lutheran. This
would mean that he would read furtively the Brucioli translation of the Bible, disregard fast laws, and attend Mass, hiding
behind a pillar so as not actually to see the idolatry. While he
was thus employed, the Calabrian abbot Girolamo Busale, who
doubted the divinity of Christ and said that the Scriptures are
contradictory, arrived in Piacenza. Busale was employed by
Isabella as a secretary. The pair took leave, following the execution of a wandering preacher, and went to Padua. Here he

encountered ideas which he described as Anabaptist, that the
Bible is to be interpreted according to the Spirit and that Christ
was not the true Messiah. One of the circle of friends said that
God would be a tyrant if he required the death of Christ in order
to forgive sins. Laureto was rebaptized. Because of repression of
heresy at Padua, Busale and Laureto fled to Naples. Busale became deranged and we lose track of him. Laureto entered the
service of Giulia Gonzaga, but again frightened, he fled to a col-
ony of Anabaptists in Salonika by whom he was excommunicated
because he would not confine his reading to the Bible alone.

His devotion to the study of Hebrew led him to seek instruction from the rabbis and then to embrace Judaism. He was cir-
cumcised. Further biblical study convinced him that the rabbis
were wrong. To get away from them he went under the guise
of a Jew to Constantinople where he succeeded in finding passage on a boat sailing to Italy. He landed at Venice and gave himself up to the Inquisition.

From all of these associations we can make no precise inferences
as to the views of Isabella herself, but certainly, like Giulia
Gonzaga, she harbored and respected those who were radically
critical of the church and her doctrines. Isabella obviously did
not feel herself bound by papal authority and was emphatically
opposed to the methods of the Inquisition. Like the other Val-
desians she assuredly accepted the doctrine of justification, which
would make her a heretic after the pronouncement by the Council of Trent. These considerations taken together suffice to ex-
plain why she felt constrained to leave Italy.

She may also have been influenced by the flight of another
member of the Neapolitan circle whom she was later to meet in
exile. Galeazzo Caracciolo, the Marquis of Vico,[10] was a nobleman in the employ of the Emperor Charles and in his suite traveled to the north. Already detached from rigid orthodoxy by the
discussions in the Valdesian milieu and shaken by the defections
of Vermigli and Ochino, his convictions were further matured
by northern travels. In 1551 he slipped away from the imperial
train at Augsburg and went to Geneva. A cousin was sent by his
father to induce him to return lest the family be deprived of all
his properties by confiscation. He was unshaken. He desired that

his wife and family join him but he must have realized that they could scarcely have been practising Catholics in Geneva, and in any case his wife, a niece of that implacable Caraffa who became Pope Paul IV, was not willing to live with a heretic.

Under safe conduct Galeazzo had meetings in northern Italy with his father and his sons. The father persuaded the pope to concede to Galeazzo the privilege of residing in Venetian territory with his family and with freedom of religion. Galeazzo pointed out that the church keeps no faith with him who has no faith. And this very pope had said that if his own father were a heretic, he would not hesitate to bring the faggots for his pyre.[11] Since the wife had not attended any of the rendezvous, Galeazzo resolved without a safe conduct to risk the stake by returning to his estate at Vico. He was met with caresses. The wife embraced, the father exulted, the children rejoiced. But when they were made to know that he had not come to stay, but only to induce them to join him in exile the father ranted, the wife wept, and a 12-year-old daughter tightened her arms about his legs. He returned to the ship and to Geneva.

With such an example before her, Isabella decided to take a similar course. But she did not go to Geneva, the Grisons, the Italian portion of Switzerland in the Valteline, nor to Zürich or Basel, but rather to the German lands. We do not know whether she went first to Vienna or Tübingen, but probably to Vienna because, as we noted, her daughter was married there to a gentleman in the court of the Emperor Maximillian II, who was willing to allow her to stay and would accord liberty of religion, for he tolerated the Augsburg Confession in restricted areas.[12] She did not stay, presumably because her daughter and husband were still Catholic.

She went to Tübingen in 1557, the guest of Piero Paolo Vergerio, a very remarkable figure. He had been the bishop of Capo d'Istria and on several occasions had served as a papal nuncio. In this capacity he had visited Martin Luther in Wittenberg, and at the court of France had been impressed by the beauty and carriage of Marguerite of Navarre. He was a strong believer in conciliarism and pushed strenuously for a council to compose the religious dissensions. But the first session of the Council of

Trent disillusioned him utterly. He came to be suspect of disseminating Lutheran views and was deposed from his bishopric. Rather than expose himself to worse, he went to Switzerland and was there led to make a decisive break by witnessing the death struggles of Francesco Spiera. Spiera saved his body by abjuring the Protestant faith, but then became convinced of his damnation and in agonized desperation took his life.[13]

Vergerio became the ecclesiastical adviser of Duke Christoph of Württemberg. Their correspondence constitutes a large volume in print. Isabella was now his guest. A modern writer has assumed that Vergerio proposed to marry her. But his letter says that he wished her to stand *in loco matris* at his marriage to some one else. The wedding never came off. And Isabella did not remain. A messenger came from Zürich to "seduce" her away from this Lutheran stronghold, "as if," said Vergerio, "one could be saved only at Zürich." [14]

In the year 1558 she lived in the house of Frau von Schön on the Kirchgasse with a cook, four maids and her son Piero, who had joined her in exile. He was lodged with another Italian refugee.[15] The expenses were presumably met by the stipend sent by Giulia Gonzaga. Evidently Isabella was not in dire poverty, though she must have felt her estate to be vastly reduced in comparison with her former opulence.

She had the comfort of high esteem from her fellow exiles and coreligionists. Celio Secondo Curione, a professor at Basel, dedicated his edition of the works of Olympia to her in 1558. Curione relates how she had been illumined by the light from above while at Naples. As the wife of the governor of Piacenza, she had been distinguished for temperance, virtue, modesty, charity, and patience so that all mourned her departure. But she realized that she could not serve two masters, and after a stay in Milan scaled the Alps. Her husband, her brother, and her sons again and again sought to break down her resolve. She assured them that she desired nothing more in this life than to rejoin them, if only she could be guaranteed liberty of conscience. "What an amazing example not only to women but also to men!" [16]

But before long Isabella became subject to the fate which dogged the Italians in exile. They did not fit. They were un-

OLYMPIAE FVLVIAE MORATAE MVLIERIS OM-

NIVM ERVDITISSIMAE LATINA ET

Græca, quæ haberi potuerunt, monumenta,

eaq́; planè diuina, cum eruditorum

de ipsa iudicijs & laudibus.

Hippolytæ Taurellæ elegia elegantissima.

AD ILL. ISABELLAM BRESEGNAM.

BASILEÆ.

APVD PETRVM PERNAM.

M. D. L. VIII.

The title page of Curione's publication of
the works of Olympia

COELIVS SECVNDVS CVRIO

ISABELLÆ MANRICHÆ BRESEGNÆ

ILLVSTRI, AC RELIGIOSAE, FOEMI-
NAE PER CHRISTVM IESVM.

S. P. D.

VOD Socrates dixit, fœmi
nas si diligenter instituantur,
non minus aptas ac dociles
ad literas & artes liberales
omnemque virtutem , atque
adeo ad fortitudinem, quæ vi
rorum propria esse putatur,
quàm mares; id verū esse non ita paucæ, tum pa-
trum tum nostra memoria, non obscurè declára-
runt. Possem ex omni ætatum memoria exempla
proferre, nisi de claris mulieribus integra volu-
mina extarent , & omnium iam manibus versa-
rentur. verùm in eis quàm paucas legimus cum
eruditione morum castimoniam, pauciores ve-
ram religionis cognitionem , & sacrarum amo-
rem literarum coniunxisse: atque in eisdem, vix
vllam, quæ græcæ simul & latinæ linguæ faculta
te polleret . Nostra verò ætas multis rebus felix
hac etiam felicior alijs, aliquot protulit, atque in
ter eas vnam in quam Deus omnes ingenij Do-
tes contulisse videtur. Hæc OLYMPIA FVL-
VIA MORATA, appellata est, FVLVII
Mantuani viri doctissimi filia, cuius hîc vitam de-
scriberem , nisi ex sequentibus epistolis, facile

a 2

Page 1 of the first edition of Curione's
publication of the works of Olympia

acquainted with, and uninterested in, the incrustation of Protestantism beyond the Alps. What to them were the differences
between the Lutherans, Zwinglians, and the Calvinists? Their
main concern was to resist the tyranny of the Antichrist at Rome.
Some of the Italians did identify themselves with the theological
stance of the localities in which they happened to be stationed.
In that case they were divided from Italians in divergent localities. Some, disquieted by the squabbles, went in the direction of
Anabaptism and Antitrinitarianism.

At Zürich sociological considerations made the life of the exiles
highly uncomfortable. The refugees there came largely from the
town of Locarno in Italian Switzerland. This village had gone
over to the Protestant reform after the Peace of Kappel, which
in 1531 forbade Protestant minorities in the Catholic cantons.
The entire Swiss diet was now called upon to enforce the terms
and penalize the converts. Zürich absolutely refused. The other
evangelical cantons were willing to concur in banishment, lest
the Catholics inflict the death penalty. Zürich was adamant. The
outcome was banishment, and the emigrés then presented themselves at the gates of the city which had so stoutly championed
their right to espouse the true faith. Zürich took them in. She was
well aware of the risk, but manned her walls and at the same
time trod softly to avoid needless provocation. She was soon to
discover that to save a lamb from the lion may be easier than to
live with him afterwards. The Italians were too prolific and too
enterprising. They bought grain on the Zürich market, disposed
of it at a profit in Italy, used the proceeds to purchase trinkets
in Italy, and then sold them at a price undercutting the rate in
Zürich. Local merchants were irate. The town council, therefore, parceled the Italians out among the guilds and conceded
to them a church with services in their own tongue only until
such time as they could learn the Zürich dialect.[17]

Now the pastor of this Italian church was Bernardino Ochino,
lately come as a refugee from England after the accession of
"Bloody Mary." He thought to do the Zürichers a service by
defending their view of the Lord's Supper against a rabid Lutheran, who held that the body of Christ in the elements is eaten
with the teeth even by unbelievers. Ochino not only refuted this

view, but in so doing pointed out that Luther advanced in many respects from one position to another and very probably would have arrived at Zwingli's view of the Lord's Supper if Zwingli had not done so first. This thrust so angered Duke Christoph of Württemburg that he cancelled his contribution to the support of Ochino's congregation.

Colleagues were of the opinion that Bernardino had not treated the subject with proper dignity. He tried again, and this time to relieve Zürich of any responsibility, published his book at Basel. He dealt once more with the sacramentarian controversy, and this time relegated the whole dispute to the area of the non-essentials, because "the penitent thief was saved without having taken Communion, without having thought about the Lord's Supper, without ever having considered whether the body of Christ was or was not in the bread and the blood in the wine. The one thing needful is to believe with a warm faith, and in spirit to taste and feel that Jesus is Christ, the Son of God, who out of the highest love died for us. God is everywhere but his presence is of no avail if we are not enamored of him. And what good is the presence of the body of Christ unless we feel it in faith which is not attached to places?" [18]

This tract was dedicated to Isabella Bresegna. "Those in Italy," he wrote, "long have known the lustre of your eminent virtue. A spirit so exalted and a mind so clear as yours could not remain buried beneath the papist stupidity and when Christ had opened your eyes you perceived the abominable superstitions, idolatry and anti-Christian blasphemies of Rome. You decided to forsake all to embrace Christ. You elected to live amid these mountains, preferring the poverty of Christ to the riches of Egypt. All who have conversed with you recognize your patience, constancy, perseverance, and mortification and have been edified by your divine words. I have chosen to dedicate to you this tract of the Supper of the Lord which the elect are called upon to solemnize with rejoicing. May you then take fresh occasion to bless and thank God to whom be praise, honor and glory through Jesus Christ our Lord." [19]

Such a glowing commendation from an inconvenient pastor of an unwanted Italian congregation would not at this juncture have endeared Isabella to her hosts. In June of 1559 we find her at Chiavenna in Italian Switzerland. A visit by Galeazzo Caracciolo [20] before her departure must have been comforting and would not be compromising because he was held in high esteem at Geneva.

The case was different in 1561 when in the Grisons she received visits from Vergerio. He was in bad odor in that region for several reasons. One was that he sought to introduce Lutheran teaching into a region devoted to Zwinglianism. Another was that he could never forget that he had been a bishop and wanted to acquire an episcopal authority over the churches of the Valteline. He was on one occasion hailed as "a visitor extraordinary." He stoutly opposed an effort of the churches to set up a synodical organization. His motive was not merely the lust of power, but rather the desire to use the area as a port of entry for the smuggling of Protestant propaganda into Italy. But by 1560 the Counter-Reformation had won, and the hope of protestantizing Italy had become an anachronism. To further his plan he employed political means and entered the service of France in order to keep Spanish influence out of the area. The French were to guarantee religious liberty. The Grisons did not relish his machinations.[21]

To a degree Isabella suffered from his friendship. Fabricius, a minister at Chur in the Grisons, wrote to Bullinger the successor of Zwingli at Zürich saying, "The trouble with Vergerio is that he wants to run everything. He is all mixed up on the sacrament." And again "Vergerio is a perfect nuisance. He is distributing tracts in German in which he is teaching that in the Sacrament there is a crass carnal eating of the body of Christ." Then Isabella enters. Fabricius adds, "I think you know how the Lady Isabella is getting on."

Bullinger replies, "I hope Vergerio will come to a better mind. No, I don't know how Isabella is getting on. Tell me." Fabricius answers, "As for Isabella, that's a long story." And then three dots in a modern printing of the letter, followed by, "It is not an edifying tale." The three dots stood for the words, "I will write presently." Either he did not or the letter had been lost.[22]

This "unedifying tale" may have been connected with Ver-

Disputa di M.

BERNARDINO OCHINO DA SIENA INTORNO
alla presenza del corpo di Giesu
Christo nel Sacramento
della Cena.

Non mai per l'adietro stampata.

IN BASI

M. D. L

BERNARDINO OCHI
NO ALLA ILLVSTRISS. SI
gnora Donna ISABELLA MANRI
CHE Bresegna, desidera gratia & pa
ce da Dio Padre nostro, & da
Giesu Christo Signor
nostro.

AVENDO gia a dare
in luce molti Sermoni,
non gli dedicai ad alcu
no particolare: impero
che l'intēto mio era che
fusseno letti da tutti, & specialmen
te da quelli, i quali erano per cauar
ne maggior frutto, sicome sono gli
eletti di Dio: ma hora perche voglio
dedicarui questi Sermoni della Ce
na del Signore, è debito mio il mo
strare, perche. Nessuno potrà giusta
mente dire che io sia mendace, o a
dulatore, se desalcādo molto di quel
lo che io sento di vostra signoria par
camente, & con sobrietà, lauderò nō
voi, ma i doni & le gratie, le quali in
uerità vi ha concesse Dio, per pura

gerio, but again possibly with the Anabaptists of whom Fabricius goes on to speak. They were making great inroads in the Grisons under the leadership of Camillo Renato. Whether Isabella had any connection with him we do not know, but it is highly likely in view of the way in which she harbored such radicals at Piacenza. If she went to such length one can understand why Curione, when he reissued the works of Olympia Morata, omitted the dedication to Isabella and substituted one to Queen Elizabeth.

We are sure only that Isabella died on February 8, 1567.[23] She would have agreed with Ochino that exile is far from resolving the problem of religious liberty because "the wings of Babylon are everywhere." [24]

BIBLIOGRAPHY

Biographies of Isabella Bresegna

Alfredo Casadei

"Donne della Riforma Italiana: Isabella Bresegna," *Religio* XIII (1937), 6-63. This is the fullest treatment. There is one error on p. 38. Vergerio did not propose to marry Isabella.

Benedetto Nicolini

"Una Calvinista Napoletana Isabella Bresegna," *Studi Cinquecenteschi*, I. *Ideali e Passioni nell'Italia Religiosa*, pp. 1-33. On page 17, line 7 change Ginevra to Gênes.

Aldo Stella

Dall'Anabattismo al Socinianesimo nel Cinquecento Veneto (Padua, 1967). Many passing references and details on the circles in which she moved.

Documents

Deposition of Laureto with an admirable introduction:

M. E. Pommier

"L'Itineraire religieux d'un moine vagabond italien au XVIe Siècle," *Mèlanges d'Archéologie et d'Histoire* (1954), 293-322.

Deposition of Tizzano with an excellent introduction:

Domenico Berti

"Di Giovanni Valdes e di taluni suoi Discepoli secondo Nuovi documenti tolti dall'Archivio Veneto," *Atti della R. Accademia dei Lincei* III, 2 (1878), 61-81.

NOTES

1. For Curione's preface to the works of Olympia Morata see note 16, for Ochino's, note 19. Vergerio's account is in his letter to Duke Christoph in *Briefwechsel zwischen Christoph Herzog von Württemberg und Petrus Paulus Vergerius,* ed. E. von Kausler und Theod. Schott (Tübingen, 1875), p. 159.

2. Nicolini, *op. cit.,* p. 25, and Benedetto Croce, "Il Marchese di Vico Galeazzo Caracciolo, Vite d'Avventure di Fede e di Passione," *Scritti di Storia Letterarua e Politica,* XXX (Bari, 1936), 179-281. This reference p. 200, note 3.

3. For details in this paragraph Nicolini, pp. 8-12, and Casadei, p. 11.

4. Casadei, pp. 13-23, and Nicolini, p. 9.

5. Federico Chabod, *Per la Storia Religiosa dello Stato di Milano durante il Dominio di Carlo V* (Bologna, 1938), p. 144 and documents 59 and 61, pp. 228-30.

6. Stella, p. 34, note 91.

7. Laureto deposition, ed. Pommier, p. 318.

8. *Ibid.,* p. 302.

9. Deposition Tizzano, ed. Berti, doc. III, p. 73.

10. Croce, see note 2.

11. *Ibid.,* p. 223.

12. Erich Hassinger, *Das Werden des neuzeitlichen Europa 1300-1600* (Braunschweig, 1959), p. 369.
    Maximillian's letter to Vergerio in *Briefwechsel* (see note 1), No. 56a, p. 155.

13. There is much on Vergerio in Frederick C. Church, *The Italian Reformers 1534-64* (New York, 1962) and an excellent brief sketch by Benrath in the *Realencyclopdie für Protestantische Theologie,* 3rd ed.

14. *Briefwechsel* (see note 1), Nos. 51, 52, 55, 56a, 57, pp. 145-57.

15. Ferdinand Meyer, *Die evangelische Gemeinde zu Locarno* (Zürich, 1836), II, 152.

16. Curione, *Olympiae Fvlviae Moratae Mvlieris Omnivm Ervditissimae Latina et Graeca . . . Monumenta . . .* (Basel, 1558). Copy at the Newberry library in Chicago.

17. Fully covered in the work of Meyer, above note 15.

18. Roland H. Bainton, *Bernardino Ochino,* Biblioteca Storica Sansoni N.S. IV (Florence, 1940), and more briefly in English in my *Travail of Religious Liberty* (Philadelphia, 1951), from which a few paragraphs have been taken over.

19. *Disputa di M. Bernardino Ochino da Siena intorno alla presenza del corpo di Giesu Christo nel Sacramento della Cena* (Basel, 1561) with dedication *alla Illvstriss. Signora Donna Isabella Manriche Bresegna.*

20. On Caracciolo's visit Croce, *op. cit.,* p. 232.

21. Details in Church, *op. cit.* in note 13.

22. "Bullingers Korrespondenz mit den Graubündern," ed. Traugott Schiess, Vol. II, *Quellen zur Schweizer Geschichte* XXIV (Basel, 1905-06). No. 184, p. 148; No. 207, p. 164; No. 211, p. 167; No. 395, p. 347; No. 396, p. 348; No. 399, p. 352; No. 401, p. 355.

23. *Ibid.,* Vol. III, No. 10, p. 8.

24. Bainton, *Ochino* (see note 18 above), p. 117.

Renée of Ferrara

14.

Renée of Ferrara
(1510 - 1575)

"Had I had a beard I would have been the king of France. I have been defrauded by that confounded Salic law" (which forbad the succession of women to the throne). These were the words of Renée, daughter of King Louis XII of France and sister-in-law to King Francis I, who was married to her sister Claudia.

Renée was married to the Duke Ercole of Ferrara. The marriage was, of course, political—designed to link another north Italian city to France. Renée never forgot her mission and brought with her Madame Soubise, her childhood governess who spoke no Italian at all, besides an enclave of servants, gentlemen, and ladies in waiting. The Duke of Ferrara was not too happy about all of this. He did not want conflict with France and certainly did not desire to lose his wife's dowry, which consisted of parcels of French territory. Neither did he wish an exclusive attachment to France which would involve a break with the emperor or the pope, who, though they quarreled with each other, were often allied against France. Ercole tried to reduce Renée's household and succeeded in the end in having Madame Soubise shipped home.

The matter became more thorny when heresy came to be involved. Renée received religious refugees from France. She may have done so simply because they were French, but it is difficult to believe that she was unaware of the reason for their flight and

Les Petites Prières de Renée de France

Les Petites Prières de Renée de France

devoid of sympathy for their opinions. The year 1534 precipitated an exodus from France of those with Protestant leanings.
Up to this year, Francis I had pursued an ambiguous policy, on
the one hand courting Melanchthon and the German Protestants
and on the other suppressing Lutherans in Normandy. On the
whole he was moderate toward the innovators in France until
October, 1554, when on the 18th of the month, between two
and three in the morning, placards were affixed at street corners
and even on the king's chamber door, describing the Mass as
"execrable blasphemy, pretending to be a sacrifice to God,
whereas the only sacrifice was made once and for all by Christ.
The Mass is idolatry because it claims that Christ is bodily present in the bread and wine, whereas after the resurrection the
body was in heaven at the right hand of God [a Calvinist rather
than a Lutheran position]. The appalling polysyllabic word
transubstantiation is not in the New Testament, which speaks
simply of bread and wine. The Mass is as remote from the Lord's
Supper as Christ from Belial." [1]

The affront was followed by arrests. One the 21st of January,
1535, a great procession marched through the streets of Paris with
fife and drum, carrying lighted candles. The king in velvet with
bare head carried a taper. The Queen rode side saddle on a pal-
frey covered with cloth of gold. The royal princes and princesses,
cardinals, 20 archbishops, bishops, the members of parliament,
the university, the clergy, all marched carrying the sacred relics,
the crown of thorns, the holy lance, the crown of St. Louis, the
stone tables of Moses, the blood of Christ, and the milk of the
Virgin. Then, after a good dinner, they watched the burning of
six heretics. Those who escaped were proscribed. The seventh on
the list was Clement Marot. The 43rd was Leon Janet. These two
turned up at the court of Renée.[2]

We know that Marot went first to Navarre, the kingdom of
the king's sister, Marguerite. Her religious opinions were dis-
tinctly liberal. She perceived that the baying of hounds was coming too close and advised Marot to leave. One may assume that
it was she who commended him to her friend and relative, Renée
of Ferrara. What were the opinions of these two men? We know
very little about Janet, but he is alleged to have engaged in

Protestant proselytizing while at the court of Renée. We know more about Marot because he was a poet of distinction who translated the Psalms into verse for the Huguenot Psalter. He may not have been a heretic in the doctrinal sense, but he was certainly scathing in his denunciation of the venality and superstition of the church. Here is an example in one of his poems:

> Masses no end and anniversaries,
> Chants, bells, and candles dripping grease:
> It's all for a financial squeeze.
> If you've nothing left but a chemise
> There'll be no bell nor aught of these.[3]

On what basis did Renée receive these men? One author, greatly concerned to defend her Catholic orthodoxy, contends that she took them in because they were French, not because they were heretics. Strictly speaking they may not have been heretics, but they were proscribed, and she can scarcely have been ignorant of that fact. We simply do not know what her religious opinions were at this time.

The next year, that is in 1536, another Frenchman arrived. He was 26 years old. A fugitive also from France, he had published a book called *The Institutes of the Christian Religion*. His stay in Ferrara can scarcely have exceeded a month or so, yet it was sufficient to initiate a lifelong correspondence. His name was John Calvin.[4]

When rumor reached Ercole that his wife's court was contaminated by heresy, he was naturally disturbed and began to apply some pressures to his wife. Calvin was informed of this by Madame de Pons, the daughter of Madame Soubise who had been shipped back to France. Before long Madame de Pons received the same treatment. She must have had Reformed leanings to take it upon herself to inform Calvin. His letter to Renée reads: "I have heard that your domestics have been scandalized by the word of a certain preacher who says that one may go both to Mass and to the Lord's Supper. I don't want to be a detractor, but I cannot suffer a wolf in sheep's clothing. I esteem the word of this preacher no more than the song of a jackdaw. The Mass is an execrable sacrilege and an intolerable blasphemy of the death of Jesus Christ, who has made for us the one and only

sacrifice. It is an accursed and execrable idolatry. Therefore
Madame, to whom God has given in his infinite majesty the
knowledge of his name, you are to fulfill your vocation. If you
think to avoid giving offense to any, you will have to banish
Jesus Christ." [5]

If Ercole tried to interfere with the French suspects in the
entourage of his wife, she reported the matter to France and
the king of France insisted that they belonged to his jurisdiction. Ercole did get rid of Janet and Marot by letting them
escape. The case was changed when Italians also came to be
involved. We have not a little information about many of them,
and it is quite detailed with respect to Fanino Fanini of Faenza.
His trial took place in 1547, something over a decade after the
above-mentioned incidents. The trial resulted because of a re-
lapse from an earlier recantation made in response to the pleas
of his wife, sister, and two sons. Having been released, he was
seized by intense melancholy, until he reaffirmed his faith and
began to travel about the villages of Romagna converting people
to this faith. In consequence he was again arrested.

Then ensued a quarrel over jurisdiction, not with France this
time, but with the pope who wanted to have the heretic tried
on the estates of the church. Ercole insisted on Ferrara. As a
result Fanini was kept in prison for 18 months. During that time
he deeply affected his fellow prisoners. Renée besought her husband to grant "the poor Fanini" release. Two other women,
Olympia Morata and her friend Lavinia della Rovere, tried to
help him. Apparently Lavinia was the one who enlisted the
intercession of her father-in-law Orsini, a military man without
theological education, who twice addressed letters to the duke
pleading for clemency.

Then Pope Paul III was succeeded by Julius III, who demanded greater stringency. Ercole felt no longer capable of
withstanding papal encroachment and permitted the sentence
of execution to take its course. Once again Fanini's family
pleaded with him to yield, but this time he stood firm and even
rejoiced. A fellow prisoner asked, "How about your children?"
He answered, "They have the best of guardians." "And who
may he be?" "Our Lord Jesus Christ." Having been handed a

crucifix, he said, "Do I need this bit of wood to remind me of my Savior, reigning and engraved on my heart?" He was strangled and burned.[6]

Renée herself could not escape suspicion because of her efforts on behalf of not only Fanini but of many more, including Ochino.[7] She was no ultra-Protestant and would listen equally to a friar or a preacher, but her behavior was justifiably suspect. The local inquisitor began to intimidate her. "You would be astounded," wrote Renée to the queen of Navarre, "if you knew how rudely he defamed me and my house." [8] Despite her possible divergence from Roman doctrine, she had no scruple in appealing to Paul III to set her case under the jurisdiction of the Roman rather than the local inquisition. This he did in a brief dated in 1543.[9] Ercole did not mind rebuffing the local inquisitor, but hesitated to defy Rome when the Holy See became more intolerant. Yet he knew that if his wife, the daughter of the King of France, were treated as a common heretic, the king of France, now Henry II, would intervene on her behalf. Ercole made a clever move in asking the king himself to send someone to persuade her to return to the faith. His letter details all of her derelictions and his vain attempts to recall her from her errors.

"To his most sacred Christian Majesty, Sire: My wife came to me from France 25 years ago and she lived in a Christian manner becoming to one of royal blood. But lately, seduced by some Lutheran rascals, she has refused to go to confession and Mass, and when one of her servants was dying, she refused him extreme unction. She said he stood well with God and did not need any other confession. Seeing her obstinacy against the honor of God and the infamy she was bringing upon my house, I besought her a thousand times to give up her heretical fancies and follow the religion of her blessed father and mother, and her sister, your mother. I tried to cover up her delinquency for the honor of France and of my house. Not even at Christmas did she go to Mass, and she educated our two daughters, one 18 and one 16, in the false religion. I was afraid this would make difficulty in marrying them to Christian princes, because the rumor of their mother's heresy was spreading all over Italy. She told me the

Mass is idolatry and used other words which I am ashamed to quote. Against her hot arrogance I had to exercise the patience of Job. I sent my chaplain to say Mass for the daughters but she would not allow it. I beg you, Sire, to have pity on my plight and to send a good Catholic theologian who will bring the Duchess back from her enormous heresy." (March, 1554.) [10]

The king complied, and the man whom he sent was Matthew Ory, one of the most indefatigable and implacable inquisitors in France. He had ferreted out Michael Servetus less than a year before and would have had him burned at Vienne in France had he not escaped to be burned at Geneva. Another theologian ready to essay the task was the Jesuit Father Jay, for Ercole had been very helpful in establishing this new order in Ferrara. Associated with these two was the local inquisitor Papino. There was one other from France, sent by that most Catholic house, the family of Guise. The person commissioned was Leon Janet, who, as we noted, had fled from France after the affair of the placards, had served in the household of Renée, and had left under suspicion of heresy. Presumably he had made some accommodation to Catholic practice, seeing that he was able to survive in France, and may have been commissioned on the assumption that he would be a suitable person to persuade Renée to do the same. On the other hand the Guises, for family reasons, may have wished to give Renée some support, for Anne, the Duchess of Guise, was the daughter of Renée and had herself received instruction in the Reformed faith. Significantly Janet went to Ferrara by way of Geneva and brought Renée a letter from Calvin. He expressed grave distress over her plight and resolved without delay to send a minister to stand at her side. His name was Morel.[11]

Confronted by this phalanx of formidable inquisitors, Renée held her ground.[12] She indulged in no open defiance, but met the torrential eloquence of Ory with tears and calm resistance. There is no evidence of a formal condemnation, possibly because Renée invoked the bull of Paul III, which reserved jurisdiction over her case to Rome. But the duke had made her a prisoner in her own palace. She showed signs of rejoicing and told her husband that he might compel her body, but not her spirit and

conscience. Then, on the 13th of September, she capitulated and
went to confession and Mass. Was this simply a recantation? In
view of the hot language attributed to her by the duke, one
would think so. But in view of her earlier ambiguities with respect to Catholic and Reformed preaching, she appears still to
have been the liberal Catholic of the 20s who had not kept pace
with the polarization of the 50s. With her submission the duke
became lenient and allowed her to return to her quarters. But
she refused to cohabit with him.[13]

Calvin and his friends voiced dismay over her defection. "May
God be kind to her," he wrote, "and may Christ overcome the
impious synagogue of Antichrist." [14] To her he wrote more
gently saying that he was not sure of her condition, but the
quiet on the part of those who had lately persecuted her was
ominous. Let her take fresh courage, remembering her debt to
her Redeemer.[15] Again three years later he besought her to seek
instruction daily in the school of the Savior and let her recall
the word of the Lord to Peter that he would be taken where he
would not.[16]

On the death of her husband Renée decided to return to
France. The new pope advised her not to go. So also did Calvin.
"I have not had letters from you," he wrote. "Don't feel yourself
bound by your oath of recantation. Herod ought not to have
kept his oath to deliver to Salome the head of John the Baptist.
Don't think you will gain anything by going to France. All there
is in confusion. Be not beguiled by the grandeur of the world.
I wish I could talk with you in person." [17]

Calvin was only too right that Renée was throwing herself
into a welter of confusion. In two more years the wars of religion were to break out in France. Much more than religion was
involved. The struggles were partially between the noble families and the crown, and partially among the noble families
themselves. The religious issues were distributed somewhat along
family lines. Since Renée was related to them all and kept the
lines open with them all, her inner distraction was the more
acute. It was the Duke of Guise, her son-in-law, who perpetrated
the massacre of Vassy which set off the wars of religion. The
Edict of January, 1562, had granted to the Huguenots, as the

French Calvinists were called, liberty of worship in restricted areas. The duke caught a congregation worshiping in a barn at Vassy, outside the prescribed limits, according to his claim. He mowed them down.

The family most consistently dedicated to the reform was that of Chatillon, of which the outstanding representative was the Admiral Coligny.

The ruling houses of Valois and Bourbon were less consistent because of their concern for the maintenance of the throne and the stability of the land. Francis I vacillated in his attitude to the Reform. Henry II, his son, was an implacable persecutor. So, too, was his son Francis II, but he did not live long. Then the queen mother, Catherine de Medici, came into the ascendency during the reign of her son Charles IX. She did not care whether she said her prayers in Latin or in French, and at one time would abet the Huguenots and at another instigate the massacre of St. Bartholomew. Also of the house of Valois was Marguerite, the sister of Francis I. She was a leader of the liberal, evangelical Catholic reform movement. Her daughter Jeanne d'Albret was to be the very nerve of the Huguenot resistance.

The Bourbons offer a confused pattern. Anthony of Navarre, the husband of Jeanne d'Albret, vacillated and ended a Catholic. His brother Condé was a stalwart Huguenot. Henry, the son of Anthony and Jeanne, was to become Henry IV. Having long led the Huguenots, he went at last to Mass to pacify the land and then promulgated the Edict of Nantes, which granted a limited toleration to the Huguenots.

Renée was devoted to Marguerite of Navarre, had a temporary tilt with her daughter Jeanne, had young Henry of Navarre for a time under her tutelage, and became very intimate with Coligny. She did not break with Catherine de Medici, nor with her own daughter Anne, the Duchess of Guise, nor with her daughter's husband. In France Renée returned to the Reformed faith, but continued to be the liberal of the 20s. This meant that she tried to maintain neutrality and did not give direct support to the Huguenot troops.

Her role was to care for the victims of the three wars which came between 1562 and 1572, especially the Huguenot victims.

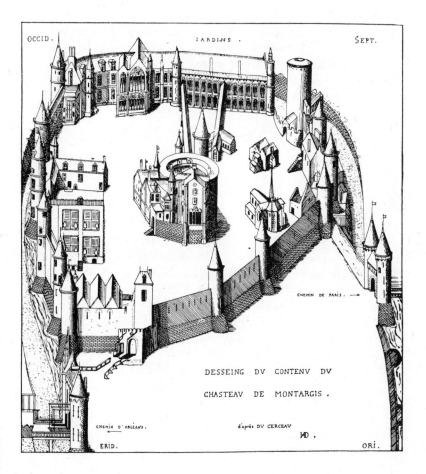

OCCID.   IARDINS.   SEPT.

CHEMIN DE PARIS .

DESSEING DV CONTENV DV

CHASTEAV DE MONTARGIS .

CHEMIN D'ORLEANS .

d'après DV CERCEAV

MERID.   ORI.

Montargis

This she was able to do in her little principality of Montargis, some 40 miles east of Orleans. It included Chartres, and she tried at first to evangelize it. To do so was contrary to the edicts. The people resisted and she stopped. In her village at Montargis there were Catholics and Huguenots. She expelled no Catholics. From the outside attempts were made to wipe out her "nest of heretics," as the Duke of Guise called it. Catherine de Medici threatened her. She replied that to help refugees was a good work because they were poor folk, whatever their religion. She was impartial and even gave assistance to monks.[18]

The increasing violence of the wars gave her intense distress. After the first war a journey through the territory ravished by the Huguenots was a tour over scorched earth. A Catholic commander recommended to Catherine de Medici that she make Poitou a desert. The Huguenots sacked churches, desecrated cemeteries, and hanged Catholics. The Catholics, in turn, massacred Huguenots. Some 400 perished at Orleans. A little incident reveals the temper of the populace. A father had baptized his child according to the Huguenot rite. Some Catholics then seized the child and administered another baptism according to the Catholic rite. At vespers the Reformed father and the Catholic godfather had an open quarrel. A drunken man clacking his sabots sounded an alarm. A crowd gathered and gave chase to the father who barricaded himself in his house. His shop was sacked, his wife maltreated and left for dead in a ditch. Eight persons, who with the father had fled to a barn, defended themselves. The tocsin sounded. The mob fired the father's house before the gendarmes arrived.[19]

The violence extended to Montargis itself. The Huguenots had their preaching service in the Catholic cathedral. Renée attended. The Catholics protested. She withdrew her presence. The Catholics were determined to suppress the preaching. She issued an ordinance forbidding assembly by day or by night on pain of hanging, but this did not stop the irate Catholics. Some 30 in corselets and with lances and arquebuses entered the cathedral. The next day the number was doubled, and when the Huguenots came for their services, the one side shouted its prayers and the other its sermons. The mob sounded the tocsin and made an attack upon a blind innkeeper with Huguenot leanings. He hid in a barn, but his wife was gouged on the chin and had a breast cut off. His house was pillaged. The gendarmes arrived. An attempt by the Reformed to desecrate a cemetery caused such a flare of indignation that Renée had to take refuge in the castle.[20]

One can understand the attempts of the Catholic party to expel her and her company. She resisted sometimes by quiet obstruction, sometimes by open defiance. The Duke of Guise sent a commander to clean out the nest. As eight companies of infantry approached she sent word that she had always been obedient to the king (somewhat of an exaggeration). She had guarded the castle well and needed no help. "If you make it a ruin," she said, "what good will it be to the Duke of Guise? If you come I will throw myself into the breach and see whether you will have the audacity to kill the daughter of the king of France." He did not come.[21] But she could not hold out indefinitely. The day came when her little garrison could not resist superior forces. On September 26, 1569, she had to dismiss 460 refugees. She provided them with 150 carriages, 8 coaches, and a large number of horses, and victuals.[22]

During the long period of her resistance spiritual care was provided by ministers from Geneva. The chief was Morel, whom Calvin had sent to her at Ferrara. He was both a support and a thorn. On two counts he made trouble. The first was that he desired to introduce the rigorous discipline of Geneva and complained to Calvin that the unworthy were admitted to the Lord's Supper. The other was that Renée, being a woman, was told that she should not meddle in ecclesiastical affairs. To Calvin he wrote, "Renée wants to attend the meetings of the synod, as does the Queen of Navarre [that is Jeanne d'Albret]. But if Paul thought that women should be silent in church, how much more should they not participate in the making of decisions! How will the Papists and the Anabaptists scoff to see us run by women! The church here is in a bad way. I refused to celebrate the Lord's Supper in September because otherwise dogs and swine would have been mixed with the sheep. Christmas is coming, when there is always a celebration, and I don't know what to do." [23]

Then came a dispute with Calvin. In the first war of religion
the Duke of Guise was assassinated. The Huguenot preachers
said he was in hell. She protested to Calvin. He told her he
feared she had been beguiled by affection for the duke. "Did
not David say [Psalm 139:21] 'Do I not hate them that hate thee,
Oh Lord? I hate them with a righteous hatred.' You say that this
applies only under the old dispensation of the Old Testament.
By that kind of interpretation you subvert the whole of Scripture. True we must be merciful, as God is merciful. But we must
defend the honor of God and the conservation of the Church.
The Duke started the fire and cannot be excused. To damn him
is too much, unless we have infallible proof of his reprobation.
There is a judge before whom we all shall stand. It won't do to
put the duke in hell and the King of Navarre in paradise, for
after all the king was an apostate. We must exercise moderation.
We must pray for the salvation of any one, but we are not to
regard all as members of the church, nor wish them prosperity.
The Queen of Navarre was perplexed whether she should allow
prayers for her husband in the churches under her jurisdiction
after his defection. I advised her to omit them and she complied,
though her husband was closer to her than your son-in-law to
you. We must hate evil, though not persons.

"I quite agree that there should be no sacking of the shops of
the Catholics. Morel does go too far. We are to render good for
evil. Hate and Christianity are incompatible. We must seek
peace with all. Those who pretend to seek reconciliation while
stuffing cannons are without excuse. I am glad you have come to
know Coligny." [24]

Renée answered on the 21st of March, 1563. "I have received
your letters of the 8th of January and also of the 24th in response to mine when I was at Fountainbleau [she had been at
court]. I left because I was forbidden to have preaching not only
in the lodge of the king but also in the house which I had purchased. Coligny and his wife came but stayed only for a week.
I have received your admonitions with regard to my household
and am trying to carry them out. I have made an effort to assist
Morel. At first he invited me to attend the consistory of elders
chosen by himself. Then he told me that women should not

attend, although the Queen of Navarre, the wife of the Admiral [Coligny] and the queen herself attend such assemblies. But I did not press the point. I have taken counsel with Coligny on how to repress the vice and scandals among those of the Reformed religion. Nearly all of my staff are of this persuasion, and yet some of them molest my own attendants. I wish you could come and see with your own eyes.

"Monsieur Calvin, one of the ministers incited me to a diabolical hate which God has not commanded. I won't deny that David says we should hate God's enemies with a mortal hatred and if I knew that the king, my father, the queen, my mother, my lamented husband and all my children were reproved by God, I would hate them with a mortal hatred and wish them in hell. I would conform myself entirely to God's will if he gave me the grace, but when it comes to my deceased son-in-law, you should know that he made it possible for me to harbor those of the Reformed religion in this village. He prevented the confiscation of the properties of Chatillon and he saved Montargis from sack. I do not excuse the faults of my family, but when it is said that he started the fire, I would say that he had retired to his house and had not intended to budge. But now there is pestilential rage against him. I know that he persecuted, but I tell you freely that I do not know whether he is reproved by God, for he gave sign to the contrary before dying. I myself have been held in despite because he was my relative.

"As for those who would persuade the King of Navarre and Condé to take David as their model rather than Christ I would say that if there are any on earth rejected by God, it is those who pervert the truth with their insolent lies. Monsieur Calvin, I am distressed that you do not know how the half in this realm behave. They even exhort simple women to kill and strangle. This is not the rule of Christ. I say this out of the great affection which I hold for the Reformed religion. If it be said that I take this attitude out of partiality for my relative I would say that I have shown no partiality for him or for my children.

"I beg you, Monsieur Calvin, to pray God to show you the truth. When it comes to prayers I have never laid it upon my ministers to pray for me or anyone else. I have left them to pray as they choose with liberty of conscience.

"As in the past I ask you now to burn this letter. [Happily he did not.] Monsieur Calvin, may God watch over you." [25]

None of Renée's children followed her course. Alfonso, who succeeded his father as the Duke of Ferrara, was even more intolerant. Another son became a cardinal. The daughters all married Catholic princes.

After the assassination of the Duke of Guise, Anne married the Duke of Nemours, a leader of the Catholic forces. Renée's grandson, the second Duke of Guise, assassinated Coligny. Yet she would consign none of them to hell.

BIBLIOGRAPHY

Works on Renée

Bartolomeo Fontana

Renata di Francia, 3 vols. (Rome, 1893-99). This work is very valuable for the many documents incorporated, but the comments of the author must be received with circumspection because he seeks to demonstrate that Renée from the beginning to the end was an orthodox Catholic.

E. Rodocanachi

Renée de France (Paris, 1896), makes her throughout a heroine of the Reformed faith. He, too, includes important documents.

Charmarie Jenkins Webb

Royalty and Reform: The Predicament of Renée de France 1510-1575, 2 vols., unpublished dissertation at Tufts University (1969). An exceedingly valuable study based on fresh research in the archives. She regards Renée as a vestigial figure of the Catholic liberalism of the 1520s who refused to succumb to the polarization of the 1550s.

NOTES

1. On the affair of the Placards see R. Hari, "Les Placards de 1534," *Aspects de la Propagande Religieuse* (Geneva, 1957).
2. C. -Mayer, *La Religion de Marot* (Geneva, 1960).
3. *Ibid.*, p. 112.
4. On Calvin's visit to Renée see Émile Doumergue, *Jean Calvin,* Vol. II (Lausanne, 1902), Chapter II.
5. *CR* XI, No. 374 bis, p. 323, Nov. 1541.
6. A. Casadei, "Fanino Fanini da Faenza," *Nuova Rivista Storia* XVIII (1934), 168-199.
   J. Crespin, *Histoire des Martyrs* (1582), pp. 185-6.
7. Webb, a long section following p. 179.
8. Rodocanachi, p. 114.
9. *Ibid.*, p. 164.
10. Fontana II, pp. 344-50.
11. *CR* XV, No. 1993, Aug. 6, 1554.
12. Rodocanachi, p. 243.
13. *Ibid.*, p. 260.
14. *CR* XV, No. 2037 and 2041.
15. *CR* XV, No. 2105, February, 1555.
16. *CR* XV, No. 2920, July 20, 1558.
17. *CR* XVIII, No. 3228.
18. Rodocanachi, pp. 384 and 446.
19. *Ibid.*, pp. 352-6.
20. *Ibid.*, pp. 362-3 and 434.
21. *Ibid.*, pp. 373-5.
22. *Ibid.*, p. 464.
23. *CR* XX, No. 4055.
24. *CR* XX, No. 4074. No date.
25. *CR* XX, No. 4085. March 21, 1563.

15.

Olympia Morata
(1526-1555)

We would know more about Olympia Morata if most of her works had not perished in the siege of Schweinfurt. Only the fragments which she previously sent to friends survive, plus a number of letters. They would have been more numerous had the span of her life exceeded 29 years. Her father, Fulvio Pellegrino Morato, was a teacher of grammar who had tutored young Ercole, later duke of Ferrara, and his brothers until some dispute with their father caused him to transfer to Vičenza. Here between the years 1532 and 1539 he founded a veritable Calvinist cell. Recalled to Ferrara in 1539 he continued his career there as a man of letters till his death in 1548.[1] His religious views are disclosed only in a poem in which he espouses the doctrine of predestination. Of the two thieves crucified with Christ one, he points out, was saved, one damned though no worse than the other. The elect are those saved solely by faith in Christ. Fulvio early instilled in his daughter a love of classical learning. At the age of 13 she was able to give a declamation in Latin on the *Paradoxes* of Cicero.

Her reputation was already such that Renée, our friend the Duchess of Ferrara, invited her to the court as a companion to her daughter Anne, several years younger than Olympia. Both of them were placed under the tutelage of another scholar versed in the classics, a German by name Chilian Senf, in Latin Sinapius. Olympia wrote a poem in Greek voicing her enthusiasm over her studies.

Never does the same desire enlist us all.
Tastes are not conferred by Zeus on all alike.
Colts Castor tames, Pollux the boxing glove.
Yet they were hatched within the selfsame nest.
I, a woman, have dropped the symbols of my sex,
Yarn, shuttle, basket, thread.
I love but the flowered Parnassus with the choirs of joy.
Other women seek after what they choose.
These only are my pride and my delight.[2]

Such studies did not appear to her to be incompatible with Christianity, for, said she, there is much in Cicero which is not repugnant to the Christian religion.[3] Nevertheless in later years she looked upon this period of her life as marked by indifference to religion. She composed a dialogue between herself and her intimate lifelong friend, Lavinia della Rovere. We have observed in the previous sketch that Olympia and Lavinia tried ardently to save Fanini. The dialogue may thus be briefly summarized:

"LAVINIA: You are always pouring over books. Do you never let up?

OLYMPIA: I do indeed immerse myself in books that I may not waste the time which God has given me. I have been lauded to the skies because I read so many authors, but I know my ignorance. I have been in danger of forgetting God. I fell into such error that I thought human affairs subject to fate and that God does not cure mortal ills. When I was utterly abject, God displayed to me a mercy which even parents do not show to their children.

LAVINIA: You had a great reputation for virtue and piety.

OLYMPIA: Yes, adulation such as you find in courts. You yourself can testify how far I was from Christianity.

LAVINIA: Yes, I recall. But if everything said about you is not true, nevertheless you are learned in Greek and Latin.

OLYMPIA: I am diligent, but those who read my works readily recognize my deficiency.

LAVINIA: I have admired the way you stuck to your studies without being nagged by your mother or any one.

OLYMPIA: I did it out of duty to God and his glory.

LAVINIA: I would urge you to devote your attention to sacred studies. I put these above all gems. God it is who sustains all, infuses all, renews all. From my earliest years I was enamored of his beauty and desired to be united with him in spiritual marriage. If we seek riches where shall we find them better than in him? If justice, where if not in him who adorns all with virtue? I gave myself not to the delights of the flesh but prayed, 'Oh God, King, Source, Head of mercy, who hast looked with compassion on our fathers, who hast fashioned all in Christ, who hast established man as lord of the earth, grant unto me thy wisdom, enroll me among thine own, for I am a fleeting mortal devoid of prudence unless endued with thy wisdom. Our feeble human nature cannot ascend to things divine unless thy Spirit come on the wings of the wind to bestow thy wisdom.' "

For a period Olympia had to drop her studies, whether classical or Christian, in order to care for her dying father. When she returned to court, her beloved Anne had already left to become the spouse of Fancis, later the Duke of Guise. Olympia was not really needed any more. But the summary way in which she was dismissed resulted from slanderous accusations. She wrote, "I was deserted by my princess, who was alienated not only from me but from my entire family by detraction. You can imagine my grief. No one had any regard for us. If I had stayed at the court I would have imperiled my salvation. I was not allowed to read the Old and the New Testament. I began to long to depart for the house of many mansions where a day is better than a thousand in the courts of princes." [4]

Just what were the slanders and who the detractors we do not know. A friend informed Calvin that the man at the bottom of it all was Jerome Bolsec. He was an unstable, malicious person, now Reformed, now Catholic. Practising medicine at Ferrara, he was used by the duchess as an intermediary with Calvin and by the duke to spy on the duchess. While at Geneva he had tackled Calvin on predestination. That was not reprehensible, but he had accused Calvin of sodomy and that was. He was quite capable of any slander.[5] The statement of Olympia that remaining at court would have imperiled her soul and that she was not permitted to read the Old and the New Testament indicates that religion was a factor in her dismissal. Perhaps Duke Ercole put on the pressures to get rid of her.

Certainly the friends with whom she consorted were enough to render her orthodoxy dubious. One was Celio Secundo Curione. He was an old friend of her father, like him a classical scholar and also a teacher at Ferrara. In later life he showed leanings to the leftwing Protestants. He attended an Anabaptist conventicle at Vicenza and preserved manuscripts sent to him by Michael Servetus. The state of his opinions during his residence at Ferrara may be judged by two incidents prior to his coming. He had removed from the reliquary in a church the relics of saints Agapetus and Tiburtius and had substituted a Bible with the inscription, "This is the ark of the covenant, the source of the true oracles, the real relics of the saints." He was imprisoned in a cloister, but escaped. Then, when he heard a Dominican claiming that Luther destroyed good works and denied the virgin birth and the divinity of Christ, Curione jumped up and challenged the speaker to cite particular passages, which of course he could not do. Curione pulled from his cloak Luther's commentary on Galatians and read passages refuting the allegations. The congregation turned on the preacher, who fled to the bishop of Turin. Curione was in consequence imprisoned with both legs in chains. One leg developed a sore. He requested the jailor to alternate the legs, clamping only one at a time. Then Curione tucked the free leg under him, stuffed the empty tight with rubbish, pulled his high boot over the foot, covered the false leg with his cloak and at the next shift put the dummy into the clamp. Thus free, he escaped through a window and over a wall. Thereafter he wandered with temporary residences in various Italian cities, including Ferrara.

With the establishment of the Roman Inquisition in 1542, his continued residence in Italy became untenable and he escaped to Lausanne. His family was left behind and it was large, four boys and three girls. He returned to Italy to conduct them over the Alps. His presence became known and as he was at breakfast an official of the Inquisition came after him with the summons. "Surrender in the name of the pope." Curione saw the guards waiting for him and was about to give himself up. He sprang up with the breakfast knife still in his hand. He was a large man. The official took fright and stepped back. Curione saw his chance, dashed through the door, greeted the guards, ran to a stable and took to horse. Horses and hounds on his trail were impeded by a heavy storm. He did manage later to assemble his family and get them over the Alps.[6] Curione assured Olympia that none in the world was dearer to him than she, save his wife and daughters.[7] Such was the feeling which resulted from their days together in Ferrara, and such a commendation would not help her at the court of Ercole.

There were three other persons at Ferrara of doubtful orthodoxy who were close to Olympia. All were Germans from the town of Schweinfurt in Franconia. They need not have been Lutherans because they were German, but some of them certainly were. One was the tutor already mentioned, Chilian Sinapius. The second was his brother John, a medical humanist, who having delivered an oration in defense of the humanities at Heidelberg, was now pursuing a double vocation of literature and medicine at Ferrara.[8] The third was Andrea Grunthler, also a doctor with classical competence. These men, enamored of Italy, were minded to marry there and remain. John fell in love with a noble French lady in waiting to Renée, by name Françoise Boussiron.[9] He was so distracted that he could not concentrate on his studies and to persuade the lady sought the good offices of John Calvin, with whom she had corresponded since his stay at Ferrara. Calvin complied and succeeded. The choice of Grunthler fell on the very good friend of Françoise, our Olympia Morata. After her dismissal from the court of Renée she had been at home assisting her mother in the care of her sisters and little brother. Now opened a new vista. These Germans decided to return to Germany to escape the increasing religious intolerance in Italy.

Olympia, then 24 years of age, was deeply in love with her husband. She wrote in Greek a poem on marriage.

> King of kings and Lord of lords, creator of male and female,
> Thou hast given to the first man a mate that the race perish
> not.

Thou hast willed that fallen humanity be the mystical bride of
  thy Son,
Who for her has given his life,
Spread now harmony and peace over those united in this hour,
For of thine ordinance is the nuptial couch.[10]

Grunthler left his wife in the care of her friend Lavinia della
Rovere and went alone to Germany to secure a post. Olympia
wrote to him: "I grieve over your absence. 'Love is full of solicitous fear.' Would, my dear, that I could be with you. Then
you would perceive more fully how great is my love for you.
The delay in seeing you is unbearable, for true love brooks no
delays. I could more readily endure anything else for your sake
than this. Therefore I beg you to do everything you can with
hands and feet that we may be together this summer, as you
promised. If you love me, as I you, I know you will do your
best." [11]

Olympia wrote a dialogue of an indeterminate date with fic-
titious characters. It is placed here not because of identical circumstances, because a young wife is lamenting not the absence,
but the alienation of her husband. Still, the general theme is
the bearing of adversity, and in that sense it is appropriate at
this point. The interlocutors are Theophila and Philotina.

"PHILOTINA: I turn to you because I am distressed by the frequent absence of my husband. As a young girl I greatly desired
to marry some one with like manners and nature, whose sight I
could always enjoy. I thought there would be no greater blessing
in life than to have a loving husband. That is why I married,
but it has not worked out that way and I am grieving.

THEOPHILA: If you will read the Bible, you will find that things
do not always turn out as we like. There is no greater grief than
for a father to have to punish a son.

PHILOTINA: I know that my sins deserve chastisement, but I see
others who are no worse than I am getting along very well.

THEOPHILA: Do you think they are better off because they live
in luxury? Look at the women at Ferrara and elsewhere in Italy
with their golden earrings, not to please their husbands, but
other men. God has not punished them, but do you think they
are better off?

PHILOTINA: Well, I'd like to be loved by my husband and to have horses and carriages worthy of my station and beautiful beds and tapestries. I'd like to be able to set a table for my lady friends.

THEOPHILA: What is more silly than to see a woman adorned with gems and her whole face buried in the table!

PHILOTINA: Yes, that is idiotic.

THEOPHILA: Consider what is more splendid and magnificent than the celestial kingdom.

PHILOTINA: I know, but there were some saintly women who had the good things of this life as well, for example Hester and Abigail.

THEOPHILA: God gives to some and withholds from others, and it is not for us to judge. His greatest gift is himself. See how much has been suffered by the Duke of Saxony. He was taken captive, deprived of his goods, despised, rejected, in the power of his enemy. His calamity exceeds yours. Think of all the ignominy and shame endured for Christ! I can give you no better counsel than to endure with patience. Remember, there is no thirst which shall not be assuaged.

PHILOTINA: These troubles of mine seem little to you. You'd feel different in my shoes.

THEOPHILA: I am not talking about myself. Those who know us intimately can say whether I am out of the range of the arrows. To any of us may come sickness, ignominy, poverty, hate, dissension, torments of the spirit greater than those of the flesh. The Christian must be ready to bear his cross.

PHILOTINA: I would rather suffer here than hereafter.

THEOPHILA: Anything is more tolerable if it is brief and this life is short.

PHILOTINA: I know you're right, but I fear I cannot follow you because of the odor of my frightful sins.

THEOPHILA: Fear not. Pray and your labor shall not be in vain. May God give you a tranquil spirit."

Grunthler secured a post in his native city of Schweinfurt and took his wife over the mountains. They stopped on the way at Würzburg to visit their old friend John Sinapius, engaged there in the practice of medicine. Olympia brought with her the eight-year-old brother Emilio and assumed the care of Sinapius' daughter when he lost his wife Françoise. When Grunthler received an invitation from the staunch Catholic, Ferdinand of Austria, to assume a chair of medicine at Linz, Olympia replied to the intermediary: "We greatly appreciate your generous offer and would gladly accept it if there were no obstacle, but you must know that we are enrolled under the banner of Christ and cannot desert on pain of eternal damnation. Please let us know whether Antichrist rages at Linz, as we have heard. I have followed my husband over the Alps and would gladly hasten by sail and oar to the inhospitable Caucusus or the limits of the west, for every land is our fatherland, provided only the rites of Rome are not required." Husband and wife in accord declined the call.[12]

Schweinfurt was considerably north of Basel, where Curione was now situated. He wrote suggesting that if she were to return to Italy she should pay him a visit on the way. She answered: "I have no intention of returning to Italy. You must know how difficult it is to be a Christian there in the midst of Antichrist. I think you will have heard of Fanini, who was constant in faith throughout an imprisonment of nearly two years, not overcome by the fear of death nor by the love of his wife and children. His body was burned and his ashes were thrown into the Po. I'd rather go to the ends of the earth than to live in such a place. If we were leaving I'd like nothing better than to come to see you. If my husband could get a post at Basel, to practice medicine, lecture, and earn a living, nothing would be more agreeable. I would be closer to Italy and could communicate more frequently with my mother and sisters, who are daily in my thoughts. An interchange of letters from here is quite difficult. As for my sisters, Lavinia has taken one of them with her to Rome. My little brother is with me. He fell from a high window unto stones, but was no more hurt than if he had landed on soft earth." [13]

Correspondence with her friends in Italy never ceased, despite the difficulty of getting letters through, especially in winter.[14] Lavinia was the recipient of a number. "My one consolation for being away from you," wrote Olympia, "is that here I can obtain theological works. I have composed a dialogue for you. Since there is war in France, your husband will be gone and you will be tormented. There may be something in the dialogue which will speak to your condition. I am sending you some of Martin Luther's writings. They have delighted me and I am sure will bring you refreshment of spirit. Give yourself to God in these studies. Do you think that God can lie? Why would he make so many promises to all who call upon his name if he did not intend to fulfill them? He invites all the distressed to come to him without exception. So give up that old error that we cannot turn to him unless we know that he has elected us from eternity. Let us rather implore his mercy and be sure that we are of the number of the elect." [15]

Olympia is here breaking with the rigidity of Calvinism, though Calvin, too, warned against worry about salvation. Olympia goes further and is not far from the universalism of her friend Curione. He wrote a book *On the Amplitude of God's Mercy* in which he voiced the tremendous optimism that all the world would be saved by adopting the Reformed religion and God would use an angel to convert the Turks and the American Indians. [16]

Naturally Olympia kept in touch with the Italians in exile. A number of her letters are addressed to Curione. She communicated also with Vergerio and urged him to translate Luther's *Large Catechism* into Italian. We recall that Vergerio, in Lutheran Tübingen, was at variance with the Swiss over the doctrine of the Lord's Supper. Olympia commented: "I know there is a great controversy about the sacrament. I think it could easily be resolved if men would consider not their own glory but that of Christ and the salvation of the church, which includes concord." In other words, like so many of the Italian exiles, she could not warm up to the disputes raging beyond the mountains. Happily she did not become embroiled in their feuds with one another. Vergerio was at odds with Curione because of the universalism of *The Amplitude of God's Mercy*. Continuing in the letter to Vergerio, Olympia refers to the capitulation of Renée. "It did not surprise me greatly for I know her inside and out. I was more surprised by some others. I am glad my mother stood firm. I have prayed that she and my sisters might be able to come to us here away from that Babylon." [17]

There is a letter to Anne, now the Duchess of Guise. "Dear Anne, though we are separated by a great distance, you are never absent from my thoughts. You recall how close we were to one another when we pursued our common studies. I sincerely hope that you will devote yourself to sacred studies, which alone are able to join us to God and to console us in this vale of tears. By God's singular mercy I have withdrawn from the idolatry of Italy. I am married to a German doctor, Andrea Grunthler. The way God has changed my heart is incredible. Whereas once I had a distaste for divine letters, now there is nothing in which I so delight. Riches, honors and the favors of kings are nothing. Only that faith which we have in Christ can save us from eternal death. It is not enough to know the history of Christ. The devil knows that. It must be the sort of faith which is active in love. Without such faith there would never be any martyrs. You know, my sweet princess, how many innocent persons now are burned and crucified for the gospel of Christ. Surely it is your office to speak up on their behalf. If you are silent you conspire in their death. You may say that if you speak out you will offend the king and your husband and you will make many enemies. Consider whether it is better to incur the hatred of men or of God. I have written this to you in very great love." [18]

When after the conspiracy of Amboise atrocious reprisals were visited upon the captives, one sole woman addressed the court and the queen mother, Catherine, in execration of such cruelty and predicted irreparable damage to France if she did not abstain from the shedding of innocent blood. This woman was Anne of Guise.[19]

For a time Olympia was able to solace herself with her studies, but disaster speedily fell on the city of Schweinfurt. That Albert Alciabides whom we encountered in the story of Elisabeth of Braunschweig was already on the rampage prior to his alliance with Erich. Having shifted his allegiance from France to the Empire, he was undertaking to reward himself by taking territories away from the bishops of Bamberg and Würzburg. The city of Nürnberg, also menaced, leagued with them in opposition.

Moritz of Saxony turned against Albert because he was disrupting the Peace of Passau, and Heinz of Wolfenbütel joined because he needed the help of Moritz in legal quarrels with the other part of Braunschweig. As the combined forces closed in on him, Albert ensconced himself with his troops, among them Spaniards, within the city of Schweinfurt, although it was a free imperial city. As the net closed, he evacuated the site and went west to link up with Erich of Braunschweig.[20] The sequel at the battle of Sieverhausen has already been described.

What all of this meant to the people of Schweinfurt was related by Olympia in Latin to Curione, in Italian to Cherubina Orsini and in both languages to her sister Vittoria.[21] Combining the accounts we have this narrative. "When Albert [Alciabides] occupied Schweinfurt, his enemies closed in on him and besieged the city. By day and by night they bombarded the walls. A soldier said that in no war had there ever been such heavy bombardment. In the meantime within the walls we were ravaged by the soldiers of Albert and his Spaniards. Not a home was safe. When Albert ran out of money, he despoiled the citizens. With so many soldiers to be fed the city was simply exhausted. Diseases spread from the army to the people, and many were afflicted with nervous disorders. Half the population died. My husband was co-opted for medical services and fell sick himself, so that we despaired of his life. He was cured by God, not by drugs, because there were none. But, as he remarked, one ill leads to another. He was barely recovered when the enemy began to throw fires into the city. Often at night you would have thought the whole town was in flames. We had to sleep in wine cellars.

"When Albert and his troops evacuated by night we expected a respite, but then the troops of the bishops and of Nürnberg entered and treacherously rekindled the fires. God saved us from the flames when, as we were about to seek shelter in the church, an enemy soldier warned us to flee the city altogether. Those who did take refuge in the church were consumed. We left without an *obol*. On the way we were stripped of our clothes. I was left with nothing but an undershirt. I lost my head covering and my shoes and had to walk barefoot over the rocks. I walked 10 miles the first day. I said to myself, 'This is all I can take. I am going

Tombstone of Olympia Morata

to lie down here and die.' Then I said, 'Lord, if it is thy will that I live give thine angels charge over me that they may lift me up upon their wings. I just can't make it.' As we got out of the city my husband was captured by the enemy, and I had nothing with which to ransom him. I could only pray God to deliver him and he did.

"We did not know where to go and started for Hammelburg, a town about three German miles from Schweinfurt. The inhabitants were loath to receive us because they had been forbidden to harbor anyone. I felt like the queen of beggars. I entered the town with bare feet, hair dissheveled, shirt in tatters, and it was not mine but had been given me by a woman on the way. The Hammelburgers would not let us stay long, and we had to move on, though I had malaria. My husband was captured by the prefect of the bishop. This most compassionate prelate had ordered all those escaping from Schweinfurt to be killed. We were detained between fear and hope until instructions came from the bishop to release us. Then God smiled upon us, and we arrived at the estate of Duke Erbach, who had suffered much for the sake of religion. He conducts daily family prayers. Would that other princes were like him. His wife is the daughter of the count Palatine. We were given clothes. When I was ill the countess waited on me with her own hands. I was given a fine robe and a thousand *sesterces*. Another nobleman, whom we had never known before, gave us some money. We came then to Heidelberg where the Count Palatine has made my husband a professor of medicine." This appointment undoubtedly was brought about through the intervention of Duke Erbach, because earlier Grunthler had heard from a friend that there was no place for him at Heidelberg.[22]

The letters containing the above account end with personal notes. To Curione she writes that she loves his books. All of hers have perished in the siege. When Curione received this news he solicited replacements from the stocks of all the great publishers in the area. Responses came from Herold, Isigrin, Oporinus, Herwagius, Froben, and Episcopius.[23]

Olympia's letter to her sister Vittoria concluded: "There is trouble everywhere. Germany is raped. England suffers persecution. Ochino has fled from there to Geneva. Oh my dear sister, may I be able to pray with David in the 90th Psalm, 'Teach us to number of days that we may get us a heart of wisdom.' Remembering that the span of our life is but toil and trouble and we soon fly away, may I give myself to the contemplation of things eternal. Emilio sends you a kiss."

The letter to Cherubina Orsini concludes: "All the Christians are persecuted in Italy. There is idolatry here too. I wish I could have my mother with me, but war is everywhere. I am consoled only by the expectation of seeing her in the life to come. The godly here must bear the cross. May God give faith and constancy that we may overcome the world."

From Heidelberg she wrote to Sinapius saying: "My husband is preparing his lectures. I am busy buying furniture for our new quarters." [24] To Lavinia she wrote: "We are fighting against domestic enemies, the sin which doth so easily beset us. God is a light to our feet. Let us not be troubled by men, for what is man if not a fleeting shadow, a wind-blown leaf, a fading flower, and vanishing smoke! Be of good cheer." [25] To Curione she said: "I am sorry to hear of your daughter's illness. My days will be but brief. This may be my last letter. I have no taste for food. Catarrh and fever rack me. Heidelberg is deserted because of the plague. I am sending you some of my poems." [26] Her health had been undermined by the 14 month siege of Schweinfurt and the rigors of the escape. This letter was her last.

Curione then collected whatever he could of her works and letters and published them. The first edition was dedicated to Isabella Bresegna; the second edition to Queen Elizabeth. Olympia was interred in the St. Peter's church at Heidelberg. A monument was erected to her by a Frenchman named Guillaume Roscalon.[27] Since he was French, the conjecture is pleasant and plausible that the expense was defrayed by Anne, the Duchess of Guise.

BIBLIOGRAPHY

Works of or about Olympia
Jules Bonnet
Vie d'Olympia (Paris, 1856), contains much well documented material.
The edition of her works which I have used is the third of 1570 in the
Beinecke Library of Yale University, entitled: *Olympiae Fvlviae Moratae Foeminae Doctissimae ac plane Divinae Orationes, Dialogi, Epistolae, Carmina, tam Latina quam Graeca* (Basel, 1570). The first edition
of 1558 has a dedication to Isabella Bresegna, the second of 1562 and
all succeeding to Queen Elizabeth.

The letters of Olympia and Curione are published in Giuseppe Paladino, *Opuscoli e Lettere di Riformatori Italiani del Cinquecento* II
(Bari, 1927). There is a critical edition of her letters with redating
and the addition of a few by Lanfranco Caretti, "Olimpia Morata Epis-
tolario (1540-1555)," *R. Deputazione di Storia Patria per l'Emilia e la
Romagna, Sezione di Ferrara* (1940). In the notes the first reference to
the letters is to Paladino in Roman numerals, and the second to Caretti
in Arabic numerals.

Passing references to Olympia are to be found in the works on Renée
by Fontana, Rodocanachi and Mrs. Webb, listed in the previous
sketch.

Fuller information on her stay in Germany is given by Dorothea Vorländer,
"Olympia Fulvia Morata—eine evangelische Humanistin in Schweinfurt,"
Zeitschrift für Bayerische Kirchengeschichte XXXIX (1970), 95-113.

NOTES

1. There is a sketch of the life of Fulvio Pellegrino Morato with the poem on justification and predestination by Giuseppe Compori, "Fulvio Pellegrino Morato," *Atti e Memorie delle R.R. Deputazini di Storia Patria per le Provincie Modenesi e Parmensi*, VIII (Modena, 1876), 361-71. His activity in the dissemination of Calvinism in the area of Vicenze is described by Achille Olivieri, "Alessandro Trissino e il movimento calvinista vicentine nel Cinquecento," *Rivista di Storia delle chiesa in Italia* XXI (1967), 54-117, in particular p. 58, note 5. The Beinecke Library at Yale has a tract by him on the symbolism of color entitled *Significatio dei Colori* (Venice, 1606).
2. *Carmina* in the *Opera* in Greek, French translation in Bonnet, p. 38.
3. *Proemia* in Cicero's *Paradoxia* in the *Opera*.
4. *Ep.* XIV, pp. 180-181. Caretti 16.
5. Sinapius to Calvin, *Ep.* 1865, *Calvini Opera*. *Corpus Reformatorum* XIV, pp. 188-89, with notes. Cf. Fontana II, 297-9 and Rodocanachi, p. 187.
6. Markus Kutter, *Celio Secondo Curione* (Basel, 1955), pp. 14 and 53-54.
7. Curio's letter IV in Paladino.
8. On the Sinapi brothers and the Ferrara circle see Eugénie Droz, *Chemin de L'Heresie*, I (Geneva, 1970), p. 133 and note 3. For John's medical career see Ladislao Münster, "L'antico ateneo di Ferrara e i suoi rapporti con gli scolari e i laureati della 'nazione alemanna' nel secoli XV e XVI,'" *Quaderni di Storia della Scienza e della Medicina VIII* (Ferrara, 1966), 34-38.
9. Aimé L. Herminjard, *Correspondance des Réformateurs* IV, 204-06.
10. *Carmina* I, Bonnet, p. 79. Caretti dates the marriage on June 12, 1550 and the arrival in Germany in July to August of the same year.
11. *Ep.* V, Caretti 9, dated by Paladino Feb. 1, 1549, but corrected by Caretti to April, 1550.
12. *Ep.* XX, XXV, XXVI, Caretti 24, 25, 26.
13. *Ep.* XV, pp. 182-3, Caretti 22.
14. *Ep.* XVII, Caretti 21.
15. *Ep.* XVI, Caretti 23.
16. Roland H. Bainton, *Castellio Concerning Heretics* (New York, 1935, reprint 1965), section on Curione.
17. *Ep.* XL, Caretti 49.
18. *Ep.* XXXII, Caretti 45.
19. Bonnet, pp. 156-7.
20. Leopold von Ranke, *Deutsche Geschichte im Zeitalter der Reformation* II (Wiesbaden, 1957), pp. 546 ff.
21. *Ep.* XLII, XLVII (Latin), XLVIII, Caretti 36, 40 (Italian), 41.
22. Bonnet, p. 143.
23. *Ep.* XLIV, Caretti 44.
24. *Ep.* XXXV, Caretti 47.
25. *Ep.* XLVI, Caretti 38.
26. *Ep.* L, Caretti 52.
27. Bonnet, p. 169.

Illustrations

page

page

Index